For
Susanne
and
Wayne

COOKING WITH HONEY

BY HAZEL BERTO

GRAMERCY PUBLISHING COMPANY
NEW YORK

acknowledgments

The author is indebted to the following for recipes, information, and suggestions: Mona Schafer, California Honey Advisory Board; Mary Lou Stubbins, American Honey Institute; Chester R. Unruh, Inez Pass, John A. Johnson, Donald Miller, and Jonathan W. White, Jr., Kansas State University; Vern Sisson, *American Bee Journal*; and Jack Happ, *Gleanings in Bee Culture*. Others, too numerous to mention, have contributed their knowledge, which is deeply appreciated.

To my husband, Vilas John Berto,
whose knowledge and encouragement helped
make this book possible.

contents

introduction THE HERITAGE OF HONEY 1

one MAIN DISHES TO TREASURE 7

two VEGETABLES WITH A DIFFERENCE 43

three SALADS FOR EVERY OCCASION 69

four BREADS, TODAY'S AND YESTERDAY'S 97

five CAKES AND COOKIES 123

six PASTRIES, DESSERTS, AND CANDIES 163

seven BEVERAGES PAST AND PRESENT 199

INDEX 228

INTRODUCTION

THE HERITAGE OF HONEY

UNLIKE MEN, HONEYBEES HAVE NEVER FALTERED IN THEIR design for organized living. Shuffled about by men and their civilizations, bees live as they did thousands of years before Christ. They continue to build perfectly engineered six-sided cells with wax oozed from their own bodies; to convert larva from worker bee into queen if needed; to feed and caress and even die for their queen; to air-condition her nursery; to houseclean; guard her entry, and at last to graduate into nectar-gathering workers.

Even as man robs her of her harvest, the bee continues to be the main source of pollination for over fifty of the vital agricultural crops without which his dinner table would indeed be poor. Even as man shifts her from field to meadow to orchard, she continues to provide him with a delectable,

1

natural sweet that is second to none in flavor and in the variety of ways it may be used. Even as man kills her with deadly insecticides, surviving bees continue to provide a food gaining in ever-widening usage by a health-conscious nation.

The use of honey is not new. Discovered by food-foraging prehistoric man some eight to ten thousand years ago, it became the first sweet known to him. But in the thousands of years to come, it was destined to play more unusual and dramatic roles in man's life than possibly any other food item.

As a religious symbol and as a medication, as well as a food, honey followed man on his global migrations. It figured in his ancient rituals of birth, marriage, and death, and in his pagan superstitions.

That ancient man knew of honey and thought the knowledge important enough to record is shown in a carving of about 7000 B.C. On the walls of a cave near Valencia, Spain, it shows a man gathering honey from a hole with bees flying around him. Ancient carvings along the Nile include pictures of the bee. Ruins in Turkey dating from about 6500 B.C. contain the remains of hives made of clay (pots, vessels, and pipes) and of coiled straw. Woven baskets, thought to have been used as hives, dating from about 3000 to 2000 B.C. have been found in Egypt.

Man gave prominence to the honeybee in most great books of religion, including the Sacred Book of the East written in Sanskrit about 3000 to 2000 B.C. As man became poet, sage, essayist, romanticist, humorist, or nursery-rhyme creator, he continued to record his love of honey and the bee.

Perhaps man's early preoccupation with honey stemmed from his lack of knowledge about how honey was produced. This ignorance led him into a mystical belief that honey was sacred and as such he worshipped it. Holy places and temple ground were consecrated with it. Great heroes such as Achilles were buried in it. Assyrians buried their dead in honey after first smearing the body with beeswax. Honey was left beside the body or at the grave as an offering to the gods by the Babylonians, Chaldeans, Phoenicians, and Egyptians.

Combined with milk, honey was fed to newborn babies by

the Hebrews, Greeks, and Romans. When sickly infants were exposed to die by Spartan mothers, honey was left with bread and water to appease Pluto, the ruler of the underworld. It anointed the lips and bodies of the priests, and was offered as food and sacrifice to the sun by the Incas of Peru.

Zeus, the father of the Greek gods, was raised on honey and goat's milk. He poured honey from the skies to resurrect the dead. Greek brides were anointed with it to assure their happiness.

Thus honey held an important place in early civilization: cleansing the spirit, heart, mind, and the body in life, and bringing the slumber of peace in death.

During the savage wars of the early ages, honey played still another role. It was carried by armies, across mountain, river, and desert, sustaining them in heat and cold. It gave them quick energy as a food and served as poultices for wounds, sores, and infections. During vast expeditions such as those of Alexander the Great, honey's healing powers for the wounded and the sick were unquestioned.

During more contemplative intervals, man turned his curiosity on the mystical producer of honey. Literature is filled with references to man's association and curiosity and esteem for this sometimes belligerent but useful insect. Aristotle, Cato, and Pliny studied the honeybee. Shakespeare, Victor Hugo, Tennyson, and Keats wrote of it, often in terms of praise or nostalgia.

Centuries passed. Great migrations of people crossed unknown seas to new lands, and they carried the honeybee with them. Although the aura of sacredness had diminished, the magic of honey continued as an important ingredient in the daily lives of most of these people, which included our own forefathers who arrived in America.

To these adventuresome, self-reliant people, honey was acclaimed for its medicinal qualities as well as for food and sweetening, much as it had been in the countries from which these people came. It helped sustain the elderly, the young, the sick, the weary. It was used as a medicine for everything from burns to croup, from sore throats to diphtheria. It was the primary ingredient in salves, gargles, packs, bandages, and dressings. Whether honey was as effective a cure as our fore-fathers thought it to be is a matter of doubt. However, it is a medical fact that honey has mild antiseptic qualities, because it will not support bacteria.

Honey combined with tea, the early Germans believed, gave them long life. Mixed with water and fermented, it be-came one of man's earliest alcoholic drinks, and was called "mead" or honey wine. Mead is still brewed today throughout the land from recipes often handed down from generation to generation.

Honey's role as an ingredient in cosmetics was known to Madame Du Barry, the mistress of King Louis XV. Its many uses covered a wide area: not only did our forefathers apply it as skin softeners, facial packs, and cures for warts and freckles, they also used it to soften horses' hoofs. Today, honey is included in many of our cosmetics, some mixtures sounding much like those great-grandma may have used.

Honey and beeswax were incorporated into household clean-ers by the housewives of yesterday. Beeswax was used in early artwork in many forms for centuries; in church candles, and in writing tablets. It is used today for decorative and creative purposes by artists.

Although many early uses of honey have been abandoned, many others are as valid today as ever. This is especially true in sports. Football players, swimmers, and runners use honey for quick energy. Sir Edmund Hillary included it on his Mount Everest expedition. The skin divers who undertook a survey of the sunken *Lusitania* readied themselves by taking honey. Thus, modern sportsmen and the Spartans of long ago have something in common.

When you consider its long association with man, it is amazing that most of the technological information about honey and the honeybee has been developed during the twen-tieth century. For ages, beekeepers thought the queen bee was a king bee. Not until the sixteenth century did man discover that the queen was a female that laid eggs. A description of this was published in Spain, in 1586. And in 1609, *Feminine Monarchie* was published in England, showing for the first time that the drones were the male bees.

Now, however, with research continuing to build new information about them, new importance has been attached to this "white man's fly," as the Indians called the bee when it arrived in this country, about 1622. It has now become most important to our food and agricultural economies. Knowing this, we are making ever greater strides in learning about the care of this insect and how best to use it.

With approximately 1,200 commercial beekeepers in our country, and over 300,000 bee hobbyists and sideliners, we produce about one third of the world's 900 million pounds of honey per annum. Aside from this, beekeepers now rent out thousands of hives of bees to the growers of fruits, vegetables, seed, and hay crops during the pollination periods.

Depending on where you live and the nectar the bees gather, you may choose from many flavors of honey to use. Twenty to thirty floral flavors make up most of the honey sold. They include such flavors as orange, locust, sage, maple, blueberry, blackberry, buckwheat, clover, and fireweed. The lighter colored honeys such as clover, sage, and fireweed are milder than many others and are good for general cooking use, alone or blended.

Five general types of honey are on the market: liquid, which is used in most recipes; granulated or solid, sometimes called candied, creamed or spread; comb; cut comb which comes in bars; and chunk which has small pieces of comb honey in liquid honey.

Because honey's two main sugars, levulose and dextrose, are absorbed quickly by the body, it gives quick energy to your whole family, regardless of age. Furthermore, honey contains protein, and its minerals and vitamins assure its perfect digestion.

Honey is easy to care for—it is simply stored at room temperature. It never spoils, doesn't need refrigeration, preservatives, or additives. Should it crystallize, a normal occurrence, it can be reliquefied by simply placing the container in warm water, or in a 200-degree oven until clear.

Now that you know the heritage of honey, use it with confidence and pleasure. The ensuing chapters are arranged with basic main dishes first, followed by vegetables, salads, breads, desserts, and beverages.

You'll find meats prepared succulently and differently,

breads that will fill your kitchen with great-grandma's baking-day fragrance, cakes and cookies more moist than any you've ever baked, and salads that will bring praise from your guests. Even beverages can be different made with honey, and we give you a few old recipes like honey beer, fun to read about, even if you never get around to making it.

Adventures with honey wouldn't be complete without recipes and suggestions from our past. Some of these you may want to try. Others you will enjoy as glimpses of times past. Other bits of information may evoke memories—some are humorous, some whimsical, others quaint, or surprising, but all are guaranteed to add a special flavor as you go adventuring with honey.

---
o n e

MAIN DISHES TO
TREASURE

"TREAT YOUR HUSBAND WITH HONEY AND YOU WILL POSSESS
his heart," Roman housewives were told thousands of years
ago. Mindful of that, and of Pollio's boast to his friend
Caesar that he'd preserved himself to such a hale and hearty
old age by using honey internally and oil externally, we've
given you a variety of delicious and hearty main dishes, all
using honey, and all recommended to hold your husband's
heart.

Many considerations will dictate your choice: time, cost,
convenience, purpose, ease of preparation, and personal pref-
erences. Whatever your choice, you will want to be able to
serve it with distinction and pride, certain of its delectable
flavor, and the simple elegance that marks superbly prepared
food. These recipes are offered with that assurance, and your

7

guests will feel complimented that you have given a special touch to what otherwise might have been a conventional dish.

Should you choose pork, you'll find it one of the most delicious of main dishes. The Romans of imperial times, after learning to prefer it to mutton, reveled in preparing the hams, whether fresh, smoked, or dried, with great finesse. Apicius, a great cookbook writer in the first century A.D., rolled his ham in a crust of oil and flour after first filling gashes in the skin with a mixture of honey, dried figs, bay leaves, and other condiments of his day. Roman sauces were both sweet and sour, like ours: honey, grapes, carrots, vinegar, oil, wine, musk, and nuts. Great eaters that they were, they used grape syrup and honey lavishly throughout their meals.

Honeyed chicken, duck, and turkey offer tempting and different dishes. Served on any occasion, they are easy to prepare and satisfying.

Steak on the grill or lamb with honey may bring memories of long, lazy country days, loud with the hum of bees; or of walking barefoot, carefully skirting bee-laden clover, or of warm honey fresh from the hive.

As you stir up sauces, mix glazes, or add ingredients, you will be using items known for centuries: honey, oil, vinegar, and wines. How they are used makes the difference.

Ham

When in doubt, thousands of cooks across the land choose ham for their main dish. Why? Because it is one of the easiest meats to prepare successfully, and it lends itself to a variety of delicious menus whether for guests or family. Here are hams in every category, including canned, whole, tenderized, and sliced. Choose any one, and try our various glazes for still more taste thrills.

✥ HONEY-ORANGE GLAZED HAM

It took Great-grandma hours to prepare dinner for her large family. You can do it the easy way with a fully prepared ham.

```
    1 canned ham (6–10 pounds)
1¾ cups water
    1 6-ounce can unthawed frozen orange juice concentrate
  ½ cup honey
  ¾ to 1 teaspoon dry mustard
  ½ teaspoon salt
  ⅛ teaspoon nutmeg
    1 cinnamon stick
    3 tablespoons cornstarch
    2 medium oranges
Whole cloves
```

Score the ham and stud it with cloves. Bake in a 350° oven about 10 minutes per pound. Make the glaze as follows: Combine water, orange juice, honey, mustard, salt, nutmeg, and cinnamon in a saucepan. Blend the cornstarch with ½ cup of the mixture. Heat over a medium flame, stirring constantly until the mixture thickens and comes to a boil. Boil for 1 minute, and cool. During the last 30 minutes of baking time, brush the glaze over the ham two or three times. Reheat the sauce with sectioned oranges and serve. Allow 3 to 4 servings per pound.

✥ CRUNCHY HAM

```
    1 3-pound canned ham
    1 cup honey
2½ tablespoons lemon juice
  ½ cup nuts, chopped
  ¼ cup corn flakes, crushed
```

Bake the ham according to the directions on the can. One half hour before cooking time is up, spread the ham with a mixture of the other ingredients. Bake 30 minutes longer. Serves 8.

✿ *WHOLE HAM, HONEY GLAZED*

    1 fully cooked ham (10 pounds)
    2 cups cider
    ½ teaspoon whole allspice
    1½ sticks cinnamon
    ½ teaspoon cracked ginger
    1 teaspoon whole cloves
    1 cup honey

Bake the ham, fat side up, on a rack in a shallow pan. Heat the cider and spices, and boil for 5 minutes in a covered saucepan. Bake the ham in a 325° oven, 15 to 18 minutes per pound. Baste with the sauce about every 15 minutes until 1 hour before the ham is done. When basting is done, drizzle half of the honey over the ham. Bake another ½ hour, and then drizzle the remaining honey. Bake 30 minutes longer, or until the ham is brown and glistening. If you are using a meat thermometer, it should register 160°. Remove the ham from the oven, let it cool for 20 minutes, score the fat, and stud with cloves. Garnish as desired. Serves 12 to 14.

✿ *HONEY-SPICED GLAZED HAM*

One company alone used 6,000 pounds of honey this year in curing and processing their small precooked hams, but this recipe calls for only half a cup.

    1 ready-to-eat ham (6–8 pounds)
    Whole cloves
    1 cup fresh orange juice
    1 stick cinnamon
    1 ginger root
    ½ teaspoon whole allspice
    ½ teaspoon whole cloves
    ½ cup strained honey (approx.)

Score the fat and insert a clove in each square. Bake the ham in a shallow pan in a 325° oven, allowing 15 to 18 minutes per pound. Combine the remaining ingredients, except the honey, and boil for 5 minutes in a covered pan. Baste the ham with this orange sauce at 15-minute intervals until 40 mintes before cooking time is up. Drizzle with half the honey, and bake another 20 minutes. Drizzle with remaining honey and bake another 20 minutes or until ham is brown and glistening. Serves 8.

❈ SOME MORE GLAZES

As in Great-grandma's day, there are many kinds of glazes to add zip to your ham. Here are a few you can try:

- Combine 1¼ cups brown sugar, ½ cup honey, and ½ cup orange juice. Apply to ham as above.

- After scoring the fat into squares, rub surface with mustard, then pour over 1 cup honey. Bake another 30 minutes, basting frequently.

- Mix 1 cup honey with ½ cup port wine and ⅓ teaspoon cinnamon. Brush over the ham which has been spread with prepared mustard.

- Mix 1¼ cups honey with ½ orange marmalade and a few drops of liquid hot pepper seasoning, and baste.

- Mix ½ cup sugar, ½ cup honey, ½ cup pineapple juice, ½ cup orange juice, and baste ham frequently with this.

❈ BROILED HAM SLICES WITH HONEY

Heat broiler, and arrange ham slices in the pan, with the top of the meat 2 to 3 inches below heat, depending on the thickness of the slices. Snip the fat to prevent the meat from curling. If the slices are the ready-to-eat kind, broil from 2 to 5 minutes. Turn, spread lightly with honey, and broil till golden. If the slices are not tenderized, allow 5 to 15 minutes, depending on thickness.

CURING AND SMOKING

Long before Great-grandma could serve ham, she had many chores to do. She cured the hams, either by dry or wet salting or pickling which took approximately two weeks, and then smoked them for as many days as was necessary to get the right degree of smokiness her family loved.

One curing recipe that Great-grandma used called for a mixture of 1 pound of salt and 1 ounce of saltpeter to be rubbed on the hams, which were then allowed to drain for 3 to 4 days. Then, they were immersed in brine strong enough to float an egg. For each half-barrel or 100 pounds of meat, she added 2 quarts of molasses, 4 ounces of saltpeter, and 2 ounces of soda. This was allowed to pickle for 6 to 8 weeks before smoking.

Great-grandma never faltered when it came to hard work in preparing food for the family, and this included smoking the cured hams. She took an old hogshead, stopped up all the crevices, and fixed a stick crosswise near the bottom. She cut a hole in the side, near the top. Then she turned the whole thing upside down, after tying a ham to the cross-stick. Through the hole, which was now near the bottom, she stuck an iron pan filled with hickory-wood sawdust and small pieces of green wood. She put a piece of red-hot iron in the pan, covered that with sawdust, and let the ham smoke for ten days. Besides hickory chips or wood, she sometimes used beechwood or corncobs to smoke the hams.

After smoking the hams, Great-grandma had to store them safely. Insects and their eggs were one of her worries. Sometimes she immersed the hams for two or three minutes in boiling water to cover them with a coating of grease and also to kill any bacteria or insect eggs. She might then coat them with a paste of flour, water, and cayenne pepper, and hang them in direct sunlight until the paste dried. Then she sewed them up in coarse cloth and coated the outside with shellac, varnish, or whitewash. Another way she kept insects away from her cured hams was to suspend them in a loose bag or a barrel surrounded by finely chopped straw to a thickness of 2 or 3 inches.

✤ HAM LOAF, MUFFIN STYLE

½ pound ham, ground
½ pound pork, ground
½ pound lean beef or veal, ground
 2 cups bran flakes, crushed
⅓ cup honey
½ teaspoon salt
½ teaspoon paprika
 1 teaspoon prepared mustard
 2 unbeaten eggs

Mix all the ingredients together until well blended. Shape into 12 balls and place in 2-inch muffin pans. Bake at 325°

(slow) about 1 hour. Makes 6 servings. *Note:* Ham loaf may be baked in an oblong pan 8 x 12 inches and cut into serving squares before baking.

GOURMET HAM BALLS

It might have taken Great-grandma two days to make this simple dish. After soaking her ham 24 hours in cold, weak borax water, she simmered it over the shining black wood stove, adding about 12 whole cloves, a bay leaf, 12 peppercorns, a bunch of celery, onions, garlic, chopped carrots and turnips, 2 blades of mace, 12 allspice berries, and a quart of cider or a half cup vinegar. Then she was ready to grind the meat.

    1½ cups raisin bran
    ½ cup milk
    ½ pound ground smoked ham
    ½ pound ground lean beef
    1 egg, beaten lightly
    2 tablespoons each, chopped onion and celery
    1½ teaspoons prepared mustard
    ½ cup chopped nuts
    ½ teaspoon salt

Combine milk and bran, add all other ingredients, and mix well. Shape into balls, place in shallow baking pans lined with foil, and bake at 350° for approximately 20 minutes or until partially done. Combine 3 tablespoons honey, ¼ cup packed brown sugar, and 1 tablespoon orange juice. Baste the meat balls with this mixture, and continue to bake 15 minutes or until done. Serve with rice or noodles. Or, if the balls are made small, they may be served as hors d'oeuvres. Makes about 3½ dozen, 1 inch in diameter.

LAZY DAY HAM

    1 thick-cut ready-to-eat ham slice
    2 teaspoons dry mustard
    ⅓ cup honey
    ⅓ cup port wine (or more as needed)

Rub ham slice with dry mustard, using 1 teaspoon of mustard for each side. Place in a shallow baking pan. Combine honey and wine; pour over ham. Bake uncovered in a moderate oven (350°) for 35 to 40 minutes. Makes about 4 servings.

❀ EASY HAM AND RICE

     2 cups uncooked rice
     5 tablespoons butter or margarine
1¼ pounds cooked, chopped ham
     ¼ cup honey
     1 small onion, chopped
     ¼ cup chopped parsley
Salt to taste

Cook the rice according to package directions. Melt the butter in a skillet, and add the ham. When hot, add the rice and all other ingredients, except salt, stirring gently. Add salt to taste. Serves 8.

Great-grandma used smoked shoulder butts in much the same way as she did hams.

❀ BONELESS GLAZED SHOULDER BUTT

Place a 2- to 2½-pound boneless smoked shoulder butt in a deep kettle and cover with boiling water. Simmer until tender, about 2 hours. Spoon any of the glazes for baked ham over the butt, and bake at 450° for 15 minutes. Serves 4. A delicious variation: Add a medium-sized onion and a stalk of celery to the water before simmering. Drain when tender. Mix ½ cup orange juice, ¼ cup honey, and 1 tablespoon prepared mustard and pour over butt. Turn and baste the meat with this for 10 to 15 minutes, or until glazed.

Pork

SUCKLING PIG

Pork and honey make an irresistible combination. One of its most sumptuous forms, from Roman times to the present day, is whole roast suckling pig.

Great-grandma prepared the slaughtered pig in her own big kitchen, cleaning it, scraping out ears, mouth, and eyes, and scrubbing the whole inside and out. She then soaked it in cold water for 15 minutes, drained it, and wiped it dry. Often, Great-grandma used the same stuffing she used for turkey before sewing the pig up. She bent the forelegs backward, and the hind legs forward under him and skewered him into shape (some cooks stretched the legs in opposite directions). She then dredged the whole with flour, put it into a covered roaster with a little salt water added. After twenty minutes, she removed the cover and rubbed the pig with butter, and returned it to the oven. When it was done, she would drizzle equal parts of brown sugar and honey over the whole.

Before serving, she often placed a green wreath around the neck and tucked a sprig of celery in his mouth. When serving it, Great-grandpa cut off the head first, slit the back, cut off hams and shoulders, and separated the ribs. What a fine feast lay before them!

CANADIAN BACON, HONEYED

    ½ cup raisins
    1¾ cups cider or water
    ⅓ cup honey
    1 tablespoon cornstarch
    ¾ teaspoon dry mustard
    ½ teaspoon salt
    6 slices Canadian-style bacon
    6 slices pineapple

Combine raisins and cider (or water) and simmer 10 minutes. Add honey. Combine all other ingredients, stir into cider and raisins and cook 3 minutes longer, stirring constantly. Bake bacon in shallow baking pan in 350° oven until done, about 30 minutes if sliced ½ inch thick. During last 15 minutes of baking, remove from oven, place pineapple slice on each, pour sauce over, and return to oven. Serves 6.

SALTING DOWN

In the absence of refrigeration, Great-grandma was often forced to salt down her meats in order to make them keep. First, she let the blood drain thoroughly if, as was usual, the meat was freshly killed. She then cut it up in readiness for the frying pan or the oven. This meant separating and trimming chops, steaks, roasts, and other cuts.

Her recipe for salting down was simple but time consuming. For every pound of meat, she used 1½ teaspoons each of salt and sugar, ½ teaspoon of saltpeter, and ¼ teaspoon of black or white pepper. These ingredients were used dry and in combination. Often she had to reduce them to a powder with a mortar and pestle.

The bottom of the crock was sprinkled with a thin layer of this mixture; then a layer of meat of uniform thickness was packed tightly over it. She put in layer after layer, seasoning each with as much of the "antiseptics" as one would use at the table.

When the crock was full she covered the top with a layer of cotton batting soaked in a solution of the same mixture of salt, sugar, and saltpeter dissolved in water. A lid was put on, and the whole set in a cellar, spring house, or other cold place.

When Great-grandma was ready to use her salted-down meat, she removed the portion she needed, rinsed, and scalded it. The cotton batting was soaked in the salt, sugar, and saltpeter solution once more and packed down closely over the remaining meat. Sometimes, the crock was covered with a layer of melted tallow, lard, or paraffin instead, to keep out the air.

APPLE-TOPPED PORK CHOPS

    6 loin chops (¾ inch thick)
    Salt and pepper
    2 tart red apples, unpeeled
    1 tablespoon butter
    ¼ cup honey
    Maraschino cherries

Brown chops slowly in a skillet. Transfer them to a shallow baking pan and season. Core and slice the unpeeled apples into ½-inch rings. Add butter to the skillet in which chops were browned and sauté apple rings until slightly tender. Place one ring on each chop. Cover and bake at 300° (slow) for 30 minutes. Drizzle honey over the apples and chops. Baste with drippings. Cover and bake another 15 minutes or until done. Place cherry in center of apple rings before serving. Makes 6 servings.

MANDARIN PORK CHOPS

2 pork tenderloins
½ cup oil
⅛ teaspoon garlic powder or 1 garlic clove, minced
3 tablespoons honey
1 tablespoon ginger
1 tablespoon dry mustard
1 cup soy sauce
Frozen french fries

Place the meat in a shallow pan. Combine the oil, garlic, honey, spices, and soy sauce for a marinade, and pour over the meat. Refrigerate, turning occasionally, for 24 hours. Remove from marinade and grill over coals for about 35 minutes, or until well done, turning the meat as it browns. Reserve the marinade and brush the potatoes with it. Heat them in a foil pan over the coals. Serves 8.

Serve with *Sweet and Sour Sauce.* Mix and heat 1 cup orange marmalade, 4 tablespoons vinegar, 2 tablespoons chopped pimiento, and ¼ teaspoon paprika.

HONEY-FRUITED PORK CHOPS

4 double loin pork chops
1 can (8½ ounce) sliced pineapple, drained and reserved
½ cup honey
¼ cup pineapple syrup
1 tablespoon prepared mustard
Maraschino cherries

Cut a pocket into each chop and insert ½ slice of pineapple. Combine honey, syrup, and mustard and spoon a little over each chop. Bake at 350° for 1½ hours, drizzling honey sauce over the chops frequently. Remove chops from oven; top each with ½ slice of pineapple and a cherry. Return to oven for a minute or two to warm the fruit. Heat any remaining honey sauce and serve with chops. Makes 4 servings.

✿ PORK CHOPS SUPREME

6 pork chops, ½ inch thick
1 cup hot catsup
6 tablespoons honey
1 large lemon, sliced

Blend catsup and honey and pour over each pork chop. Then top each chop with a slice of fresh lemon. Bake uncovered at 325° (slow) 1 hour or until done. *Note:* The same honey sauce is delicious over chicken pieces.

✿ ORIENTAL PORK WITH VEGETABLES

1 pound pork, sliced thin
5 tablespoons oil
2½ green peppers, sliced
1 large can water chestnuts, cut up
1 16-ounce can pineapple tidbits
1 cup water
2 tablespoons cornstarch
3 tablespoons honey
4 tablespoons soy sauce
½ cup water

Brown the pork in heated oil. Add peppers and sauté briefly. Add chestnuts, pineapple, and the 1 cup water, and bring to a boil. Mix the remaining ingredients and stir into the pork. Simmer, stirring, until mixture is thick and clear. Serves 8.

SAUSAGE-MAKING

No part of a hog's carcass was wasted a century ago. Extra fat went into soap, the head became headcheese, the feet were either boiled while fresh, or pickled. The trimmings of the carcass were ground into sausage meat, the proportions being ¼ to ⅓ fat combined with ¾ to ⅔ lean meat. Sausage was packed in casings made from hog's intestines, casings of muslin, or in airtight containers such as earthenware crocks. When sausage meat was packed in crocks, melted lard or tallow was poured on top to seal out air.

If Great-grandma decided to use pork intestines for her ground meat casings, she removed loose fat and outer membranes, turned them inside out and cleaned them thoroughly in borax water. They were then bleached for 24 hours or more in water mixed with 1 ounce of chloride of lime to the gallon. After rinsing the intestines thoroughly, she then scraped or tore off a part of the inner lining until they were as thin as they could be without tearing or puncturing them, and washed them thoroughly once more.

A lot of work went into Great-grandma's sausages. And to give them their pungent flavor, a lot of spices went in, too: salt, pepper, sage, allspice, ginger, and summer savory.

❋ SPARERIBS, OH SO SIMPLE

    2½ to 3 pounds small spareribs
     1 cup canned, crushed pineapple, undrained
    ⅓ cup soy sauce
    ¼ cup honey

Cut the spareribs into serving-sized pieces. Cover with water and parboil 15 minutes. Remove from water and drain thoroughly. Arrange in a shallow pan and brush both sides of ribs with soy sauce. Bake uncovered in a moderate oven, 350°, for 30 minutes. Combine crushed pineapple with ⅓ cup soy sauce and honey. Spoon over ribs and continue baking for 30 minutes longer. Makes about 4 servings.

❋ SPARERIBS ON THE GRILL

Cut three pounds of spareribs into serving-sized pieces; place them in a large pot of boiling water. Cover; simmer 1 hour. Meanwhile, prepare the sauce. Drain the spareribs; place them on a grill 6 inches above glowing coals. Cook for 30 minutes or until tender, basting with sauce and turning every few minutes. Makes 2 to 3 servings.

    ROSY HONEY BARBECUE SAUCE

     1 can (10 ¾ ounce) condensed tomato soup
    ¼ cup minced onion
     2 tablespoons vinegar
     1 tablespoon brown sugar
     1 tablespoon honey
    ½ teaspoon Worcestershire sauce
    Combine all ingredients

BARBECUED SPARERIBS SUPREME

¼ cup oil
1 large onion, chopped fine
1 6-ounce can tomato paste
¼ cup vinegar
½ cup water
¼ cup honey
½ cup Worcestershire sauce
1 teaspoon salt
1 teaspoon thyme
⅛ teaspoon garlic powder
1 teaspoon dry mustard
4 pounds spareribs

Heat oil in a large skillet, add onion and stir 3 to 4 minutes without allowing onion to brown. Mix tomato paste and vinegar and add to skillet, stir in all other ingredients except pork, and simmer uncovered for 10 to 15 minutes. Place ribs, fat side up, on a rack in a 400 °oven. Brush meat with sauce, and bake for 45 minutes to 1 hour or until tender, basting every 10 to 15 minutes. Meat should be crisp and brown. Cut into portions and serve at once. Serves 4 to 6.

Beef

SUCCULENT ROLLED-BEEF ROAST

5 tablespoons oil
4 or 5 pounds rolled rump roast
1 teaspoon seasoned salt
⅛ teaspoon garlic powder
¼ cup soy sauce
¾ cup water
1½ tablespoons honey
1 tablespoon vinegar
½ teaspoon ginger
2½ tablespoons cornstarch

In heavy kettle, heat oil and brown meat on all sides, sprinkle with seasoned salt mixed with garlic powder. Mix half the soy sauce with water, add honey, vinegar, and ginger, and pour over meat. Cover. Simmer gently about 3 hours or until very tender, turning meat about every 30 minutes, and adding water if necessary. When done, lift the meat from the pan, cut the strings, and keep warm while making gravy. Skim fat from juices. Mix remainder of soy sauce with cornstarch, add to pan juices, and cook until thickened, stirring constantly. Serves 8.

❀ DRESSED-UP STEAK

3 pounds round steak
1 teaspoon salt
2 tablespoons salad oil or drippings
1 large onion, sliced
1½ cups chopped celery
1 medium green pepper, diced
1 can (1 pound 4½ ounces) pineapple chunks
1 fresh tomato, cubed
1 tablespoon cornstarch
¼ cup honey
1 tablespoon soy sauce or Worcestershire

Cut meat in cubes; add salt. Brown in oil; remove meat; set aside. In same skillet, sauté onion, celery, and green pepper about 5 minutes. Drain pineapple; reserve ½ cup liquid. Add pineapple chunks and tomato to vegetables. Moisten cornstarch with pineapple juice; add honey and soy sauce. Blend into vegetables, add meat. Cover and cook at 325° (slow) 2 hours or until tender. Stir occasionally to blend and prevent sticking. Makes 6 servings.

❀ GRILLED STEAK

Place 1- to 1½-inch-thick tender steaks on preheated grill. Broil with high heat 12 to 15 minutes (for medium rare), turning once. Serve with:

FLUFFY SAUCE

½ cup dairy sour cream
2 tablespoons prepared horseradish, drained
1 tablespoon lemon juice
1 tablespoon honey
2 teaspoons freeze-dried chives

Combine ingredients; blend well. Cover and refrigerate 3 to 4 hours to blend flavors. Makes ⅔ cup.

✿ STEAK AND HONEY

1 steak per person, scored

Marinate in a mixture of crushed red peppers, salt, sliced onions, and honey. Set aside for 8 hours. Remove meat from marinade and grill over open fire if desired. Heat marinade and pour over grilled meat when serving.

✿ ORIENTAL POT ROAST

    1 teaspoon garlic salt
    ½ teaspoon dry mustard
Dash black pepper
    4 pounds chuck roast
    3 tablespoons shortening
    ⅓ cup soy sauce
    1 cup water
1½ tablespoons honey
    1 tablespoon vinegar
    ⅓ teaspoon ginger
    2 tablespoons chopped onions
    ¼ teaspoon celery seeds
    2 tablespoons cornstarch dissolved in 3 tablespoons water

Combine salt, mustard, and pepper and rub on roast. Brown meat in shortening over medium heat. Place on rack in roasting pan. Combine soy sauce, water, honey, vinegar, ginger, onions, and celery seeds. Pour over meat. Cover and simmer 2 hours or until tender. Remove meat to warm platter, skim fat from drippings. Add cornstarch to 2 cups drippings, cook over medium heat, stirring constantly until thickened. Serves 6 to 8.

PRESERVING BEEF IN GREAT-GRANDMA'S DAY

Beef was as great a favorite of the early settlers as it is today. But what a difference between the way we browse through the meat departments of huge, brightly lighted stores, choose our precut, prewrapped portion, ready for the kitchen, and what Great-grandma had to go through.

An entire beef was slaughtered and butchered on the farm, and came to the kitchen for Great-grandma to do the rest. For days following, she was busy trying to preserve all the meat for future use; this, in addition to all her other chores:

canning, preserving, extracting honey for the winter, helping neighbors, tending the sick, as well as sewing, mending, ironing, and washing endless tubs of clothes.

Even so, she successfully took care of her meat, whether or not ice or an ice house was available (and often it wasn't). She knew that joints of meat with the cut side up and the knuckle downward (so as not to bleed) might keep two to four days in the shade. Or, if running water was handy from a spring or pump, she laid the meat in a box or tub and let the water flow through it. When the meat began to rise from the bottom of the box, the meat had to be used.

With skim milk, sour milk, and buttermilk usually in abundant supply, Great-grandma often preserved cuts of meat for short periods by placing them in large stone jars, covering with milk, and then weighting the meat with a clean stone to keep it under the surface. The containers were then put in a cold cellar or in running water from a spring for a week to ten days. When the meat was used, she fed the milk to the pigs.

If she had stored steaks in milk, she washed them thoroughly, then soaked them a few minutes in water containing a tablespoon of soda to the gallon. This neutralized the acid of the milk and was thought to make the meat more tender.

Great-grandma had other ways to preserve her meat for short periods. She often placed 2- or 3-pound pieces between layers of dry cornmeal or bran, or, after covering the meat thickly with these, she hung it in a shady place with good ventilation. She also preserved meat for short periods by soaking it for three to five minutes in a solution of one tablespoon of borax to a gallon of water, then rinsing with clear water before using it.

Because Great-grandma thought that fresh powdered charcoal had powerful antiseptic properties, she often rubbed fresh meat with it for short-time preservation. Before using the meat, she rinsed off the charcoal.

Charcoal helped to sweeten tainted meat and was used either in lumps or pulverized. Great-grandma put about a dozen egg-sized lumps into the water that meat was to be boiled in or, if she used pulverized charcoal, a cheesecloth bag kept it within bounds until all odors were absorbed.

If charcoal wasn't handy, Great-grandma might hang the

meat inside an inverted box or barrel. Beneath the meat, she placed an earthenware bowl with a half cupful of table salt in it. She gradually added two ounces of sulfuric acid to the salt at the rate of ½ ounce every 15 or 20 minutes. Taking care not to breathe the fumes as they disinfected the meat, she rinsed it with a soda or borax solution after the process was completed.

Great-grandma had to protect her meat from the flies that laid their eggs in the meat and later hatched into maggots. She wrapped the meat in a cloth moistened with vinegar. She also kept flies and other insects away from her fresh meat by rubbing it with ground pepper or ginger, or by coating it with waxed paper. She prepared this paper herself. First, she melted five ounces of stearic acid over low heat. Then she stirred in 2 ounces of carbolic acid and added, in a thin stream, 5 ounces of melted paraffin, stirring constantly. She removed it from the fire and continued to stir until the mixture was set. Again, she melted it with gentle heat, applied it with a brush to suitable paper, cooled it, then wrapped the meat and sealed it.

When Great-grandma's fresh meat needed immediate attention, she cooked great quantities of it, each day placing it on the stove to boil. Thus, she thought, the germs that caused decay would be killed and the process would be arrested yet another day.

❀ HONEY GLAZED SHORT RIBS

    4 to 5 pounds short ribs
    ½ cup each, orange or pineapple juice and honey
    ¼ cup each, soy sauce and lemon juice
    3 tablespoons chopped green onion
    1 teaspoon each chili powder and garlic powder
    ½ teaspoon salt

Place meat in shallow pan. Combine remaining ingredients thoroughly, and pour over the short ribs. Cover and refrigerate 2 to 3 hours, turning the meat often. Drain the meat and place in a foil tray, and place on a grill over coals. Cook the ribs until tender, 1½ to 2 hours, turning 3 or 4 times during cooking, and brushing with marinade. When done, remove ribs and serve. Serves 6 to 8.

✿ HAMBURGERS ROYAL

1 pound ground beef
Salt to taste
Chopped onion to taste
1 egg, beaten, or a bit of water
¼ cup bread crumbs

TOPPING

½ cup honey
2 teaspoons soy sauce
1 tablespoon pickle relish

Blend salt and onion into meat, add egg or a little water, and the bread crumbs. Shape into hamburgers and grill. As they cook, add topping mixture, well blended.

✿ ZESTY MEAT LOAF, MUFFIN STYLE

1 egg
½ cup milk
1½ teaspoons salt
¼ teaspoon ground pepper
¾ cup white or wheat bread crumbs
1 pound ground chuck or round
Zesty Sauce

In a large bowl, beat egg slightly with fork. Add milk, seasonings and bread crumbs. Blend together lightly. Put 1 teaspoon of Zesty Sauce in bottom of 6 (3-inch) muffin cups. Divide meat loaf into each cup. Shape lightly to resemble muffin. Bake at 350° 20 to 25 minutes or according to how you like your meat. Serve hot with balance of Zesty Sauce.

ZESTY SAUCE

(*This is good with beef, chicken, or shrimp.*)

1 can (15 ounces) or 2 cans (8 ounces each) tomato sauce with tomato bits
2 tablespoons honey
2 tablespoons wine vinegar
1 clove garlic, finely minced
2 green onions, thinly sliced (tops included)
2 tablespoons canned green chilies (or a few drops red pepper sauce)

Combine all ingredients. Heat to use as meat loaf sauce. May be used hot, or chill to serve as dip. Makes 2 cups.

✿ CHILI, GOURMET STYLE

    1½ pounds ground beef
     1 cup water
    1½ cups celery, diced
     1 medium onion, minced
     1 can (20 ounces) red kidney beans, drained
    1⅓ cup tomato puree
     2 teaspoons chili powder or to taste
     2 teaspoons salt
     2 tablespoons wine vinegar
     ¼ cup honey

Sauté meat until red color disappears, stirring. Add remaining ingredients except vinegar and honey. Taste for salt. Stir and bring to a boil. Simmer, covered, about an hour, stirring occasionally. Add vinegar and honey; stir to mix. Serves 6.

Lamb

If you've never tried lamb, glazed and succulent with honey, you've a treat in store. Tender, juicy, aromatic, either the breast or the shoulder roast will bring the compliments every cook appreciates.

✿ BAKED LAMB, WESTERN STYLE

     6 pounds lamb breast (spareribs)
    Salt and pepper
     1 can (9 ounces) crushed pineapple
     ¼ cup honey
     1 teaspoon salt
     ½ teaspoon cinnamon
     ¼ teaspoon allspice
     2 medium oranges, peeled and sliced

Cut lamb breast into serving pieces; season. Place on rack in a shallow roasting pan. Bake at 325° (slow) for 1 hour. Drain off drippings; combine remaining ingredients; spread over lamb. Bake 30 to 45 minutes or until lamb is tender and glazed. Makes 6 servings.

PRESERVING LAMB

Mutton and lamb, like other meats that had to be preserved for long periods of time by Great-grandma, were dried, canned, pickled, or smoked. Pickling called for large containers such as tubs or casks which were sterilized. Meat was cut into strips of equal thickness. The pieces were then rubbed thoroughly with fine salt or powdered saltpeter, or a mixture of these dried in a slow oven.

While the meat drained from slats, the pickling liquid was made with salt, saltpeter, sugar, molasses, and baking soda by bringing the mixture to a boil, skimming, and cooling it. After scalding the barrels or casks, salt was sprinkled over the bottom about half an inch thick, and the meat packed in tight layers with salt sprinkled between them When the meat was packed, the cold pickling liquid was poured over all, a clean piece of wood put over the meat, and over this a heavy stone to weight the meat below the level of the liquid.

❀ BAKED LAMB SHOULDER

    5 to 6 pounds shoulder of lamb
    ½ cup honey
    ½ cup lemon juice
    Salt to taste
    Dried crushed mint leaves

Marinate meat in combined honey and juice, turning to coat, and refrigerate overnight or for several hours. Turn occasionally. Drain meat, reserving marinade. Place in roasting pan. Score meat, add salt. Roast, uncovered, in a 325° oven about 40 minutes to the pound, basting frequently with marinade. When half done, sprinkle on mint leaves, and continue roasting. Serves 8.

Game

Wild game such as venison and elk were great favorites of earlier day menus. Often, such meat made a welcome change from the domestic animal meat diet. Brought fresh from the snowy mountains by packhorse or by men trudging mile after mile, such meat was often hung for days to ripen into tenderness and good flavor.

 HONEYED VENISON ROAST

  3 to 4 pounds venison or elk
  ¾ to 1 cup salad oil
  3½ tablespoons honey
  3½ tablespoons vinegar
  ½ cup soy sauce
  2 onions, chopped
  ⅓ teaspoon garlic powder, or 1 or 2 cloves garlic, crushed
  ½ teaspoon ginger

Place meat in shallow pan. Combine remaining ingredients and pour over meat. Refrigerate several hour or overnight. Remove meat, drain, reserving marinade. Roast at 325° for 2 to 3 hours or until tender, basting frequently with marinade. Serves 6.

BARBECUED BEAR

  1 bear roast, 2 to 3 pounds
  Salt and pepper
  ¾ teaspoon garlic powder
  2½ tablespoons honey
  1½ tablespoons paprika
  1 teaspoon dry mustard
  Dash of cayenne pepper
  2¼ tablespoons Worcestershire sauce
  1 teaspoon salt
  ¼ cup vinegar
  1 cup tomato juice
  ¼ cup catsup
  ½ cup water

Season roast with salt, pepper, and garlic powder, and roast at 350° for 1 hour or until well done. Slice thin. Mix remaining ingredients in skillet, simmer for 15 minutes, add meat. Cook 1 hour or until meat is tender. Makes 6 servings.

*   *   *

Wildfowl, too, made a welcome addition to the table. "Pheasants," said Great-grandma, "should be selected with the spur but little developed; the tenderness of the bird is known by trying the flesh of the pinion." Woodcocks and waterfowl such as wild ducks, teal, and widgeon, could be tested by pinching the pinion and breast. The age of partridges could be told by examining the long feathers of the wing, round at the tip in an old bird, and pointed in a young one.

Cooks were warned to keep the fire brisk and well kept up when roasting fowl. In preparing the birds, such as pigeons, the cook cleaned them and stuffed them as she did chickens; sometimes she left the feet on and dipped them into scalding water. The skin was then stripped off the feet, the feet crossed and tied together below the breastbone. If the head was left on (it was becoming less fashionable to do so at the turn of the century), it was dipped in scalding water, picked clean, and tucked under the left wing. The liver was put under the right wing. Snipe, woodcock, and plover were basted with lard or fresh butter, served on toast, and garnished with sliced orange or orange jelly. Prairie chicken, pheasant, and grouse were larded, or wide strips of bacon or pork placed over the breast before roasting. The gravies might be seasoned with the juice of a lemon and a tablespoon of currant jelly, then thickened.

In the case of ortolans, reedbirds, rail, and soras, they might be roasted or broiled. An oyster was often rolled in melted butter, then in bread crumbs seasoned with pepper and salt, and put into each bird before roasting.

To keep fowl from becoming tainted, a piece of charcoal was often put in the cavity of each, the birds then hung in a cool, dark place with a cloth thrown over them.

Grouse, quail, partridge, and pheasant are cooked much like chicken. Because they are lean, they require extra fat during cooking to prevent them from drying out.

ROAST QUAIL

Wash and wipe quail. Cover with slices of salt pork and tie in place. Place quail, breast side up, in shallow baking pan in 450° oven. Brush with butter. Roast uncovered 15 to 20 minutes, or until done as desired. Mix together 2 to 4 table-spoons butter, 4 tablespoons honey, and 1 tablespoon soy sauce or 2 tablespoons lemon juice. Baste during the final 5 to 10 minutes of roasting. Allow one bird per person.

- Young birds may be barbecued much as chicken is cooked. Great-grandma larded them well with corned ham or pork. She put lemon juice and a glass of wine in her sauces. Butter rolled in flour and put on top during baking was one of her secrets. These balls were also put in broth to thicken it.

- Rubbing fowl with ginger imparts a delightful flavor. Orange juice with a bit of honey, or currant jelly spread on the bird for a glaze brightens the dinner table.

- A sweet-sour sauce for wild meats combines ½ cup of honey with 2 teaspoons of mustard and 2 table-spoons of vinegar. Use for roasts or steaks, basting with it.

- Try a sauce made by mixing 2 tablespoons of prepared mustard with 1 teaspoon honey, ½ teaspoon of ginger, and 1 cup of orange marmalade. Baste roasting fowl during the last 15 minutes. Serve remaining mixture with the bird.

Chicken

CHICKEN, HONEY-ROASTED

1 3-pound broiler
Salt to season
¼ cup butter, melted
½ cup honey
¼ cup lemon juice

Salt chicken, and roast in 350° oven for approximately 1 hour. Baste with mixture of butter, honey, and lemon juice and continue roasting for 50 to 60 minutes, basting frequently until done. Serve with drippings from pan. Serves 4.

CHICKEN DELICIOUS

    1 cup margarine
    1 3-pound fryer, cut up
1½ cups pancake mix
1½ teaspoons salt or to taste
1½ tablespoons paprika
Pepper if desired
    4 tablespoons honey
    4 tablespoons lemon juice
    ½ cup butter (or margarine) melted

Melt the 1 cup of margarine in 13 x 9 x 2-inch pan. Dredge the chicken in combined pancake flour, salt, paprika, and pepper, place in pan and turn to coat chicken. Bake in a 400° oven, skin side down, for half the baking time, or about 30 minutes. Turn the chicken, and spoon over combined honey, lemon juice and melted butter. Bake about 30 minutes more or until tender, basting frequently with sauce. Serves 8.

CHICKEN BREAST WITH SESAME SEED

    6 chicken breasts, boned
Salt to taste
    2 tablespoons margarine or butter
    4 tablespoons honey
    1 tablespoon soy sauce
1¼ tablespoons sesame seed

Flatten breasts slightly and season. Place, skin side down, in shallow greased baking pan. Melt butter, add honey and soy sauce, pour over chicken. Bake in 325° oven 45 to 50 minutes, basting every 15 minutes. Sprinkle with sesame seeds, and continue baking in 450° oven 10 minutes or until well browned and tender. Serves 6.

CHICKENS—FROM BARNYARD TO POT

If Great-grandma ever ran short of fresh or "put up" meat, or simply for variety, she would catch a chicken, kill it, and quickly scald, pluck, clean, and cool it for company or for a large family Sunday dinner. She was a whiz at cutting up a chicken, either for creamed chicken and dumplings or for fricassee with hot biscuits and honey. Combining equal amounts of honey and soft butter produced a delicious spread for sour milk biscuits. A bit of grated orange rind, if she had it, gave extra pungency.

After plucking off the larger feathers, she had to pick out the pinfeathers with a fine-pointed knife, or pinch them out with a strawberry huller. Then, the chicken had to be singed over a flame to get rid of fine down and hairs. She removed the head and the oil sac, just ahead of the tail. When she cleaned the chicken, she was very careful not to break the gall bladder which would give the flesh a hopelessly bitter taste. She set aside the liver, heart, and neck for giblet gravy, and also the gizzard, which Great-grandpa liked fried.

If she intended to fry the chicken, she made sure she selected a young bird. She checked the feet and breastbone for softness, and the skin for smoothness.

In the late summer or fall, Great-grandma butchered chickens for winter food, and to cull the flock. After cleaning and plucking the birds (she saved the feathers for stuffing pillows and featherbeds), she cooked the meat and canned it in glass jars or cans. If she used cans, she surrounded them with hot water, packed them with cooked meat, and the jelly from the meat was then poured into the can. The cover was then soldered in place, a small hole was punctured in the cover, and the water was boiled until it steamed from the aperture. The opening was then sealed with solder.

GLAZED BAKED CHICKEN

2 fryer-broiler chickens, cut up (about 2½ pounds each)

MOON GLOW SAUCE

¾ cup fresh orange juice
2 tablespoons fresh lemon juice
¼ cup salad oil
¼ cup honey
1 teaspoon salt
½ teaspoon pepper
1 teaspoon dry mustard or curry powder
½ teaspoon paprika

Combine all ingredients and shake or blend until well mixed. In a large bowl, place chicken pieces skin side down. Pour Moon Glow Sauce over the chicken and rotate pieces to coat completely. Cover bowl and marinate in refrigerator for several hours or overnight. Remove chicken from sauce and place, skin side down, in pan on rack. Line the bottom of pan with foil to catch drippings. Baste chicken with Moon Glow Sauce. Bake at 400° (hot) 30 minutes. Turn chicken and baste with remaining sauce. Bake 30 minutes more or until done. If chicken browns too fast, cover with foil. *Note:* If desired, the recipe may be cut in half and cooked in skillet. Serves 8.

CHICKEN DIABLO

    1 cut-up fryer
    1 cube margarine, melted in baking pan
    ½ cup honey
    ¼ cup mustard
    1 teaspoon salt
    ¾ teaspoon curry powder

Combine the honey, mustard, salt, and curry powder. Roll the clean, dry chicken in the mixture and bake at 350° for 1½ hours, turning once or twice. Serves 4 to 6.

OVEN-BARBECUED CHICKEN

    2 to 3 pounds frying chicken
    Salt and pepper
    ¼ cup butter, melted
    1 tablespoon lemon juice
    ½ cup salad dressing
    ¼ cup hot catsup
    2 tablespoons honey
    1 teaspoon paprika

Season chicken. Combine all ingredients in baking pan. Arrange chicken in single layer turning once to coat. Bake at 350° (moderate) 45 to 60 minutes or until done, basting every 15 minutes. Serves 4 to 6.

HARVESTING HONEY

To Great-grandma, having honey on her cupboard shelves was as important as having spices, jellies, and jams. Practical and realistic, she had no time to romanticize about honey as the poets and other writers did. It was a food that added flavor and delicacy, and was healthy besides.

With Great-grandpa often working many miles from home, plowing fields, sowing, planting, and harvesting, it was up to Great-grandma to harvest her own honey. Donning his overalls and making them bee-proof by tying the bottoms of the legs over her high-button shoes, putting on gloves and veil, she lighted the smoker which quieted the bees as she robbed them. Lifting off the top of the hive, she brought out the filled combs of honey, put them into her dishpan, and hastily retreated to her kitchen. The odor of the gunnysack scraps burning in the smoker smoked out more than bees. The children began to infiltrate the kitchen, surreptitiously poking their fingers into the dishpan when they thought Great-grandma wasn't looking. Tonight, they knew, there would be pans of hot sour cream biscuits, spread with the first of the honey.

For two or three days, Great-grandma's sugar-sack filled with comb honey hung from a nail and drained into a deep bucket. Some of the comb was left whole for spreading on hot breads and pancakes—Great-grandpa particularly liked it this way.

The strained honey was poured into sterilized jars, covered, and kept in the pantry. Should it crystallize, she merely put the jar into hot water, never boiling it, until it returned to its original texture.

BROILED CHICKEN, WINED

Another simple, different taste treat

    3 pounds chicken breasts
    1 cup honey
    ⅓ cup Madeira wine, or more if desired
    Salt to taste

Season the chicken with salt, place on broiler, and cook until tender, about 35 minutes; turn and baste frequently with the sauce of mixed honey and wine. Serves 4.

HONEY BARBECUE CHICKEN

¼ cup butter
½ cup orange juice
½ cup honey
2 tablespoons lemon juice
2 tablespoons chopped parsley
2 tablespoons soy sauce
1 tablespoon dry mustard
2 broiler-fryers (2½ to 3 pounds each), split in half

Melt the butter in a small saucepan. Blend in the remaining ingredients and simmer 2 to 3 minutes. Cool. Put the chicken halves in a shallow pan and pour the sauce over them. Allow to marinate a few hours before cooking. Place the chicken halves, cavity side down, on the grill. Cook slowly, 40 to 45 minutes, basting frequently with sauce. Turn and cook, meat side down, for an additional 10 minutes. Serves 4 to 6.

HONEY GLAZED CHICKEN

Another quick, easy, delicious way to serve chicken is to cover it with a honey glaze. Simply brown the chicken pieces about 15 minutes. While chicken is browning, combine ⅓ cup butter, melted, ½ cup honey, ¼ cup lemon juice. Pour over chicken, cover, and cook over low heat for 30 to 35 minutes, basting it occasionally.

HOLIDAYS AT GREAT-GRANDMA'S

Thanksgiving and Christmas were occasions that brought the family together, days of prayer and giving thanks for the simple things of life: love and health, shelter and food, and for friends and family. The house, whether chinked log or slabbed raw timber, was shining. Floors gleamed with fresh wax, and beds were fresh for the incoming family, the sheets smelling of lavender. Bouquets of dried flowers glowed for Thanksgiving, with bright pumpkins, apples, nuts, and berries from meadows, now dry and brown, and from along the creek banks.

Young and old arrived by buggy, wagon, or sleigh, often singing, "Over the river and through the woods, to Grandmother's house we go. . . ." Was ever a song more nostalgic and beloved? They were greeted by great fires blazing in the fireplaces and the round-bellied iron stoves. White tablecloths gleamed from hours of expert ironing with heavy irons kept hot on the range. Pies, freshly churned butter, breads, cranberry sauce, and steamed puddings stood on pantry shelves. Excited voices echoed through the house, and the fragrance of roasting turkey filled the air.

Days before, Great-grandma had chosen the turkey carefully. She felt the breastbone to make sure that it was as soft as cartilage. The feet were soft and not covered with coarse scales. She made sure the skin was soft and smooth. After cleaning the bird, she would stuff it with a dressing rich with chestnuts and redolent of sage.

After the big feast was over, Great-grandma would put all the bones, skin, and leftovers into a big pot of water, add seasonings, and then push the big kettle to the back of the stove to simmer for about four hours. She'd enrich the soup with whatever she had on hand, such as rice or potatoes, and scraps of dressing, and a few herbs. Hot and steaming, with fresh biscuits and honey, the soup warmed every child before he left for the cold trip home.

If there was enough turkey left over, this is the kind of dish that might have been served before the final favorite grandchild departed.

✿ *TURKEY WITH RICE*

    6 cups cooked, diced turkey
    ¾ cup honey
    6 tablespoons prepared mustard
    Salt
    1½ teaspoons curry powder
    6 tablespoons turkey drippings
    3 cups cooked rice

Mix honey, mustard, salt, curry powder, and drippings thoroughly. Combine lightly with diced turkey, and heat, stirring lightly. Serve over hot cooked rice. Serves 8.

*   *   *

Although Great-grandma often had turkey, other fowl from her barnyard might add to the fragrance of her kitchen. If she chose duck or goose, the bird was plucked carefully, reserving the down which would one day go into her finest pillows. Singed, drawn, and washed, the fowl was then ready to be stuffed with dressing or perhaps a combination of ingredients, such as celery, onions, or pared, quartered apples. Orange juice or lemon juice plus honey with a little mustard produced a succulent glaze.

 ## HONEYED DUCKLING

    1 5-pound duckling
    1¼ teaspoons poultry seasoning
    1 teaspoon salt
    1¼ teaspoons seasoned salt
    ¾ teaspoon paprika
    ⅓ cup lemon juice
    ½ cup honey
    1½ teaspoons dry mustard
    Onion slices
    Lemon slices

Prick cleaned duck to allow fat to drain when cooking. Combine poultry seasoning, salt, seasoned salt, and paprika and rub the inside and outside of the duck. Roast in 450° oven 15 minutes, drain off fat. Reduce oven heat to 350° and bake 1 hour, draining off fat as necessary. Combine juice, honey, and mustard, brush duck. Place onion and lemon slices on duck, using toothpicks to secure them. Continue to bake duck for 45 minutes, brushing occasionally with honey glaze.

*   *   *

Christmas at Great-grandma's house meant soft lamplight, tinsel flashing like tiny stars, a huge, fragrant, freshly cut tree hauled from the "back forty," and strung with little angels and very old and beautiful balls. It meant real candles, held with tiny clips to the thick branches and flickering with each breath of cold air that came with another arriving relative or guest. It meant popcorn and store-bought candy and nuts and oranges. It meant gifts that, somehow, Great-grandma and all the family had found time to knit, to sew, to embroider. But most of all, it meant the warmth, the glow, the kindliness of going to Great-grandma's house that everyone felt deep within his heart.

HIVE SOCIETY

Great-grandma filled her honey jars for winter as diligently as she filled her jelly and preserve glasses. In order to do this, she kept her eye on the beehives out in the orchard, feeding the bees sugar syrup in the early spring if their own supply of winter food was gone and nectar had not yet formed in the flowers. Later in the spring, she probed deep into the hives to check on the heart of the colony, the queen bee, and her household. She had to know almost as much about the life of the bee as she did about life in her own home.

She knew that if the queen was gone, the worker bees must immediately convert an egg or a larva not over three days old into a queen bee. To do this, the larva must be fed royal jelly constantly for five days by young nurse bees. During this time a bee may make 2,000 to 3,000 visits to rear each larva.

The workers then seal the larva inside the cell, and she weaves a cocoon around herself, remaining about seven or eight days more. When the new queen is ready to come out, workers help by thinning the end of the queen cell.

For the next five or six days, she stretches, runs over the combs, and hunts out and destroys any other queen cell or queen that may be anywhere else in the hive.

The dozens of idle, indolent drones, coddled for weeks by the workers, suddenly sense that the virgin queen is nearing her nuptial flight. They preen, prance, and clean their huge eyes which have about 13,000 little eyes in each globe to enable them better to see the virgin queen as she soars high into the sky.

Dashing after her, they join thousands of other drones, but only the swiftest and strongest one will catch and fertilize her. He pays with his life for his brief romance. All other drones returning to the hives are ruthlessly pushed from the hive where they starve or succumb to chill. The queen, if she survives cold winds, predatory insects, birds, and rain, returns to the hive and goes to work, laying, in two or three days,

1,500 to 2,000 eggs a day (about twice her own weight). During her life of about five years, she may lay a million eggs.

Pushing her abdomen into an empty cell and attaching an egg to the bottom of it, she can produce either worker or drone eggs. Eggs deposited in a worker cell are fertilized by the male cells received during her nuptial flight which are contained in a sac. Eggs deposited in drone cells are not fertilized and will produce only drones.

Queens are cherished by their retinue of twenty-two feeders and by the entire household while she is performing her egg-laying job proficiently. She is constantly attended by body-guards who caress her so devotedly that they may rub her thorax bare of fuzz. However, laws are brutal in the insect world, and should she fail, she is immediately replaced by a new queen. Fifteen or twenty workers will cluster about the queen in a tight ball and remain there until she starves. This "balling," as it is called, is also done to dispose of a newly introduced or extra queen.

When the queen is laying, attendants, facing her like spokes in a wheel, feed her royal jelly every time she rests, usually about every twenty minutes, each meal lasting three minutes. This revitalizes her so that her egg-laying may continue. Since only young bees, not over twelve days old, can manufacture this royal jelly in their heads, she is always attended by the young.

Great-grandma might well envy the queen's lack of worries about the care of her nursery and household. The queen's children take complete charge, becoming air conditioners if necessary, to keep the temperature of the brood nest at about 93 to 95 degrees. By fanning with their wings and bringing water for evaporation, they control summer heat and humidity. In winter, they mass close together for warmth, the queen being protected and fed first even if it means all the other bees must die.

All other chores except egg-laying are also taken care of by the worker bees. The newly hatched babies devote their first three weeks of life to household duties, cleaning the brood cells, feeding the larvae, making wax, building comb, storing pollen, taking nectar from arriving bees and storing it, guarding the entryway from enemies, and cleaning refuse from the hive. At last, they graduate into field bees. They may average ten flights a day to gather nectar, more if they gather pollen, since it is lighter.

A honeybee can fly between ten and fifteen miles an hour and carry a load equaling her own weight. By comparison, an efficient airplane can carry only a quarter of its weight in cargo.

As did Great-grandma, the bee knows the value of honey for energy. A pinhead-sized drop will whirl her wings for a quarter of a mile. If nectar flow is good, she can suck up a load in a minute, and fill the pollen baskets on her legs in three minutes.

When she returns to the hive, she may eat a bit and rest briefly, or a house bee may feed her and send her on her way. She could fly about 4 million miles at about seven miles an hour on the energy produced from a gallon of honey if she were able to live long enough. However, she will fly fourteen miles an hour with her honey sack full and her two pollen baskets loaded.

She may visit hundreds of flowers to obtain one load of nectar, and during her lifetime she may contribute the sum total of half a teaspoon of honey, that lifetime lasting, during the peak of work, only four to six weeks.

However, bees do not go out for the day's work without first receiving news from scout bees who fly to locate fields, meadows, or orchards filled with nectar or pollen-bearing flowers, which may be miles away. And as in any human household, good news means excitement and the bees excitedly communicate their good news by dancing. According to many scientists who have studied the dancing of the bees, concise information is given about the newly discovered nectar. By furiously wriggling their abdomens, or by weaving or turning in dizzying circles, or by walking either fast or slow in certain directions, the bee is believed to be telling her co-workers how great the nectar flow is, in which direction, and how far away the supply is. The Austrian scientist Karl von Frisch believes the bee marks the favored flower by opening scent glands in her abdomen and leaving the pleasing fragrance for other bees to find.

Like Great-grandma, a worker bee does not neglect the

food storage problem. She gathers pollen by dashing into the flower and practically rolling in it to fill the pollen-carrying hairs. Then, leaving the flower, she scrapes the pollen from her body (even the eyes have special hairs and are cleaned with special brushes) and mixes it with a drop of honey, presses, molds, and rolls it into a tight ball, and pushes it into her back-leg baskets. Rows of hairs hold it there, with a rigid one upright in the middle for added safety. This "bee-bread' 'is fed to the young, and may be eaten by mature bees, but Great-grandma always avoided getting it into her honey as its flavor was disliked.

It takes 556 worker bees flying 35,584 miles or 1⅓ the distance around the earth to produce one pound of honey. Little wonder that millions of bees literally wear their wings to shreds providing 285,000,000 pounds a year for Americans.

If Great-grandma's hives had uneven surfaces or crevices, the bees immediately smoothed or sealed them with propolis, a glue or varnish made from resinous gummy buds of trees such as elm. They also glue their hives together with this, making them hard to separate without a knife or "hive tool."

To be sure her honey wouldn't ferment later, Great-grandma robbed her bees of their honey only when most of the honey cells had been capped by the bees. These cells, only 1/350 of an inch thick and perfectly engineered into hexagonal shape, are made from wax produced by the young bees. After gorging on honey, they hang in a living curtain, claw to claw, and as their temperature rises, flakes of wax like fish scales ooze from platelets on their bodies. When the young bees feel them oozing, they may reach for the wax, and drop to the floor with it and begin building the cell. Bees from the top of the curtain let their wax fall and retrieve it later.

Royal jelly, another product of young bees only, is a glandular secretion marvelously capable of turning a sexless short-lived worker in its larval stage into a mature queen who may live ten to twenty times as long as the worker.

Great-grandma, ever on the alert for swarming possibilities, learned to hunt for queen-bee cells deep within a hive and cut them out. If one queen cell escaped her knife and if the hive was overcrowded (80,000 is a very full house, 35,000 to 45,000 being an average), she knew that soon the old queen would swarm, taking perhaps 35,000 workers with her and enough honey from Great-grandma's store to begin a new home.

Great-grandma avoided antagonizing her bees by staying away from them on cool, cloudy days, or after a chilly rain, or after a honey flow had been suddenly interrupted. She knew light-colored clothes bothered them less than dark, that strong odors irritated them; that when one bee stung her, its odor drew many more bees who also would sting. Quick movements in front of the hive or in the workers' flight path always brought quick reactions as horses with switching tails learned.

In Great-grandma's day, bee plants such as dandelion, maple, elm, willow, and clovers were abundant, and insecticides which now kill millions of bees were virtually unknown. Today's beekeepers must be ever on the alert to find new bee pasturages in cultivated crop areas, or to grow nectar-bearing plants if possible. In spite of the world need for food which the bee makes possible to satisfy through pollination, the life of the honeybee is precarious.

However, given a chance, she will continue to gather nectar and pollen for her household's use during the long, cold days of winter, huddling ever closer to the queen to warm her and give her food.

When spring comes again, and the buds break from their long nap, and the sap runs clear, the survivors will venture forth once more as they have done for thousands of years. The queen will once more glue tiny eggs to the bottom of fragile cells; drones will hatch once more and bide their time, and the organized life of the honeybee will repeat itself, giving man abundant crops and a healthful, energy-filled sweet.

two

VEGETABLES WITH A DIFFERENCE

IN THE WINTER, GREAT-GRANDMA WAS OFTEN HARD PUT TO find new ways to prepare her home-grown and preserved vegetables, and her numerous chores left little time to experiment.

With spring, fresh sunshine opened a whole new world of renewed faith. The fragrance of freshly plowed fields, of garden areas, surged through tired bodies like a freshet. No time was lost in planting the dark, rich earth.

When the first young plants appeared, Great-grandma was out in her garden before the early dewdrops had vanished, filling her enormous apron with sweet young peas, crisp lettuce, golden baby carrots, or the earliest tender leaves of spinach or beets. Sometimes she wandered across the new meadow grass where golden mustard waved in the breeze and gathered a mess for the family's spring tonic.

Tiny baby beets, new peas cooked in their young pods, red shiny radishes, and slender onions added fragrance and color to a table grown weary with winter's food.

Spring on the farm was a time of renewal, a time for gladness and joy, but a time when work came with the dawn and ceased long after the sun had sunk from sight.

Adding honey to vegetables harvested early for that fragrant first spring taste added a flavor and aroma that appealed to all. Carrots not liked any other way disappeared quickly if cooked with a touch of honey.

❀ CARROTS AND HONEY

> 5 to 6 carrots, peeled and cut into ½-inch slices
> ¼ cup margarine or butter
> ½ cup honey
> 2 to 3 tablespoons chopped parsley
> Salt and pepper to taste

Drop the carrots in boiling salted water, cook till tender, drain. Melt margarine and add remaining ingredients, blending well. Heat carrots in sauce and serve. Or carrots may be put into a greased casserole, the sauce poured over, and baked, covered, in a 350° oven 20 to 30 minutes. *Variation:* ¼ cup of prepared mustard may be added to sauce if desired. Serves 8.

*   *   *

Great-grandma never peeled a young carrot. Scrubbing off their soft coating was all that was necessary. She figured the young carrots needed 30 minutes to cook, old ones 45. Seasonings such as parsley and chives grew at her doorstep. Sometimes she added a gill of meat stock to every pint of cooked carrots.

❀ HONEY-ALMOND CARROTS

> 1 pound carrots
> 2 tablespoons butter or margarine
> 1⅓ tablespoons flour
> ⅔ cup milk
> 2 tablespoons honey
> Salt to taste
> Toasted almonds

Cook carrots in boiling water until tender, drain. To make the sauce, melt margarine, add flour and stir until smooth, add milk slowly. Add honey and salt, cook until thickened, continuing to stir. Add to carrots, sprinkle with nuts, and serve. Serves 8.

*   *   *

The most delectable carrots of the year a century ago were those that were thinned from the rows of growing carrots. Young, succulent, they helped in two ways: by giving remaining carrots a chance to grow larger, and giving the family an earlier-than-usual treat.

Ginger, honey, lemon juice, sugar, butter, orange juice or peel all may give a gourmet touch to recipes for carrots.

CARROTS, GOURMET STYLE

    3 dozen small whole carrots, scrubbed
    ⅔ teaspoon salt
    ½ teaspoon ginger
    ⅓ cup margarine or butter
    2 tablespoons honey
    ⅓ cup frozen orange juice concentrate, thawed
    Grated orange peel
    Parsley

Cook carrots in boiling water until tender, drain. Mix salt with ginger. To make the sauce, melt margarine in a skillet and add all the other ingredients. Add carrots and heat, turning often to glaze. Serves 6.

*   *   *

Now and then especially fine flavored butter was needed for vegetables. After Great-grandma "worked" out the buttermilk from freshly churned butter, she put in one teaspoon of clear honey to about 3 pounds of butter. She could not taste the honey, but it improved the flavor.

✿ CARROTS, DELICIOUS

    3 cans carrots, cut up, drained, and slightly mashed
    1½ cans (8-ounce) crushed pineapple
    3½ tablespoons butter or margarine
    3½ tablespoons honey
    2 tablespoons brandy
    Salt to taste
    Dash of lemonade
    Sprinkle of mace

Heat carrots, and add all remaining ingredients. Serves 6.

✿ HONEY-BUTTERED CARROTS

    2 pounds carrots
    ½ cup (¼ pound) butter
    ¼ cup honey
    1 to 1½ teaspoons grated orange peel

Cook carrots until tender in salted water, drain. Whip the butter until light and fluffy. Gradually add the honey, beat smooth. Stir in orange peel. Serve over carrots. This sauce is also delicious over cooked beets, waffles, or pancakes.

✿ HONEY BUN CARROTS

    2 10-ounce packages carrot nuggets frozen in butter sauce
       in cooking pouches
    2 tablespoons honey
    ¼ teaspoon parsley

Slip frozen cooking pouches of carrot nuggets in butter sauce into about 3 cups boiling water. Bring to second boil. Cook 16 minutes, turning several times to ensure complete cooking. Do not cover pan. Remove flavor-tight cooking pouches by grasping extra-long flaps. Open, drain butter sauce into serving dish, quickly stir in honey and parsley. Add hot carrot nuggets, tossing lightly to coat. Serves 4 to 6.

*   *   *

While we now freeze, can, or buy fresh vegetables all year, this was impossible at the turn of the century. Aside from canning, carrots along with other root vegetables were usually stored in sunken hogsheads, casks, or large dry-goods boxes, or in dry barrels or bins. They were then filled with fine dry sand or road dust, which was shaken down around the vegetables until the container was full. Or they might be covered with a foot of meadow hay or straw over which enough earth was thrown to protect them from freezing.

❁ MORE SIMPLE HINTS FOR DELICIOUS CARROTS:

- Prepare carrots, cut in fingers or chunks, and cook in boiling, salted water until tender. Drain, arrange in a baking dish, and drizzle honey over the top. Sprinkle with chopped mint or marjoram and grated cheese. Reheat and brown under the broiler or in a very hot oven.

- To dress up leftover carrots, mix together a little melted butter, about the same amount of honey and a sprinkling of chopped parsley. Add the carrots and heat uncovered for 2 to 3 minutes, stirring carefully until the carrots are well glazed.

- Here is another glaze that you can use on carrots or onions: Combine ¼ cup honey, 2 tablespoons sugar, 1 tablespoon butter, 1 tablespoon lemon juice, 1 tablespoon Worcestershire sauce, 1 teaspoon vinegar, ¼ teaspoon salt and ⅛ teaspoon pepper; stir and boil 1 minute in skillet before adding 3 to 4 cups of cooked vegetables. Simmer vegetables in glaze until heated through.

❁ HONEY-SAUCED BEETS

2 cups diced or sliced beets, cooked or canned
1 tablespoon cornstarch
½ teaspoon salt
1 tablespoon water or beet juice
¼ cup honey
1 tablespoon butter or margarine
2 tablespoons vinegar

Heat beets, drain. Mix cornstarch and salt, blend in water. Add honey, butter, and vinegar. Cook over low heat, stirring constantly until thick. Add sauce to beets, and let stand ten minutes to absorb flavors. Reheat. Serves 4 to 6.

* * *

To Great-grandma, clean, soft cistern water and honey vinegar were two important ingredients in preparing vegetables, the one to boil them in, the other to pickle or sauce them. While making the honey vinegar, a good test for its strength was to put an egg in it. If the egg floated, breaking the surface in a spot about as large as a dime, it was about right. Aside from water and honey, fruit juice or yeast was sometimes necessary to hurry the fermentation. Then warmth and air were important, too, and the whole process was hastened by allowing the honey water to trickle slowly over cypress shavings so as to expose the mixture to the air as much as possible.

 ### GLAMOROUS BEETS

1 1-pound can diced beets, drained
3⅓ tablespoons margarine or butter
2½ tablespoons honey
2 tablespoons prepared mustard
1¼ teaspoons Worcestershire sauce
Salt to taste

Combine all ingredients except beets, and simmer over low heat until smooth. Add beets and heat. May be heated on top of range or put into a 350° oven 10 to 15 minutes. Serves 4.

ORANGE AND LEMON BEETS

3 pounds fresh beets or 2 cans (1 pound 1 ounce)
¼ cup lemon juice
½ cup orange juice
2 tablespoons wine vinegar
2 tablespoons honey
1½ tablespoons cornstarch

SEASONINGS

¼ cup butter
½ teaspoon grated orange peel (optional)
½ teaspoon grated lemon peel (optional)

Prepare, cook, drain, and slice fresh beets into ¼-inch slices. If canned sliced beets are used, drain well. In a saucepan,

combine fruit juices, vinegar, honey, cornstarch, and seasonings. Stir until smooth. Bring to boil, stirring; continue cooking until sauce is thick and clear. Add beets, butter, and fruit
peel. Heat to serving temperature. Makes 6 servings.

*   *   *

Cleaning vegetables fresh from the garden was important.
Great-grandma kept two utensils to clean root vegetables: a
small stiff brush and a square of rough burlap. The brush
scrubbed earth from every crevice. Burlap was also used as
a cleaner. For new potatoes, she merely washed them and
then gave them a good rubbing with the burlap which took
all the skin off. Carrots, parsnips, and salsify also required
scraping after the burlap treatment.

SWEET POTATOES ROYAL

6 medium sweet potatoes, unpeeled, cooked in salted water
Salt to taste
3 tablespoons margarine
4 tablespoons orange juice
4 tablespoons honey
Dash of cinnamon, if desired

Peel cooled potatoes and cut into halves or thirds lengthwise.
Add salt if necessary. Place in shallow baking pan. Combine
remaining ingredients, heat slowly, and pour over potatoes.
Bake 20 minutes in 400° oven, basting frequently with sauce
in pan. Serves 6.

ORANGED SWEET POTATOES

7 to 8 sweet potatoes
½ cup orange juice
1⅓ teaspoons orange peel
½ cup margarine or butter
¾ cup honey
¼ cup brown sugar
Salt to taste

Peel raw potatoes, slice lengthwise, and brown in butter or
margarine. Put into casserole, adding remaining butter in pan,
and pour over combined remaining ingredients. Bake at 450°,
covered, for about 30 to 40 minutes. Remove cover, baste, and
continue baking until tender, basting frequently. Serves 6
to 8.

*   *   *

Leftover sweet potatoes were never wasted a century ago. The mashed potatoes were sweetened with honey, then raisins, which had been soaked in boiling water for five minutes and drained, were added. Baked in a moderate oven until hot, they added a new taste thrill for the next meal.

HONEY-GLAZED SWEET POTATOES

>   5 or 6 sweet potatoes, boiled
> ½ cup honey
> ½ cup orange juice
> ⅓ cup butter
>   1 teaspoon salt

Arrange peeled, sliced potatoes in greased casserole, spooning the combined remaining ingredients between layers. Bake at 375° about 30 minutes, basting frequently. May also be cooked in heavy griddle on top of range. Serves 6.

COMPANY SWEET POTATOES

>   4 or 5 sweet potatoes
>   1 cup pineapple juice or 1 9-ounce can crushed pineapple
> ¼ cup margarine
> 1¾ teaspoons salt or to taste
> ¼ teaspoon cinnamon
>   1 egg, slightly beaten
>   2 teaspoons brown sugar
> 1½ tablespoons honey
>   12 dates, cut up
>   8 large or 32 small marshmallows

Cook potatoes in salted boiling water until tender. Pare and mash. Combine all remaining ingredients with potatoes except sugar, honey, and marshmallows, beating until creamy with mixer or spoon. Place in 8-inch round baking dish, sprinkle top with combined sugar and honey, press marshmallows on top, and bake in 350° oven about 30 minutes or until marshmallows are golden brown.

*   *   *

Canned sweet potatoes take on a new flavor when whipped until light and fluffy. Add honey and cinnamon to taste, spoon into a well-buttered casserole and top with slices of pineapple. Bake in a moderate oven, 350°. Or add orange juice instead of pineapple, a bit of rind, and the pulp from an orange.

Pile mashed mixture into the hollowed-out orange shells, and heat in a hot oven or under the broiler until browned. For an added treat with mashed sweet potatoes, add pecans or nuts, when prepared as above. A piece of marshmallow may top the whole.

✿ QUICK CASSEROLE

```
4 medium sweet potatoes, cooked, and halved, or leftovers
1 can luncheon meat, 12-ounce size
4 canned pineapple slices, drained
2 tablespoons brown sugar
1 cup pineapple syrup from pineapple slices
1¼ tablespoons cornstarch
Salt to taste
2 to 3 tablespoons butter
¼ cup sherry (optional)
2 tablespoons honey
```

In greased 10″ x 6″ x 2″ baking dish, arrange potatoes, meat, and pineapple in layers. Combine all remaining ingredients except butter, sherry, and honey, mixing the cornstarch with the sugar and salt, before adding to the liquid. Cook, stirring, until thick and clear, about 4 minutes. Add butter, sherry, and honey, and pour over layers in baking dish. Bake, uncovered, in 375° oven about 35 to 40 minutes, basting occasionally with sauce. Serves 4 to 6.

*   *   *

Ginger and yams make an excellent dish when you must use canned ones.

✿ HONEY GINGER YAMS

```
3 1-pound cans yams, drained
¼ cup water
1½ teaspoons orange peel
½ cup honey
1 teaspoon salt
4 tablespoons margarine
1 tablespoon lemon juice
1 teaspoon crystallized ginger, finely chopped
```

Combine all ingredients except yams and lemon juice in large skillet; heat. Add yams and cook until yams are hot, stirring gently. Add lemon juice and serve. Delicious with lamb. Serves 6.

*   *   *

Storing pumpkin and squash for winter use was a problem for Great-grandma. Unlike many vegetables, they had to be kept rather cool and dry. If they could not be packed in straw in the barn, or hung by the stem from the ceiling in a storeroom, they were stored in the attic or upstairs in the house. Cooked pumpkin was often used as a side dish, eaten either with thick cream after the sauce was seasoned with honey and spices, or without cream. Its aroma filled the kitchen with memories of Thanksgiving and pumpkin pie. Winter squash was cooked the same way, their uses interchangeable, even for baking purposes.

HUBBARD OR ACORN SQUASH, HONEYED

    3 acorn or Hubbard squash to serve 6
    ½ cup honey
    ½ cup butter, melted
    2½ tablespoons sweet chowchow
    Salt and pepper to taste
    1 clove garlic, crushed
    ¾ tablespoon chili powder

Cut acorn squash in half, remove seeds and fibers. Put in shallow baking pan, cut side down, and bake 30 minutes in 375° oven. Turn squash upright, drain, continue baking another 15 minutes or until tender. Mix remaining ingredients and put a teaspoon of sauce into hot squash hollows and serve immediately. Serves 6.

HONEYED ACORN SQUASH

    3 acorn squash
    5 tablespoons margarine, melted
    ⅓ cup honey
    ½ teaspoon salt
    ⅓ teaspoon cinnamon
    ¼ teaspoon ginger

Cut squash in half, remove seeds and fiber. Put in shallow baking pan, cut side down, add ½ inch of water, and bake 30 minutes in 375° oven. Turn squash upright, and drain liquid.

Combine remaining ingredients and pour into squash hollows. Bake 15 minutes or until tender, basting frequently with sauce. Serves 6.

✿ GLAZED WINTER SQUASH

    ½ medium-sized squash, or enough to serve 6
    2 tablespoons honey
    2 tablespoons brown sugar
    2 tablespoons lemon juice
    1 teaspoon salt or to taste
    ½ cup butter, melted

Cut squash into small pieces and peel. Place in greased shallow baking pan. Add remaining ingredients to melted butter and pour over squash. Cover and bake at 400° about 30 minutes; remove cover, and bake about 15 minutes longer, basting occasionally until tender. Serves 6.

* * *

Great-grandma cooked early tender stalks of such plants as sea kale, pokeweed, wild mustard, cowslips, burdock, chicory, and spinach for greens. She figured it took about a peck of greens for a family of six.

✿ SPINACH RING

    1 teaspoon honey
    ½ cup medium-thick cream sauce
    3 tablespoons melted butter
    Salt and pepper to taste
    Dash of nutmeg, if desired
    2 cups cooked spinach, drained

Mix honey with cream sauce, add melted butter, and seasoning. Gently combine with spinach. Fill a greased ring mold (small size) and heat in 350° oven until thoroughly heated. Turn onto platter and fill with creamed tuna or chicken, creamed eggs, mushrooms, or crabmeat. Garnish with pimiento. Serves 4.

* * *

Great-grandma's family always waited eagerly for "roasting ear" time, a time when corn could be stripped from green husks, rushed to boiling water, and served succulently sweet, dripping with freshly churned butter. When the tall plants showed signs of aging, and when rows of corn were at their peak, she often allowed the young folk to plan a husking-bee. With huge tubs of corn waiting to be husked, the young people arrived from near and far for a gala evening. Not all the corn found its way into the tubs. Some of it was flipped toward a favorite boy or girl, a familiar tune played in a different key. With final dessert, the young people might pound the yard in a quick square dance or play a favorite game. At last they trooped homeward, over meadow and trail, by horse or cart, or by foot, a happy evening behind them. And Great-grandma's golden ears of corn were waiting to be preserved, canned or pickled.

✿ FRESH CORN SAUTÉ

    3 tablespoons butter
    1 medium onion, chopped
    1 medium green pepper, diced
    4 cups fresh corn kernels, cut from cob
    ¼ cup water
    1 tablespoon honey
    1 teaspoon salt
    Freshly ground pepper
    2 tablespoons chopped pimiento
    ½ cup grated cheese or crumbled, cooked bacon

Melt the butter in a medium skillet with cover. Sauté the onion and green pepper until tender. Add corn, water, honey, seasonings, and pimiento. Cover and cook over low heat stirrings several times until corn is crisp-tender. Serve hot with cheese or crisp cooked bacon. Serves 6.

*   *   *

Drying corn for winter took many hours during harvest-time. It could be done many ways, such as cutting corn from the cob and drying it thoroughly in pans in the oven. Or it could be husked, cleaned of silk, dipped in boiling water, or steamed over a colander. Or the kernels could be shaved from the cob, laid on earthenware platters, sprinkled with ½ cup sugar to 3 quarts of corn, stirred well, then placed in a medium-hot oven for 10 minutes. It was then removed and spread to dry in a drying rack or under a hotbed sash, then sealed in tight jars or boxes in a dry place. When required for use, the corn was soaked first in lukewarm water.

Corn might also be pickled to bring a new flavor to long winter months by taking off the outer husks, leaving the corn well covered with the inner husks, and tying them tightly at the top end. The ears were then packed in a clean firkin or cask and covered with strong brine. When needed, it was soaked first in fresh water twelve or more hours before using.

CABBAGE DELIGHT

3 cups coarsely chopped cabbage
1½ cups cubed carrots, fresh or canned
½ cup chopped onion, or one small onion
1½ cups chopped celery
2 cups hot water
1 tablespoon honey
1¼ teaspoons salt
¼ cup oil

Combine vegetables (if using canned carrots, add later). Add remaining ingredients, mixing thoroughly. Cook gently until just tender, 12 to 15 minutes. Serves 8.

* * *

Not accustomed to wasting any leftovers, our forefathers often used leftover boiled cabbage for breakfast by stirring in a little melted butter, pepper and salt, and 3 to 4 tablespoons of cream. The whole was then heated in a buttered frying pan, and stirred until smoking hot. The mixture then stood just long enough to brown slightly on the underside. Sometimes a couple of beaten eggs were added, and the whole turned upside down on a flat serving dish. The cabbage was extra tender because during the boiling a generous pinch of soda was added, not only tenderizing it, but keeping it as green as when it was brought from the garden.

Onions were used fresh when young and small, dipped in salt and eaten out of hand, or combined in salads. They were also used as a main vegetable all year round.

❁ ONIONS EN CASSEROLE

    3 cups small onions
    ⅓ cup honey
    ½ cup catsup
    1½ tablespoons butter or margarine
    Salt to taste

Cook onions in salted water ten minutes. Drain and put them in a baking dish. Mix honey, catsup, and butter and pour over. Cover and bake about an hour in 350° oven, basting occasionally. Uncover for last 15 to 20 minutes if too juicy. Serves 6. *Hint:* Omit catsup and add a little sherry and slivered almonds.

*   *   *

Great-grandma believed in soda for many things, including indigestion. She also believed in putting a pinch of soda in all her green vegetables while they were boiling. This tenderized them, kept their fine color (peas especially), and caused leaf vegetables such as cabbage to cook in half the usual time.

Onions were favored for health reasons. They were especially beneficial for brainworkers and nervous invalids, the very people who, she felt, were the least likely to eat them. To kill the disagreeable odor of onions on the breath, she suggested chewing and swallowing grains of roasted coffee. To remove the odor from her pans, she used wood ashes or sal soda, potash, or lye in boiling water.

❁ BAKED BEANS, SPANISH STYLE

    ½ cup coarsely chopped onion
    1 medium green pepper, diced
    1 clove garlic, finely chopped
    2 tablespoons butter
    2 cans (1 pound 12 ounces) baked beans, undrained
    ½ cup hot or seasoned catsup
    ¼ cup honey
    1 cup grated sharp cheese
    ½ cup dry bread crumbs
    Salt, pepper, paprika

Sauté onion, green pepper, and garlic in butter until tender. Remove from heat; add to beans, catsup and honey. Pour into

2-quart casserole. Combine cheese, crumbs, and seasonings; spoon over bean mixture. Bake uncovered at 350° until mixture is hot and top is browned (about 45 minutes). Makes 8 servings. Freezes well.

*   *   *

Dried beans were one of the staples a century ago. Picked months before, when the bean shells were shriveling on the vines, when the warmth of summer had given way to the first nip of fall, when potato vines lay brown and corn stalks rustled wearily in the restless breezes, the beans filled gunny sacks until the time was found to thresh them. Pounded with flails to free the dry, crisp shells, or stamped on, the beans at last were poured from one container to another letting the wind whisk away the shells. Day after day, the beans were thus cleaned, the final picking out of foreign material done by hand. They were then put into mouse-proof buckets or jars and stored in a dry place. Should they become infected with bugs, they were put into a coarse sack or basket and dipped in boiling water for a minute or two, then hung up to dry.

TASTY HONEY BEANS

1½ pounds dried white beans, thoroughly washed
3 tablespoons margarine
⅔ cup honey
2½ to 3 teaspoons salt, or to taste

Bring beans to a boil in 8 to 10 cups of water and boil 3 minutes. Turn off heat and let beans stand one hour, covered. Continue cooking until tender, adding more water if necessary, so that at the end of cooking time there will be about one cup of water remaining. Add remaining ingredients, mix gently, and simmer until most of liquid is absorbed, leaving beans juicy, about 15 to 20 minutes. Serves 8.

Other suggestions: Add honey, mustard, and a bit of ground ginger to canned baked beans.

In your regular baked bean recipe, substitute honey for the molasses or for part of the brown sugar.

✿ HONEY BAKED BEANS

¼ cup fat or salad oil
2 cups chopped onion
1 pound ground beef
1 teaspoon salt
1 cup tomato catsup
2 tablespoons prepared mustard
2 teaspoons cider vinegar
½ cup honey
2 cans pork and beans in tomato sauce
1 can kidney beans, drained

Heat fat in skillet. Add onions, simmer until golden yellow. Add ground beef. Stir with a fork while onions brown slightly. Add remaining ingredients. Pour into a bean pot or a 2-quart casserole. Bake in a hot oven (400°) for 30 minutes. Makes 8 servings.

✿ LIMA BEAN CASSEROLE

½ package frozen lima beans
1 (no. 2) can kidney beans, drained
1½ (no. 303) can baked beans
½ pound pork link sausage
¼ pound ham
1½ teaspoons salt, or to taste
Pepper
¼ teaspoon mustard
¼ cup catsup
½ can (8-ounce) tomato sauce
1 tablespoon honey
1 tablespoon brown sugar
⅓ cup chopped onion

Cook lima beans ten minutes, drain, and mix with other beans. Put sausage in a small amount of water in skillet, cover, and simmer 5 minutes. Drain and brown. Dice sausage into 2 or 3 pieces each and cut ham into small cubes, add to beans. Combine all other ingredients and add to beans. Spoon into casserole, bake uncovered 1 hour in 400° oven. Serves 6.

*   *   *

Even as today, ants were troublesome when sugar and honey were around. Housewives were advised that a heavy chalk mark laid a finger's distance from the sugar box or honey jar all around, leaving no space uncovered, would prevent ants from giving further trouble.

✿ LIMA BEANS, SAUCED

2 cups lima beans
1 teaspoon mustard (dry)
1 teaspoon sugar
1 teaspoon honey
¼ cup margarine
1 teaspoon lemon juice
Salt

Cook beans in boiling salted water 20 to 30 minutes (if frozen, follow directions). Drain, reserving ½ cup of water. Combine mustard and sugar, bring to boil, and simmer 2 minutes. Add honey, beans, margarine, and lemon juice. Reheat. Serves 4 to 6.

✿ EASY LIMA BEANS

½ pound sliced bacon or ham
1 cup sliced onion
2 (1 pound 4 ounces) cans butter beans (or 4 cups cooked lima beans)
1 tablespoon honey
1 tablespoon brown sugar
⅓ cup liquid from beans
Salt to taste
Pepper if desired

Cut bacon or ham into pieces, fry till crisp in large skillet; drain, reserving 3 tablespoons fat. Add onion and sauté 5 minutes. Add beans and all remaining ingredients, and simmer uncovered 20 to 30 minutes or until most of liquid has been absorbed. Serves 6.

*　　*　　*

The first green beans of the season were simply cooked, with a bit of bacon or bacon fat or perhaps fresh butter at Great-grandma's house. As the season wore on, cream might be added or a little onion in a rich cream sauce. As the beans matured, the time came when the crop must be rescued for winter. If the beans were to be put up green, they might be packed in jars between layers of salt, and sealed. To use, they required freshening in clear water for several hours, the water changed often. Or they might be pickled, or canned. However, to save a huge crop from deteriorating in the garden, large "bean picking" or "bean stringing" parties were held. This meant rollicking young folks full of laughter and fun stripping the vines, lugging gunny sacks from the garden to the yard where, in a huge circle, they strung and broke the beans, hardly realizing they worked as they joked, told stories, and threw bits of beans at each other. Great-grandma knew all about such fun as she scurried to set out food for the starving young. It was like living a bit of her own life over again.

SWEET AND SOUR GREEN BEANS

2 pounds green beans
2 cups boiling water
1 teaspoon salt
Bacon or bacon fat to season
4 tablespoons sugar
¼ cup honey
2 tablespoons soy sauce
2½ teaspoons cornstarch
⅓ cup vinegar
3 to 4 tablespoons pickle relish
½ cup cold water

Place beans, broken in 1-inch pieces, in saucepan, add boiling water, salt, and bacon fat. Cover, and cook until tender, about 15 to 20 minutes. Combine remaining ingredients and add to undrained beans. Cook until slightly thickened, stirring gently. Serves 8.

*   *   *

Parsnips were a great boon as a winter vegtable a century ago. They needed no last-minute storing as did so many vegetables. If the climate was moderate, parsnips were left in the garden all winter as freezing tended to improve their flavor. If the winter was severe, they could either be buried in a deep pit in the garden or pulled late and laid side by side in rows and covered with six to eight inches of coarse straw, leaves, or chaff.

❁ HONEYED PARSNIPS

    5 to 6 medium parsnips (about 1½ pounds), peeled, sliced
        lengthwise, then cut in small pieces
1¼ teaspoons salt, or to taste
    4 tablespoons honey
    4 tablespoons margarine, melted

Place parsnips in boiling salted water and cook until tender, about 15 to 20 minutes. Drain. Add honey to margarine in large skillet, cook until bubbly, stirring constantly. Add parsnips and simmer, covered, over low heat, for 4 to 5 minutes. Turn if necessary. Serves 6.

GREAT-GRANDMA, THE CANNY CANNER

The garden in Great-grandma's day yielded herbs which also were a part of winter's store. Gathered early, at their peak and in dry weather, herbs were picked over and dried as quickly as possible, either in a slow oven or under a hot-bed sash. After drying on thin sheets of blotting paper and turned occasionally, they were screened through a sieve to remove dust and other impurities, the stems removed, and the leaves stored in glass bottles.

Roots of plants, many to be used for medicinal purposes, were usually gathered in the spring, dried after being brushed free of dust and rinsed in cold water, and then strung together. The drying might be done in the sun or in a slow oven. Nasturtium seeds from the flower gardens joined the winter harvest. Seasoned with mace and white peppercorns, sweetened slightly, and covered with scalding vinegar, they substituted for capers.

Canning was an endless summer chore. If Great-grandma ran out of jars, she could make her own by selecting the largest bottles she had, washing them in coal ashes and soapy water. In an emergency, rubber jar rings were replaced by rings cut from blotting pads. If she needed waterproof paper to use for covering fruit jars, she made them by brushing linseed oil over paper, then suspending it over a line to dry. Almost-worn-out rubber rings were often doubly sealed around the jar by a mixture of melted black rosin, beeswax, and fine ivory black.

Containers for jellies or preserves were often made by dipping a piece of tarred rope, or other large soft cord, into coal-oil, and tying it around a bottle about an inch below the neck. After wiping off any surplus oil, she lit a match to the string, and the top of the bottle broke off at once. She used brandied papers or cotton batting for jar covers to keep out all "life germs," then pasted over a sheet of notepaper to prevent mold and fermentation. The brandied paper was made by dipping a piece of tissue paper in brandy and laying it close to the surface of the contents of the jar.

Because Great-grandma believed brass kettles contained acetate of copper, a dangerous poison, she avoided using them for preserves, especially if the product was allowed to stand in them. To test for this brass canker, she put a teaspoon of the preserves in a cup, and poured 30 drops of vinegar over it, stirring well with a bright, clean knitting or darning needle. If poisoned, the needle turned red where it touched the preserves. To be further assured, she allowed the needle to stand in the preserves six to eight hours.

When boiling fruit like apples, she often placed grape leaves in the bottom of the kettle to "green" the fruit.

At last, come winter, Great-grandma could eye her precious food for months ahead—the shining jars in the pantry, the cool dry vegetables and fruits in the root celler, the orange squash and pumpkin in the storeroom or attic, the golden honey in the cupboard—and know that, at last, she was ready for the cold blasts of winter, the chill of sharp winds.

HONEY IN GREAT-GRANDMA'S MEDICATIONS

Great-grandma's life seldom included doctors. Their arrival meant a life hovering near death, or an emergency that defied the neighborhood women's advice, Great-great-grandma's treatments, and medications that might include a pumpkin-seed emulsion or a tea made from the roots of the wild cherry.

Not that she didn't believe in doctors. They simply weren't nearby or on call, neither when needed in childbirth nor usually in the event of death itself. Neighbors helped neighbors during upsets, long illnesses, or the last throes of life.

"Sitting up" was a household word. It meant that when emergencies came, women took turns sitting up all night with the ill, giving the mother rest. It also meant sitting up with the dead in the darkened, closed-off room of the house; applying a cloth wrung with vinegar to the still face in an effort to ward off the dark color; it meant dressing the body, placing it in the newly hewn coffin (Great-grandpa helped here), draping the sheet over, and placing pennies on the eyes to keep them closed.

Keeping her family well was a demanding though rewarding task. In her cupboards were such items as finger stalls, bags for poultices, court plasters, as well as castor oil, calomel, cascara sagrada, Epsom salts, limewater, Jamaica ginger, paregoric, ipecac, quinine, flowers of sulfur, and sweet spirits of niter. Other important drugs included alum, carbolic acid, borax, charcoal, arnica, turpentine, and peroxide. Mustard, oil silk, flaxseed, linseed oil, and bran were needed for poultices. Ammonia, sweet oil, whiskey, and brandy were kept handy.

Children's ailments were a chief worry. For their stomach cough, as digestive upsets were called, Great-grandma dug down to the roots of a wild cherry tree, peeled off a handful of bark, put it into two cups of water, and boiled it down to a teacupful. This tea was then added to a quart of honey, and given to the patient every hour or two, a teaspoonful each time. If the child had worms also (which was often thought to be the case) the worms were pretty apt to be disposed of, as they were thought to have no love for the wild-cherry flavor.

For tapeworm, pumpkin seeds were peeled and an emulsion made by adding them to honey and water. Half the dose was taken in the morning while the patient fasted, and the remainder, half an hour later. After three hours, castor oil was given to bring about results.

The honey croup remedy was considered infallible in all cases of mucous and spasmodic croup. It called for 2 ounces of raw linseed oil, 2 drams of tincture of bloodroot, 2 drams of tincture of lobelia, ½ dram of tincture of aconite, and 4 ounces of honey. This was given every 15 to 20 minutes by the half or whole teaspoon.

For whooping cough, regular coughs, or colds, Great-grandma was likely to turn to horehound leaves boiled in soft water in a bell-metal kettle until the liquor was strong. After straining, the desired amount of honey was added, then the whole boiled until the water had evaporated. It was then cooled in a shallow vessel or pulled like taffy. For the relief of whooping cough paroxysms, fumes of carbolic acid and turpentine were inhaled.

Honey was considered a natural foe of dyspepsia and indigestion, and against constipation in babies, children, and adults if taken regularly.

For a constant tickling in the pit of the throat, just where the Adam's apple projects (this was called "old people's cough," caused by phlegm), Great-grandma took a fair-sized onion—a good, strong one, was advised—and let it simmer in a quart of honey for several hours, and then strained it. She administered a teaspoonful frequently. Relief was dramatic.

Honey and tar made a good cough medicine. A tablespoon of liquid tar was put into a shallow dish and placed in boiling water until the tar was hot. A pint of honey was added and the mixture stirred well for half an hour, adding a teaspoonful of pulverized borax meanwhile. Corked well, it kept until used.

Ulcerated chilblains and chaps of the "teats" were treated with a preparation of olive or cottonseed oil, rosin of Swiss turpentine, beeswax from Great-grandma's own bees, powdered root of alkanet, *balsamum peruvianum*, and gum camphor.

Boils, bruises, and burns were common ailments. Honey, mixed with equal parts of flour and a bit of water, became a gentle poultice or salve to keep out air and to heal.

Because colds were often thought to be "swallowed" down the throat instead of coming from contact with someone else with a cold, various recipes were in the repertoire. A cup of honey mixed with the juice of a lemon and a tablespoon of sweet oil was given by the teaspoon for a cough. If, however, the cold settled on the chest, a much-feared complication, Great-grandma might boil a quart of pure spring water, add as much camomile as could be grasped in three fingers, add three teaspoonfuls of honey, and cover the whole tightly. While hot, it was put on a table for the patient to inhale its fumes after a woolen cloth had been placed over his head and the vessel. After the mixture had cooled, the patient was put into a warm bed.

Another cold recipe called for alum and honey to be dissolved in sage tea for sore throat; slices of fat bacon or salt pork boiled in hot vinegar and applied to the throat were also recommended. When the throat felt better, it was wrapped in soft flannel. Powdered borax sniffed up the nostrils was also good for a cold in the head.

If lung trouble developed, a strong decoction of horehound herb sweetened with honey was used. And for consumptive night sweats, the body was sponged nightly in salt water. Hemorrhages of the lungs or stomach were checked by small doses of salt.

Beeswax was used in preparations for various kinds of wounds. For inflamed wounds, the wax was dissolved in sweet almond oil or in olive oil, or in cottonseed oil. In an emergency, the beeswax was dissolved with fresh, unsalted butter. For other types of wounds, wax was mixed with turpentine and essence of turpentine.

In the long, cold winters, frostbite was common. Ears, fingers, or toes were wrapped in honey which rapidly reduced the swelling and no danger was supposed to occur.

Chapped lips came with the winds and the sun. For this, white wax, spermaceti, and honey were heated and mixed well. Oil of almonds was added in a thin stream, and the mixture was removed from the fire and stirred until almost cold. It was then perfumed with any essence oil according to taste. If necessary, only honey, perfumed, might be used on the lips.

For a lip salve, beeswax and sweet almond oil were mixed, and for cold sores, unsalted butter, grated beeswax, juice and pulp from ripe grapes, and a chopped apple were simmered until all were dissolved; benjamin and storax and alkanet root were then incorporated, the whole strained through fine linen, remelted, and finally poured into jars or molds for use.

Corns on feet were as painful a century ago as now. One remedy called for beeswax melted with white pitch, then acetate of copper mixed with Venice turpentine was added.

Bees' stings were treated with such things as common earth mixed with water to the consistency of mud and then bound on as a bandage. Or crushed plantain leaves were applied when no water was near. Soda, moistened, might also be used.

Bees' stings were, however, used for various ailments in Great-grandma's day. Rheumatism, leprosy, and eczema were all believed to be relieved by direct bees' stings administered as medication. Such stings were also thought to be effective in drunkenness and hard drinking. Intoxicated persons, it is said, were quickly sobered by bees' stings.

Mouthwashes were deemed necessary as an antiseptic and recommended especially after the use of a silk thread, tooth-pick, or toothbrush for cleansing the teeth. Honey was an important ingredient in both toothpaste and mouthwashes. Pastes were made by rubbing up the dry materials to a fine powder in a mortar and moistening them slightly with alcohol or perfumed toilet water before adding honey to form a paste of the right consistency. The mixture was then either beaten with an eggbeater or mixed on a piece of glass or marble.

Mouthwash ingredients might include cuttlefish bone, borax, tannic acid, camphor, alum, castile soap, orris root, saltpeter, mucilage, aqua ammonia, tincture of soap bark, and red coral, plus essential oils or essences. The latter prevented fermentation or effervescence. In an emergency, Great-grandma filled tooth cavities with a temporary filling of gutta-percha after first cleaning the cavity with boric acid water or a solution of peroxide of hydrogen. Great-grandma was prepared for every type of emergency.

Tooth tartar was removed by mixing muriatic acid, water, and honey. To use, a toothbrush was wet with the prepara-tion and briskly rubbed on the blackened teeth. In a mo-ment's time they whitened, and the mouth was then instantly washed out so that the acid would not act on the enamel of the teeth. This was to be done only occasionally.

Girls disliked freckles then as now. Great-grandma took equal parts of honey and cream from the pantry, mixed well, and spread it on her face and hands. If she put it on her hands at night, she wore gloves to bed.

Children's warts were treated by washing the hands with

water sweetened with honey, or by applying a honey plaster.

Because of constant work, Great-grandma's hands became rough, chapped, and dry. Just as modern women do, she tried various methods to soften them. Sometimes she eased them after a day's family washing by moistening them and then rubbing in honey. A final wash in bran water gave further relief. Finding little time for daytime care, she often rubbed honey on her hands at night, put on large gloves, and in the morning washed them with soap followed by a gentle rubbing of oatmeal or cornmeal.

Her hand-softening recipes included a simple one of honey and sal soda, heated with water. Or she might mix a quarter of a pound of butter, a wineglassful of rose water, the yolks of two eggs, and a tablespoon of honey. Ground oatmeal was added to make a paste the consistency of butter. Applied at night, she wore gloves to protect her handmade quilt.

If honey were in short supply, beeswax was used, mixing it with equal parts of white mutton tallow, unsalted butter, and stoned raisins. This was simmered until the raisins were dried up but not burned, then strained into molds to cool. Even though it smarted when applied, it healed work-worn, burning hands.

With so many uses of honey in her medications, Great-grandma would doubtlessly have agreed with Sir J. More, London, who in 1707 wrote:

> Honey is of subtil parts, and therefore doth pierce as oyl, and easily passeth the parts of the body; it openeth obstructions, and cleareth the heart and lights of those humors which fall from the head; it purgeth the foulness of the body, cureth phlegmatick matter, and sharpeneth the stomach; it purgeth those things which hurt the clearness of the eye, breedeth good blood, stirreth up natural heat, and prolongeth life; it keepeth all things uncorrupt which are put into it, and is a solid medicament, both for outward and inward maladies; it helpeth the grief of the jaws, the kernels growing within the mouth, and the squinancy; it is drank against the biting of a serpent or a mad dog; it is good for such as have eaten mushrooms, for the falling sickness, and against the surfeit. Being boiled, it is lighter of digestion, and more nourishing.

There were certain precautions, however, that Great-grandma believed should be observed. A person should not enter a sickroom while perspiring because open pores absorbed germs as the body cooled. Nor should he sit near a person with a contagious disease if he had an empty stomach. Furthermore, sitting between a fire and an ill person would transmit the disease because the fire attracts the vapors.

She had other hints too. Hot bags of sand relieved neuralgia, while powdered rosin stopped bleeding from cuts. An application of mustard relieved pains in the side promptly, and warm borax water removed dandruff. Cod-liver oil's flavor could be changed to the delicious flavor of fresh oysters if the ill person would drink a large glass of water poured from a vessel in which nails had been allowed to rust.

Obviously, the word "specialization" had never been heard of a century ago. Day-to-day living required diagnosing, medicating, and nursing whenever the need arose. Great-grandma was the comforting presence, giving all the energy she had in a day that ended only when she slept.

three

SALADS FOR EVERY OCCASION

WHILE IT MAY SURPRISE SOME OF US, SALADS WERE AN IM-
portant part of Great-grandma's busy life. Winter salads
made use of canned and perhaps leftover foods, as well as
stored root vegetables from the root cellar or storeroom;
springtime meant eagerly awaited leaf lettuce, red radishes,
tiny onions, the first crisp leaves of dandelions, mustard, beets,
and spinach. Gathering a basketful of the dewy plants, she
plunged them into cool water freshly pumped, or drawn up
from the well beside her kitchen door.

With honey from her beehives, herbs sprouting fresh from
the small herb garden, and vinegars made flavorful with chervil, nasturtium, cucumber, sweet basil, chives, summer savory,
garlic and peppers, she transformed simple ingredients into
delectable foods.

✽ TOSSED SALAD, DIVINE

3 quarts mixed greens, washed, drained, and dried. Break into
   bite-sized pieces
1 cup cauliflower, raw
4 tomatoes, wedged
½ cup crumbled blue cheese
Salt and pepper to taste
4 slices cooked bacon, crumbled
Honey French dressing (see below)

Combine all ingredients except seasonings and dressing, refrigerate. When ready to serve, add seasonings, dressing, and toss lightly. Serves 8 to 10.

HONEY FRENCH DRESSING

.1 teaspoon dry mustard
1 teaspoon salt or to taste
Dash of pepper
2 tablespoons honey
⅓ cup vinegar
1 cup oil

Combine dry ingredients, blend in honey and vinegar. Slowly add oil, beating constantly. Makes 1⅓ cups.

*   *   *

Pollination of vegetables by honeybees was as important long ago as today. If the weather turned cold or wet, bees would not be able to visit the flowering plants. Cucumbers, squash, and pumpkins, among other plants, require bees to transfer the pollen from plant to plant. Otherwise the crop would fail, something Great-grandma could ill afford. Today, thousands of bee colonies are hauled from one place to another, and from state to state, to ensure crop successes.

✽ TOSSED SALAD WITH SESAME

2 quarts salad greens, washed, and broken into pieces
3 to 4 tomatoes, wedged
1 medium sweet onion, sliced
3 to 4 tablespoons toasted sesame seeds
¾ teaspoon salt
Dash of pepper
1 to 2 cups garlic croutons
Honey French Dressing (see above)

Mix greens with tomatoes, onion, and sesame seeds. Refrigerate. When ready to serve, add seasoning and dressing and top with croutons. Serves 8 to 10.

* * *

Other crops that require visits by bees in order to produce heavy crops are cabbages, tomatoes, carrots, cauliflowers, radishes, beans, and such vegetables as celery, asparagus, and peppers. In fact, bees were and still are the most efficient and only dependable pollinators, because they visit flowers more methodically than any other insect, never leaving one kind in the garden or orchard until all nectar and pollen are gone. Neither do they destroy the plant by eating it as other kinds of insects often do.

PIQUANT SALAD

Salad vegetables such as tomatoes, asparagus, cauliflowers, cucumbers, lettuce, raw carrots
½ cup mayonnaise
½ cup fresh lemon juice
¼ cup honey
¼ teaspoon prepared mustard
Paprika
Extra seasonings if desired

Combine all ingredients except vegetables, and shake or blend well. Spoon over vegetables. Makes 1¼ cups dressing.

SPRING SALAD BOWL

Salad vegetables such as broken lettuce, sliced radishes, wedged tomatoes, chopped parsley, shredded carrots
1 teaspoon salt

Sprinkle salt over vegetables, and toss with following dressing:

Juice of 1 lemon
1 tablespoon vinegar
1 tablespoon Worcestershire sauce
½ cup catsup
1 cup salad oil
½ teaspoon salt
½ teaspoon paprika
1½ teaspoons celery seed
¼ chopped onion
¼ cup honey

Combine all ingredients, adding honey last. Beat thoroughly and chill. Makes 2 cups.

SPINACH GARDEN TOSS

>1 head lettuce, broken into pieces
>1 cup spinach, washed and broken
>1½ cups shredded carrots
>⅓ cup celery, diced
>1 bunch radishes, sliced
>2 or 3 sliced green onions
>Tangy French Dressing below

>*TANGY FRENCH DRESSING*

>1 10½-ounce can condensed tomato soup
>¼ cup lemon juice
>2 teaspoons prepared mustard
>2 tablespoons vinegar
>2 teaspoons Worcestershire sauce
>⅓ cup honey
>1 teaspoon salt
>¾ teaspoon paprika
>1 tablespoon grated onion
>¾ cup salad oil
>1 clove garlic, crushed

Combine all ingredients except oil and garlic and beat well. Slowly add oil, beating constantly. Add garlic and chill. Toss lightly with vegetables when ready to serve. Makes 1½ pints.

 EARLIEST SPRING SALAD

4 cups shredded fresh spinach, ½ cup sliced green onions, 1 cup sliced radishes, and salt to taste. Toss with above dressing or your own favorite.

*   *   *

Vinegars were special ingredients at the turn of the century. Great-grandma made her own, both for table use and for pickling. One method was to mix 2 gallons of good cider with 2 pounds of new honey, pouring it into a cask and letting it stand 4 to 6 months. If she had a shortage of honey by spring, she put 4 gallons of warm rainwater (or cider, if she had it), 1 gallon of molasses, and 2 quarts of yeast in an open cask. The top was then covered with thin muslin and the whole left in the sun, covering only at night or when it rained. With water, the vinegar was ready in three to four weeks. With cider, it was ready in a week.

AVOCADO SALAD

1 head lettuce, washed and broken
3 tomatoes, wedged
1 bunch scallions, chopped
1 bunch watercress, broken
1 to 2 cucumbers, sliced
8 to 10 radishes, sliced
1 avocado, cut in wedges
Salt to taste

Combine all ingredients except salt (taste for salt). Toss with *Tangy French Dressing* opposite, or a favorite one. Serves 8.

* * *

Fresh chervil leaves, considered one of the finest herbs, were often added to a breakfast salad to give a delicious flavor. Chervil vinegar was made by filling a bottle half full with fresh or dry leaves, then filling it with good vinegar and putting it in warm water. After bringing the water to the boiling point, the bottle was removed, cooled, and corked. It was ready for use in two weeks. Other vinegars such as nasturtium, sweet basil, summer savory, garlic, and pepper were also made by the above method.

CRISP SALAD BOWL

Salad greens such as lettuce, chicory, endive, and watercress, broken into bite-size pieces
Tomatoes, wedged
Sliced cucumbers
Sliced radishes

Combine and serve with *French Dressing*, below.

FRENCH DRESSING

1 teaspoon salt
¼ teaspoon dry mustard
Dash of pepper
⅓ cup vinegar
2 tablespoons honey
2 tablespoons catsup
1 clove garlic
¾ cup salad oil

Place all ingredients in a jar or bottle, cover, and shake vigorously. Yield, 1⅓ cups.

SALAD GREENS WITH YOGURT DRESSING

Tear salad greens into bite-size pieces and toss with *Yogurt Dressing*. Season to taste.

YOGURT DRESSING

1 cup plain yogurt
2 tablespoons lemon juice
2 tablespoons honey

Beat thoroughly.

*   *   *

Great-grandma served salad not only for texture and flavor, but also for the medicinal value the vegetables were thought to have. Spinach, she felt, had a direct effect upon the complaints of the kidneys as did dandelion. Asparagus purified the blood, and celery acted admirably upon the nervous system and was a cure for rheumatism and neuralgia. Furthermore, tomatoes acted on the liver while onions, garlic, leeks, chives, and shallots stimulated the circulatory system, and the consequent increase of the saliva and gastric juices promoted digestion.

VEGETABLE SALAD WITH SOUR CREAM

1½ cups sliced cucumber
1½ cups sliced onion
1½ cups sliced tomatoes
1 cup sour cream
1½ tablespoons vinegar
1½ tablespoons horseradish
1½ teaspoons honey
3 teaspoons sugar
1½ teaspoons salt

Place the vegetables in a bowl. Combine the remaining ingredients and beat thoroughly. Serve on escarole. Serves 8.

SWEET-SOUR SALAD

Salad greens

DRESSING

4 slices bacon
¼ cup honey
⅓ cup vinegar
Dash of salt and pepper

Dice and cook the bacon. Remove from skillet and add honey, vinegar, and seasonings. Heat to boiling. Return browned bacon to skillet. Pour over salad greens and toss.

* * *

A century ago (and perhaps much later), red onions were considered an excellent diuretic, and the white ones helped in cases of insomnia. Both were thought to be a tonic and to be nutritious. Onion poultices were common. Thus did conservative Great-grandma use her produce for "complaints."

COLORFUL VEGETABLE SALAD

1 cup shredded red cabbage
1 cup shredded green cabbage
1 cup baby beets raw, sliced
1 cup baby carrots, sliced
1 cup chopped onions
1 cup diced green pepper
1½ cups chopped celery

Serve with the following dressing:

¼ cup vinegar
2 garlic cloves, sliced
1 10½-ounce can condensed tomato soup
2 tablespoons honey
1 cup chili sauce
1½ teaspoons salt
1 teaspoon dry mustard
½ teaspoon paprika
Dash of red pepper
2 tablespoons sugar
½ cup salad oil

Pour vinegar over garlic cloves, cover, let stand 1 hour, remove garlic. Add remaining ingredients, shake well. Yield, 2¾ cups.

✿ COLESLAW PIQUANT

    3 to 4 cups chopped green cabbage
    ½ cup diced green pepper
    1½ tablespoons diced pimiento
    1 teaspoon celery salt
    1 teaspoon grated onion
    ⅓ cup vinegar
    3 tablespoons oil
    1 teaspoon salt
Dash of pepper
    ½ teaspoon dry mustard
    1 tablespoon sugar
    1 tablespoon honey

Combine cabbage, green pepper and pimiento in bowl. Combine remaining ingredients in jar and shake thoroughly. Pour over vegetables and toss. Serves 6. Salad may also be used to stuff tomatoes.

*   *   *

Great-grandma's salad repertoire wasn't confined to the simpler efforts. Her oxcheek salad was an example. After the bones were removed, the oxcheek was rubbed thoroughly with salt and put into a deep dish in salt for a week. It was then boiled with vegetables and a sprig of parsley for five hours on her wood-fired range. Keeping the liquor for soup, she diced the meat with potatoes, beet root, and celeriac blanched for five minutes in salt water. She then added dressing, and a spoonful of capers.

✿ GREEN BEANS DELICIOUS

    1 can (1 pound) whole green beans
    ⅓ cup white wine vinegar
    2 tablespoons honey
    ½ clove garlic
    ½ teaspoon seasoned salt
    1 teaspoon minced onion
    1 tablespoon butter

In a saucepan, combine liquid from beans with vinegar, honey, garlic, salt, and onion. Simmer 5 minutes, add beans, heat; just before serving, add butter. To serve cold, add 1 tablespoon salad oil and cool in liquid. Serves 4.

COOKOUT BEAN SALAD

  1 can (1 pound) cut yellow wax beans (2 cups)
  1 can (1 pound) green beans
  1 can (1 pound) green lima beans
  1 can (1 pound) red kidney beans
  1 medium green pepper, thinly sliced
  1 medium red onion, thinly sliced in rings

  ½ cup honey
  ½ cup red wine vinegar
  1 teaspoon seasoned salt
  ½ teaspoon dry mustard
  1 tablespoon freeze-dried chives

Drain all beans thoroughly; add green pepper and onion. In a large jar with lid, combine balance of ingredients. Shake well to blend, toss lightly into bean mixture. Cover; marinate overnight, stirring once or twice. Drain and serve. Makes 12 servings.

*   *   *

Radishes were not always added to salads. Oftentimes they were scraped and then put on the table in glasses of ice water to keep them fresh-tasting and crisp.

HARVEST MOON SALAD

  1 clove garlic
  1 head lettuce or romaine
  2 cups cooked ham and turkey strips
  ½ pound sharp Cheddar cheese, cut in strips
  4 hard-cooked eggs, cut in rounds
  1 green pepper, cut in strips
  1 bunch radishes, sliced
  ½ teaspoon salt
Freshly ground pepper

Rub salad bowl with cut clove of garlic. Separate leaves of romaine or head lettuce. Arrange in bowl as lining. Arrange on top of lettuce: ham, turkey and cheese, hard-cooked eggs, green pepper, and radishes. Sprinkle with salt and pepper. Serves 4 to 6. Serve with dressing (recipe on next page).

PERK-UP SALAD DRESSING
(low calorie)

1 can (10½-ounce) tomato soup, undiluted
1 clove garlic, minced
2 tablespoons honey
½ teaspoon salt
¼ teaspoon crushed dill or tarragon
⅓ cup fresh lemon juice or white wine vinegar

In blender container, combine all ingredients. Cover and blend 5 seconds. Chill before serving over salads. Yield, 1½ cups.

* * *

When Great-grandma wanted prepared mustard, she added a few drops of oil or sweet oil to the mustard. This prevented the unsightly black surface that forms inside the jar and the paste retained its bright yellow color to the end.

ZIPPY DIP DRESSING

(*Complements garden vegetables.*)

2 tablespoons honey
2 tablespoons prepared mustard
4 tablespoons wine vinegar
1 cup undiluted evaporated milk
1 teaspoon salt
¼ teaspoon pepper

Stir all ingredients briskly in a bowl. Let stand for 15 minutes to thicken. Makes about 1¼ cups of dressing. For variety, mix with tuna or hard-cooked eggs. Set out chilled raw vegetables, and dunk.

FRUIT SALADS AND DRESSINGS

Although Great-grandma painstakingly preserved and stored large quantities of fruit for winter, by spring her jars and crocks were nearly empty.

With the advent of the first wild strawberries she went with a tin pail or lard bucket to collect fruit to replenish her stores. Throughout the summer and late into fall she gathered and preserved blackberries, wild blueberries, red raspberries and blackcaps, red and black currants, and gooseberries from her kitchen garden, juicy red cherries, plums, pears and apples.

By fall she was burned by sun and wind, her hands deeply stained from handling fruit, but well satisfied that her storeroom and bins were full of delicious fruit that would supply her family with summer's bounty throughout the long winter ahead.

❈ FRUIT SALAD, SUPREME

Strawberries
Fresh pineapple, cut in spears
Blueberries, washed and stemmed
Bananas, peeled and sliced
Lettuce

When ready to serve, line serving plate with lettuce and arrange fruits in attractive pattern. Serve with:

POPPY SEED DRESSING

3 tablespoons honey
1 tablespoon lemon juice
1 tablespoon poppy seed
¾ cup dairy sour cream

Fold first three ingredients into sour cream. Chill several hours. Makes 1 cup.

❈ A TASTE OF ISLAND DRESSING

1 cup pineapple yogurt
3 tablespoons honey
1 tablespoon fresh lemon juice
3 small, firm-ripe bananas, peeled and sliced

In blender, combine yogurt with honey, lemon juice, and banana slices. Cover and blend at low speed about 10 seconds. Makes about 2½ cups. Keeps one day, refrigerated. If blender is not used, combine yogurt with honey and lemon juice. Grate bananas directly into yogurt mixture and stir to blend thoroughly. *Variety hint:* Makes a wonderful dip for chunks of fruit.

ZIPPY HONEY DRESSING

>1 cup bottled oil and vinegar dressing
>¼ cup honey
>¼ cup catsup

Combine all ingredients in jar or cruet; cover tightly and shake until well blended. Refrigerate unused portion and shake again before using. Makes about 1½ cups.

AVOCADO-ORANGE-GRAPEFRUIT SALAD

>Wedges of avocado
>Orange sections
>Grapefruit sections
>Romaine lettuce

Alternate fruit on plate. Serve with *Honey Fruit Dressing*, below. Garnish with watercress.

HONEY FRUIT DRESSING

>1 tablespoon honey
>½ to 1 teaspoon grated orange rind
>½ teaspoon salt
>1 3-ounce package cream cheese
>1 tablespoon lemon juice
>¼ cup orange juice
>Dash of paprika and cayenne

Add honey, rind, and salt to softened cream cheese. Blend thoroughly. Add fruit juice slowly, stirring constantly. Add paprika and cayenne. Makes ¾ cup.

*   *   *

Great-grandma's cream cheese was made from "loppered" (clabber) cream to which she added salt. Poured into a linen bag, it drained three days, the bag being changed every day. Then she packed it into a wooden cup or mold with holes in the bottom, and pressed it for two hours.

❁ FRUIT WITH FLUFFY DRESSING

Bite-size fruits in a big salad bowl
Lettuce

Top any combination of fruits with:

FLUFFY HONEY DRESSING

2 eggs
½ cup honey
¼ cup lemon juice
2 tablespoons frozen orange juice concentrate, thawed
Dash of salt
½ cup heavy cream, whipped
2 teaspoons lemon peel

Combine beaten eggs with honey, lemon juice, orange juice concentrate, and salt. Cook over low heat until thickened and cool. Fold in whipped cream and lemon peel. Serve over fresh fruits. Makes 2 cups.

❁ FRUIT RING SALAD

Slice rings from peeled honeydew or cantaloupe. Place on nasturtium leaves or other greens, and fill centers with fresh fruits such as oranges, grapefruit, strawberries, pineapple, fresh or canned, apples, melon balls, bananas, and grapes. Garnish with a strawberry or Bing cherry, and serve with:

WHIPPED CREAM DRESSING

1 cup whipping cream
2 tablespoons honey
½ cup sour cream
Vanilla if desired

Whip cream until almost stiff, continue whipping and add honey in a fine stream. Fold in sour cream and vanilla. May be refrigerated for two days.
Or: Whip ½ cup heavy cream sweetened with honey as above, fold into 1 cup mayonnaise.
Or: To 1 cup mayonnaise add 2 tablespoons each of orange and pineapple juice, first mixed with 2 tablespoons honey.

*   *   *

Keeping milk sweet was often a struggle at Great-grandma's house. A bit of grated horseradish helped. In order to have cream, she poured milk into broad shallow pans, set them upon swing shelves to avoid the possibilities of drowned mice, and kept the cellar dark to discourage flies. In twelve hours she skimmed cream from the milk for the table. In twelve hours more she skimmed again unless she was short of milk and this went into the stone jar or crock for churning. She churned as soon as possible after the cream "loppered" or thickened. She was particularly cautious about allowing strong-flavored substances near her milk or butter as odors were absorbed so quickly.

BANANA FRUIT SALAD

Salad greens
Bananas peeled and sliced lengthwise
Fruit combinations such as melons, strawberries, oranges, pineapple

Serve with:

FRUIT SALAD DRESSING

½ cup creamed cottage cheese
1 tablespoon honey
¼ cup pineapple juice
Dash of salt
¼ teaspoon celery seed

Blend all ingredients together until smooth.

*   *   *

Great-grandma remembered the children in making her salads. They especially enjoyed those fixed with her cottage cheese which was often made while her range was burning low. The pan of sour or loppered milk was put on the back of the stove where it was not too hot and left to scald until the whey rose to the top. Care was taken that the milk never reached the boiling point as this made the curd hard and tough. Then, a clean cloth or towel was placed over a sieve, the whey and curd poured into it where, covered, it drained for two or three hours. The curd was removed to a bowl, chopped fine, and salt, butter, and enough sweet cream added to suit her taste. The consistency was that of putty. With her hands, she made the cheese into little flattened balls or put the whole into a deep bowl, and added more cream to thin it. Often it was eaten sweetened and with milk.

In some kinds of cheese making, rennet was used. In making her own, she followed this formula: Clean the stomach of a calf as soon as it is killed, scouring inside and out with salt. When perfectly clean, tack upon a frame to dry in the sun for a day. Cut in squares and pack down in salt or keep in wine or brandy. When ready to use, it must be soaked half an hour in cold water, washed well, and put into the milk to be "turned" or soured, tied on the end of a string.

SALAD FOR CHILDREN

Drained peach halves
Salad greens
Cottage cheese
Banana, split lengthwise
Peanut butter

Place peach halves on greens and fill with cheese. Spread banana with peanut butter, cut into pieces, and arrange. Serve with:

HONEY FRENCH DRESSING

1 tablespoon honey
2 teaspoons lemon juice
1 teaspoon lemon peel
½ cup bottled French dressing

Mix thoroughly.

Other children's favorites to try: Pears, bananas, blueberries drizzled with honey, warmed to thin it, then topped with a dressing made by adding ¼ cup honey to 1 cup mayonnaise and folding in ½ cup cream, whipped.
Or: Pineapple chunks, strawberries, white grapes and bananas, served with a dressing made with 1 cup heavy cream whipped, adding gradually 1 tablespoon honey and 1 tablespoon mayonnaise. Or blend in 1 tablespoon prepared mustard, omitting

mayonnaise. Or blend ¼ cup honey with ¾ cup dairy sour cream. Or try ½ cup shredded coconut blended with 2 table-spoons honey and 1 cup sour cream; add cut-up marshmal-lows to the fruit. Nuts may also be added.

✿ HEAVENLY SALAD

    8 tart apples, peeled and diced
   16 marshmallows, quartered
Maraschino cherries, drained and quartered
    1 pint whipping cream
Juice of ½ lemon
    1 tablespoon mayonnaise
    1 tablespoon honey

Combine the first three ingredients, add sugar if desired. Whip cream and fold in remaining ingredients. Toss with fruit, saving a little dressing for garnishing. Serves 8.

✿ FROZEN FRUIT DELICIOUS

    1 can (1 pound) or 2 cups fruit cocktail, drained
 1½ banana, peeled and sliced
    1 orange, peeled and sectioned (⅓ cup)
   ¼ cup halved maraschino cherries, drained
   ¼ cup nuts

Combine all ingredients, and prepare the following dressing:

    2 tablespoons sugar
   ½ cup honey
    1 tablespoon flour
   ⅓ cup lemon juice
    1 egg beaten
    1 cup heavy cream whipped
Maraschino cherries (optional)

Combine sugar, honey, and flour, bring to boil. Cook 1 min-ute, stirring constantly. Gradually stir lemon juice into egg, add a small amount of honey mixture, blend, and add the re-maining mixture. Bring to boiling point, stirring constantly, remove from heat and cool. Add salad mixture above, and fold in heavy whipped cream. Pour into tray and freeze firm, about 3 or 4 hours. Cut into serving pieces and garnish with maraschino halves. Serves 6 to 8.

FROSTED FRUIT

> 1 can (1 pound, 13 ounces) cling peach halves
> 1 cup halved, seeded Tokay grapes
> Several tiny clusters Tokays
> 1 tablespoon coarsely grated orange peel
> 3 oranges
> ¾ cup lemon juice
> ¾ cup honey
> Watercress

Drain peaches; place in large refrigerator tray or shallow pan. Add halved grapes and grape clusters. Sprinkle with orange peel. Pare and section oranges. Add to fruit in tray. Combine lemon juice and honey and pour over all. Set in freezing compartment until fruit is almost icy and the syrup mushy (about 30 minutes). Arrange watercress in shallow glass salad bowls or on plates. Arrange fruit on cress; top with the frosty syrup. Serve immediately. Makes 6 to 8 servings.

SUMMER FRUIT SPECIAL

Alternate thin lengthwise slices of peeled cantaloupe, honeydew melon, and papaya on chilled salad plates. Add wedges of fresh peeled pears and strawberries. Serve with:

AVOCADO SALAD DRESSING

> 1 fully ripe avocado
> 2 tablespoons lemon juice
> ½ teaspoon salt
> ½ cup orange juice
> 2 tablespoons honey
> ½ cup mayonnaise
> Dash of tabasco if desired

Remove skin from avocado; dice or mash, and blend with lemon juice. Add remaining ingredients. Beat, or whirl in blender until smooth. Makes 1½ cups.

*   *   *

Great-grandma battled many enemies to protect her bees and their crop. Bears, skunks, mice, yellow jackets, ants, and wax moths were a few of them. The bees themselves helped by stinging intruders. Or in some cases they balled up small enemies like mice in propolis, the gummy substance they used to seal their houses or to fill cracks. This balling not only killed the intruder, but it also eliminated all odors, thus assuring clean, fragrant honey.

ORANGE PINEAPPLE RING

    1 tablespoon unflavored gelatin
    ¼ cup fresh lemon juice
    ⅔ cup very hot water
    ⅓ cup honey
    ¼ teaspoon salt
    1 package (3 ounces) cream cheese
    1 cup fresh orange juice
    ½ cup crushed pineapple, drained (save juice for dressing
       below)

Soften gelatin in lemon juice. Add hot water, honey, and salt; stir until gelatin dissolves. Blend cheese and orange juice; stir into gelatin mixture. Chill until slightly thickened; fold in drained pineapple; spoon into 8-inch ring mold. Chill until firm. Unmold, fill center with fruit or cubes of cranberry jelly. Makes 6 servings. Serve with:

ORANGE PINEAPPLE DRESSING

    2 eggs, slightly beaten
    ¼ cup honey
    ½ cup canned pineapple juice
    ½ cup fresh orange juice
    1 tablespoon grated orange peel
    ½ cup dairy sour cream

Combine all ingredients except cream. Cook over low heat, stirring constantly until thickened. Chill thoroughly before folding in dairy sour cream. Makes 1 cup. Keeps well under refrigeration.

✿ DELECTABLE FRUIT SALAD MOLD

    1 tablespoon gelatin
    ¼ cup cold water
    ¼ cup lemon juice
    1 cup pineapple juice
    2 tablespoons honey
    ½ cup crushed pineapple, drained
    ½ cup fresh raspberries or other fruit
    ½ cup apple, diced
    ½ cup orange sections
    ½ cup heavy cream, whipped
    Dash of salt

Soften gelatin in cold water; stir over boiling water until dissolved. Add juices and chill until partially set. Add honey to fruit and fold in. Add salt to whipped cream and fold in. Chill in mold until firm. Serve with Orange Pineapple Dressing (above) or your favorite salad dressing.

* * *

Great-grandma often preferred making her gelatin from calf's feet. To do this, she cleaned them carefully, then boiled them in water (four feet to four quarts of water) until the water was reduced by one-half. Then she strained the liquor and let it stand ten to twelve hours before skimming off all fat. This gelatin was also used to make jelly.

✿ HONEY GRAPEFRUIT MOLD

    2 tablespoons gelatin
    ¼ cup cold water
    1 cup boiling water
    ½ cup honey
    ½ teaspoon salt
    1 cup grapefruit juice
    ½ cup orange juice
    ¼ cup lemon juice
    ½ cup chopped nuts
    1 grapefruit (canned grapefruit may be used)

Soak gelatin in cold water 5 minutes; add boiling water and stir until dissolved. Add honey, salt, grapefruit juice, orange juice, and lemon juice. Cool. When mixture is slightly thickened, fold in nuts and grapefruit sections. Turn into mold and chill.

❈ HONEY AVOCADO RING

    2 3-ounce packages lime-flavored gelatin
    1¾ cups boiling water
    1 teaspoon salt
    2½ tablespoons lemon juice
    1½ cups cold water
    ¼ cup mayonnaise
    2 avocados, peeled and mashed
    3 cups fresh fruit in season, if desired
    ½ cup chopped nuts

Dissolve gelatin in boiling water, add salt, lemon juice and cold water. Chill until partially set. Combine mayonnaise with avocado and nuts, add to gelatin. Pour into desired mold.

Serve with fresh fruit and *Honey Dressing 1*. Combine ½ cup dairy sour cream with ¼ cup honey and ¼ teaspoon nutmeg. Serves 8.

❈ YULETIDE SALAD

Good during holidays. No dressing needed.

    1 package (3 ounces) lemon-flavored gelatin
    1¾ cups boiling water
    2 tablespoons white wine vinegar
    2 tablespoons honey
    1 cup crushed pineapple, drained
    1 cup grated sharp cheese
    1 cup heavy cream, whipped
    Salad greens
    Pimiento or cherries

Dissolve gelatin in boiling water. Add vinegar and honey; chill until slightly thickened. Fold in pineapple, cheese, and whipped cream. Pour into individual bell-shaped molds or use a quart mold. Chill until thoroughly set. Unmold on crisp salad greens. Garnish with bits of pimiento or cherries. Serves 6 to 8.

*   *   *

"Boughten" gelatine was often disdained in the early days, especially by those who preferred to make their own from calf's feet. Many declared it was inferior because they claimed it was made of horn shavings and hoofs and the like, thereby making it no more fit to be used for cooking purposes than so much glue.

SALAD DRESSINGS FOR FRUIT SALADS, SOME TART, SOME SWEET-SOUR, SOME SWEET, BUT ALL DELICIOUS

 AVOCADO FRUIT DRESSING

    1 large ripe avocado, peeled, pitted, and mashed smooth
    1 teaspoon honey
    1 tablespoon lemon juice
    ½ cup orange juice
    ½ teaspoon salt

Gradually add all ingredients to mashed avocado, beat until smooth. Chill. Makes 1 cup.

 HONEY DRESSING 2

    ¾ cup honey
    2 tablespoons salad oil
    2 tablespoons lemon juice
    1 teaspoon paprika
    ¼ teaspoon salt
    ¼ teaspoon celery seed
    ¼ teaspoon minced onion
    ⅛ teaspoon dry mustard

Combine all ingredients, stirring well to blend. Refrigerate one hour or longer. Shake before using. Makes 1 cup.

HONEY CHEESE DRESSING

    1 8-ounce and 1 3-ounce package cream cheese, softened
    ¾ teaspoon salt
Dash cayenne pepper
    1½ teaspoons lemon peel
    ½ cup honey
    ¼ cup lemon juice
    2 cups salad oil

Mix thoroughly in electric mixing bowl the cheese, salt, cayenne pepper, and peel. Gradually add honey and juice, and finally the oil a few drops at a time. Beat until smooth and creamy. Refrigerate. Makes 1 quart.

✿ DELICATE FRENCH DRESSING

To ½ cup bottled French dressing, add ¼ cup honey and ½ teaspoon celery seeds. Makes ¾ cups.
Or: Combine ¼ cup honey, ½ cup mayonnaise, ½ teaspoon celery seed, 1 tablespoon lemon juice, and a dash of paprika, blending well, Yield, ⅔ cup.

✿ LIME-MINT FRUIT SALAD DRESSING

In a small bowl, with spoon, combine 1 3-ounce package soft cream cheese, 2 tablespoons honey, ½ cup mayonnaise until smooth. Fold in ½ cup heavy cream, whipped, ⅛ teaspoon salt, 3 tablespoons lime juice, 2 tablespoons snipped mint. Serve over chilled canned pineapple slices in lettuce cups.

✿ APRICOT-NECTAR DRESSING

    ¼ cup honey
     3 drops of tabasco sauce
    Dash of dry mustard
     3 tablespoons oil
    ¼ teaspoon salt
    ¼ cup lemon juice
    ¾ cup apricot nectar

Thoroughly combine all ingredients except lemon juice and nectar. Add lemon juice gradually, beating constantly; add nectar, beating well. Chill. Delicious on avocado or fruit. Yield, 1½ cups.

✿ PERFECT SALAD DRESSING

    ⅔ cup sugar
     1 teaspoon mustard
     1 teaspoon paprika
    ¼ teaspoon salt
     1 teaspoon celery seed
    ⅓ cup honey
     1 teaspoon grated onion
     1 tablespoon lemon juice
     5 tablespoons vinegar
     1 cup oil

Mix dry ingredients in small bowl, add remaining ingredients except oil. Beat oil in gradually, Yield, 2 cups.

✿ BANANA DRESSING LUSCIOUS

1 cup mashed banana
2 tablespoons honey
1 tablespoon lemon juice
½ cup cream, whipped

Combine banana, honey, and juice thoroughly. Fold in cream. Serve at once. Yield, 1½ cups.

✿ HONEY DRESSING 3

1 tablespoon paprika
½ teaspoon dry mustard
½ teaspoon salt
½ teaspoon celery salt
½ cup honey
3 tablespoons lemon juice
¼ cup vinegar
1 cup salad oil

Mix dry ingredients. Add honey, lemon juice, and vinegar. Slowly add oil, beating until well blended. Yield, 2 cups.

✿ TART HONEY SALAD DRESSING

½ cup honey
½ teaspoon salt
⅓ cup chili sauce
⅓ cup vinegar
1 tablespoon grated onion
1 tablespoon Worcestershire sauce
1 cup salad oil

Combine all ingredients except oil. Beat in oil slowly until well blended. Makes 2 cups.

HONEY IN GREAT-GRANDMA'S HOUSEHOLD HINTS

Near the turn of the century housewives were warned not to try to simplify housework by purchasing patent washing and cleaning preparations, or to employ dressmakers and such people as laundresses. This would not only deprive their children of the educational value of learning this work, but it would also make housework dull and monotonous.

Great-grandma might have agreed with this point of view.

With so many chores confronting her each day, and without patent washing and cleaning prepartions, her daily life could not have been monotonous. But without planning and methods and schedules of the days and weeks, it might have been overwhelming. Yet with an eye on earnings and savings, she happily approached each day, wasting nothing, taking advantage of household hints handed down or newly discovered.

Wet tea leaves, saved daily, were used to sweep carpets. Dusters were made of old material including tops of stockings. Rugs were beaten on lines with a carpet beater, or, if on the floor, were sprinkled with table salt, then swept hard. Oilcloth was cleaned with lukewarm water containing skim milk or buttermilk. For longer wear, whether on the table or the floor, beeswax and turpentine were rubbed on it.

Blankets or quilts were aired before storing for summer, then folded in paper, with hemlock or arborvitae sprigs, dry sweet flags, lavender or sachet powder scattered through the folds to keep out moths and to give an agreeable odor.

To clean window corners, she might use wings from the Thanksgiving turkeys, geese, or chickens. They were also used to wash windows because they were free from dust or lint. To polish windows or lamp chimneys, pulverized pumice stone was put between folds of cloth and the cloth then stitched to hold the powder. Vinegar might also be used.

For deep scratches on furniture, beeswax prepared from honeycomb was melted and thinned with turpentine to the consistency of syrup. This was applied with a soft cloth and polished with flannel or velveteen.

Furniture and floor polish required 6½ pounds of beeswax rubbed through a coarse grater, and 3 pounds of pearl ash, made from ashes from the fireplace, and a little water, boiled and stirred until it ceased to effervesce. Three pounds of dry yellow ocher was stirred in, the whole then poured into a tin pail having a tight cover. It was used by thinning it with boiling water to the consistency of cream, applied with a soft cloth, then polished with a weighted brush, and finally wiped up with coarse flannel.

Another furniture polish contained alkanet root and melted beeswax. After straining, linseed oil and spirits of turpentine were added.

A paste for polishing light furniture was composed of beeswax and turpentine. Rosin was added for mahogany furniture. After this was melted, Venetian red was added for coloi.

Housecleaning for holidays and family gatherings meant furniture cleaning. One method was to dissolve beeswax and a bit of sugar in a quart of strong beer or vinegar. The furniture was first washed with water or tea, then the mixture was applied with a sponge or brush. After oiling, drying, and a final polishing, the furniture gleamed.

Varnishing was a tedious job for Great-grandma. She had many methods of "killing knots" in her woodwork before refinishing, one of which was to hold a hot iron against the knot until the pitch stewed out, allowing her to scrape it off. Varnish was made by mixing resin, beeswax, and boiled hot oil until the mixture was stringy. When cool, turpentine was added. Applied in several coats, it was then rubbed down with very finely pulverized pumice stone and washed off with clear water. Then, using her bare hands, Great-grandma rubbed the whole with rotten stone and sweet oil before finally wiping and polishing with a chamois or flannel.

In cleaning feather beds, she passed the feathers into another fresh tick every two or three years, although people often slept on them for a whole generation without such renovation. The old ticking was washed, rubbed inside with a mixture of equal parts of beeswax and turpentine, then gone over with a warm iron. This prevented the feathers from being soiled by perspiration or from working through the tick.

Waxing was also done with new ticks, including pillow ticks which were later filled with feathers, dried tea leaves, curled strips of newspaper, cured grass clippings, milkweed down with the seeds removed, baked cotton batting (baking finely picked over cotton batting kept it from matting), or fancier dried rose leaves.

Washdays were preceded by soap-making. Great-grandma made both soft and hard soaps. Rosin added increased weight and bulk. A favorite family recipe called for a gallon of soft water, a pound of good stone lime, 3¼ pounds of sal soda, an ounce of borax, 2½ pounds of tallow or other animal fat (she often used fat from a butchered hog), 1¾ pounds pulverized rosin, and an ounce of beeswax. The lime and soda were gradually added to the boiling water and stirred vigorously before the borax was added. When all had dissolved, the melted fat was added in a thin stream and stirred vigorously. After the rosin and beeswax were added, the mixture was boiled and stirred until thick, then cooled in molds.

Ironing day meant hours of heating irons on a wood range or on a living room heater. It meant "doing up" yards of fine laces, ruffles, fancy work, petticoats, shirtwaists, long baby clothes, children's clothes, as well as sheets and pillowcases, linens and dish towels.

To do fine ironing it was thought by some that several kinds of irons must be used, including a 6- to 7-pound polishing iron for shirt bosoms, collars, and cuffs; a puff iron for fine tucks, puffy sleeves, and other elaborate work; a fluting iron for ruffles, and perhaps a child's toy iron for tucks, fluting, or other difficult parts of clothes. Starch was prevented from sticking to the iron by putting beeswax in a little bag of cloth or between two pieces of paper and running the iron over it.

To prevent rust on irons, a piece of beeswax was laid in a cloth, the hot iron run over it, then the iron was scoured with a cloth sprinkled with salt.

Silks and ribbons were cleaned with a mixture of gin, honey, and soft soap in a bit of water. Pieces were scrubbed, and then dipped in clean water, and ironed almost immediately. If the material was very soiled, it was also passed through a warm liquor of bullock's gall and water, rinsed well, then passed through a bit of glue and boiling water before drying on a frame.

Another cleansing mixture for clothing consisted of gum camphor dissolve in alcohol, borax, saltpeter, honey, pipe clay and beef's gall, along with hard white soap, spirits of turpentine and sulfuric ether. It was stored in a black glass bottle and tightly corked. It was judged safe for woolens, silks, and all the ordinary fabrics that Great-grandma knew, and would clean practically every kind of spot or stain likely to be on her garments.

To prevent her silks or woolen goods from turning yellow when stored, pieces of white beeswax were broken up and put in loosely folded cheesecloth, and placed among the articles, after they were wrapped in old white linen or cotton cloth.

Great-grandpa, too, used beeswax. For polishing his steel tools, the wax was mixed with oil of turpentine and boiled linseed oil. His harnesses and leather goods remained soft and pliable after waxing them with this mixture.

Most types of leather goods needed waterproofing including new shoes for the family. For this, mutton tallow and perhaps neat's-foot oil or castor oil might be added to beeswax, with coloring such as ivory black added.

For seams of leather goods a stronger solution was needed. This included India rubber, and was made with neat's-foot oil and as much Indian rubber from an old pair of rubber overshoes or boots as the oil could hold, plus mutton tallow, beeswax, and coloring. Shoelaces were much easier for little fingers to thread if the shoestrings were first rubbed with beeswax, and they came untied far less often.

When harnesses needed cleaning, which they often did, Great-grandpa used beeswax and neat's-foot oil, simmered until the beeswax dissolved, then added oil of tar. Other combinations for cleaning or waxing were black rosin and beeswax, ivory black and Prussian blue, mutton tallow and beeswax with brown sugar, castile soap jelly and indigo and turpentine. Black balls for leather dressing also had beeswax as an ingredient.

Cements were made for almost any mending chore, including knives come loose from their handles, broken china, and crockery. Grafting wax for orchards was needed. By combining and melting rosin, tallow, and beeswax, then cooling it in cold water and kneading it into a mass, enough wax was made to last for years.

Even though Great-grandma's chores filled almost every waking hour, she found time to mix toilet waters, shampoos, hair curling solutions, dainty soaps, shaving creams for the men, and creams that helped them raise a luxuriant beard. Minutes were snatched from the mending, washing, ironing, canning, sewing, and housecleaning to produce these present-day items, the ingredients which might include oils of lavender, cloves, bergamot, sage, nutmeg, rose geranium, essence ambergris, musk, tincture of orris root, and honey. Other strange ingredients were tincture of cedar wood, myrrh, Krameria, oil of neroli, oil of balm, and essence of clove gillyflower, and were often measured by drams, drops, and ounces. These mixtures when completed were usually left to stand for weeks to make a better product.

Egg yolk was an important ingredient in shampoos and was thought to help prevent gray hair. Another combination for gray hair consisted of a gallon of new milk into which was put two quarts of green tendrils of the grapevine, two pounds of honey, and a handful of rosemary. This was simmered until reduced by half. Strained through a linen cloth, it was applied frequently to the hair.

Prepartions for curling the hair included some adhesive ingredient such as beeswax which was then mixed with various oils and diluted with alcohol or water. One recipe called for a piece of white beeswax about the size of a hickory nut melted in an ounce of olive oil and perfumed with a few drops of oil of neroli.

Honey was added to both shaving creams and preparations to give luster to the hair and beard when the natural oils seemed lacking. One recipe combined honey with alcohol and glycerin as an inexpensive dressing.

Great-grandpa's razor strop was kept sleek and efficient with various dressings such as fine flour of emery and beeswax. Or the grit from a fine grindstone was collected as it gathered in the form of paste on the blade of a scythe or axe, and added to the beeswax.

Thus, Great-grandma filled her days, and avoided dullness and monotony.

BREADS, TODAY'S AND YESTERDAY'S

BREADS FRESH FROM THE OVEN: HOW MANY OF US CHERISH the memory of that delicious fragrance from our youth? To-day, the fragrance is as tempting, and a slice of warm bread, a delicate crescent roll, or a sticky cinnamon roll, is perhaps even more appreciated than in bygone days when such were daily treats, not rare events.

Here are recipes for every taste, for every occasion, whether for family or guests. How many otherwise ordinary meals are made into something very special because of an added hot bread!

Honey is an excellent sweetener for bread, because it improves both the flavor and keeping quality. Homemakers may not be aware that they can use honey in place of sugar in their own favorite bread recipes by substituting equal amounts of honey for sugar.

When measuring honey, lightly grease the cup or spoon so the honey will pour more readily. Use a rubber scraper or spatula to ensure the full measure called for.

Unlike Great-grandma who often set a sponge, made with warm water, baker's yeast, lard, sugar, soda, and flour, or one using mashed potato (preferably old potatoes as new ones were not deemed successful), today we may make quick and easy doughs or those taking a longer time.

While Great-grandma exhorted her children to knead 20 to 30 minutes in what she called "useful gymnastics" (it developed strong arms and chests, they were told), we knead lightly and sometimes not at all. Furthermore, yeasts and flours have become easier to use, and automatic ovens, refrigerators, and freezers make the whole process something less than the labor of a century ago.

ENRICHED WHITE BREAD

    2 cups milk or 1 cup milk and 1 cup water
    2 teaspoons salt
    3 tablespoons honey
    3 tablespoons soft shortening
    1 cake compresssed or dry granular yeast, soaked according
        to directions on package
    5 to 6 cups all-purpose flour

Scald milk and cool to lukewarm (80°). Add salt, honey, and shortening. Add yeast. Add half the flour; beat thoroughly. Gradually add more flour to make a soft dough. Knead on floured board until smooth and elastic, approximately 8 to 10 minutes. Place in slightly greased bowl, turn over, and cover. Let rise in warm place until double in bulk. Punch down lightly and let rest 15 minutes. Form into two loaves, and place in greased pans. Let rise until double in bulk. Bake in oven at 400° for 40 minutes or until golden brown. Makes 2 loaves, 9½ x 5½ inches.

WHOLE WHEAT BREAD

    2 cups milk
    3 tablespoons honey
2½ teaspoons salt
    2 tablespoons shortening
    1 cake yeast, compressed or granular and soaked according
        to directions on package
    5 to 6 cups flour

Scald milk and cool to lukewarm. Add honey, salt, shortening, and yeast. Add enough flour to make a soft dough, mixing thoroughly. Knead into a smooth elastic dough that is relatively dry. Place in lightly greased bowl, turn once, cover, and let rise in warm place until double in bulk, about 2½ hours. Divide dough in two equal pieces, let rest 10 minutes. Form into loaves, place in greased pans and brush tops lightly with warm water. Cover to prevent crusting. Place in warm (85°) place, and let rise to about half an inch above the top of pan, approximately 50 minutes. Bake 30 to 35 minutes at 425°. If desired, 1 cup chopped nuts or raisins may be added during kneading. Yield, two loaves, 9½ x 5½ inches.

*   *   *

Great-grandma's huge bread pans baked four to six loaves at a time. She had no worry about calories as she baked the golden loaves for her family. Sliced hot, and slathered with new honey, it was an unforgettable joy.

BRAN RAISIN NUT BREAD

    1 cup whoe bran cereal
⅓ cup raisins
    2 tablespoons shortening
⅓ cup honey
¾ cup hot water
    1 egg, unbeaten
    1 cup sifted all-purpose flour
    1 teaspoon baking soda
½ teaspoon salt

Combine first four ingredients in bowl, add hot water. Stir until shortening is mixed. Add egg and beat well. Sift together the dry ingredients. Add to bran mixture, stirring only until combined. Place in greased 9¼ x 5¼" loaf pan. Bake in 350° oven about 35 minutes or until done. Remove, cool, and slice. Makes 1 loaf.

✿ HONEY RYE BREAD

¼ cup honey
1 tablespoon salt
2 tablespoons shortening or oil
1 tablespoon caraway seed (optional)
1½ cups milk, scalded
2 packages active dry or 2 compressed yeast cakes
1 cup water
3 cups light rye flour
2½ cups sifted flour (approximately)
Melted butter

Add honey, salt, shortening, and caraway seed to milk; cool to lukewarm. Soften dry yeast in warm (110°) water; or compressed yeast in lukewarm (85°) water. Combine yeast with milk mixture; add rye flour and 1 cup of flour. Beat thoroughly. Add remaining flour to make a stiff dough. Turn dough out on floured board, let rest 10 minutes. Grease fingers before kneading until the dough is smooth and elastic. Place in well-greased bowl, turn once to bring greased side up. Cover and set in warm (80° to 85°) place to rise until doubled, about 40 minutes. Without punching down, turn out on lightly floured board; divide into two equal parts. Shape into loaves. Place in two greased 9 x 5 x 3″ pans. Cover and let rise until doubled, about 30 minutes. Bake at 350° about 50 minutes. Turn out of pans on rack away from drafts. Brush tops with melted butter.

Hint: For a chewy crust, lightly brush tops of loaves with warm water after 20 minutes of baking, two or three times at 10-minute intervals.

*   *   *

Great-grandma was proud of the even texture of her bread. "Gaping holes of diverse size," she said a century ago, "are an unerring telltale of a careless cook."

SAVORY CHEESE BREAD

    1 cup milk
    ¼ cup honey
    1 tablespoon seasoned salt
    2 packages active dry yeast or 2 compressed yeast cakes
    ½ cup warm water
    ¼ pound (1 cup) sharp Cheddar cheese, grated
    1 teaspoon dry mustard
    ⅛ teaspoon cayenne pepper
    4½ to 5 cups sifted flour

In a small saucepan, heat milk just until bubbles form around edge of pan. Remove from heat. Add honey and seasoned salt, stirring until dissolved. Cool to lukewarm. Sprinkle yeast over warm water in large bowl, stirring until dissolved. Stir in milk mixture, cheese, mustard, cayenne pepper and 2 cups of flour. Beat with wooden spoon until smooth, about 2 minutes. Gradually add remaining flour; mix in last of it by hand until dough leaves sides of the bowl. Turn dough onto lightly floured board. Grease fingers before kneading until the dough is smooth, about 10 minutes. Place in lightly greased large bowl, turn once to bring greased side up and cover with towel. Let rise in warm place (85°), free from drafts, until double in size, about 2 hours. Punch down dough, turn onto lightly floured board, shape into loaf. Place in greased 9 x 5 x 3" loaf pan. Cover loaf with towel, let rise until double, about 1 hour. Bake at 400° for 30 to 35 minutes. Cover with aluminum foil for the last 10 to 15 minutes of baking. Turn out of pan and cool on rack.

*   *   *

Great-grandma felt that children especially should eat brown bread. Dyspeptics, she thought, have long been familiar with its dietetic virtues, and, she said, if the use of it were more general, we should have fewer wretches to mourn over the destroyed linings of their stomachs. It was not only wholesome and sweet but honest. Sponge was the beginning of her bread, and she used two parts graham flour and one third white and to every quart of this she allowed a handful of Indian meal, with a teaspoon of salt, and half a teacup (about 3½ ounces) of molasses.

❀ SWEDISH RYE BREAD

(Recipe for 2 loaves.)

1¾ to 2 cups milk
3 tablespoons honey
2 tablespoons molasses
1 cake yeast (or 1 package granular yeast soaked according to directions on package)
1½ tablespoons shortening
2 teaspoons salt
1 teaspoon caraway seed
4 cups white flour (approximately), mixed with
1 cup rye flour

Scald milk and cool to 80°. Add honey, molasses, and yeast and let stand 10 minutes. Add shortening, salt, caraway seed, and enough of flours to make a smooth elastic dough. Knead until smooth and dry. Rye dough should be stiffer than white bread dough. Place in lightly greased deep pan, turn once to grease, cover, and set in warm place (85°) until double or about two hours. Divide dough in two equal pieces, round, and let rest 15 minutes before shaping in loaves and placing in greased pans.

For hearth bread, prepare a lightly greased cookie sheet and sprinkle lightly with corn meal. Place the molded loaves on cookie sheet about five inches apart and put in a warm area away from drafts, and let rise. Cover dough with plastic or damp cloth, not allowing cloth to touch dough. After about ½ hour make six cuts, ¼ inch deep, across the top of each loaf with a sharp knife. Punch about a dozen holes approximately one inch apart down through the loaf with a greased meat skewer or large fork. Both of these operations are to prevent bursting. When loaves have doubled in size, wash with a mixture of equal parts of egg white and water, and bake in a 400° oven for 45 minutes.

*   *   *

Cheap flour and laziness were at the bottom of more mishaps in the bread operation than any other combination of circumstances, according to Great-grandma's theory. It was judicious, she maintained, that one should lay in two barrels of flour at a time, and use the best flour only for the semi- or tri-weekly baking.

HONEY PRUNE BREAD

  2 tablespoons shortening
  3 tablespoons sugar
  ⅓ cup honey
  2 eggs
  1 cup sifted flour
  ⅔ cup whole wheat flour
  1½ teaspoons baking powder
  ½ teaspoon salt
  ½ teaspoon soda
  ½ cup sour milk
  ½ cup chopped cooked prunes
  ⅔ cup chopped walnuts or pecans
Orange or lemon rind

Cream shortening, sugar and honey thoroughly. Add eggs; beat until well mixed. Sift together flour, whole wheat flour, baking powder, salt, and soda. Add dry ingredients and sour milk alternately to the creamed mixture and blend. Stir in prunes, nuts, and rind. Pour into greased loaf pan, 8½ x 4½ x 2½". Bake at 350° for 1 hour and 10 minutes.

*   *   *

Without thermostats on the old wood ranges of long ago, the bare arm was the test of the oven temperature. If it could not be kept in the oven while the cook counted to thirty, the oven was too quick.

APPLESAUCE NUT BREAD

  2½ cups prepared biscuit mix
  1 cup uncooked rolled oats
  ½ teaspoon salt
  2 teaspoons baking powder
  1 egg
  1 cup honey
  1 cup Gravenstein applesauce
  1 cup golden raisins
  1 cup coarsely chopped walnuts

Combine biscuit mix with oats, salt, and baking powder. Beat egg slightly: add honey and applesauce. Beat quickly into biscuit mix. Stir in raisins and nuts. Pour batter into 9 x 5 x 3" lined, greased loaf pan. Let stand 10 minutes before baking to keep fruit and nuts from sinking to bottom. Bake at 350° 60 to 70 minutes or until done in center when tested. Cool in pan 10 minutes before removing to rack. Bread will slice better on second day. Freezes well. Yield, 1 loaf.

*　　*　　*

"Grate away the burned portions of the crust should there be such," cooks long ago advised. That was preferable to chipping with a knife.

✿ FRESH ORANGE BREAD

    ¼ cup shortening
    1 cup honey
    1 egg
    1½ tablespoons grated orange peel
    2½ cups sifted flour
    2½ teaspoons baking powder
    ½ teaspoon soda
    1 teaspoon salt
    ¾ cup fresh orange juice
    ¾ cup finely chopped walnuts

Cream shortening; continue creaming while adding honey in a fine stream. Add egg and beat well; add orange peel. Sift flour once, measure; add baking powder, soda, and salt, and sift together. Add flour alternately with orange juice, a small amount at a time to first mixture, beating after each addition until smooth. Stir in nutmeats; blend. Turn into 9 x 5 x 3″ lined, greased loaf pan; bake at 325° for 1 hour or until done. Let cool in pan 10 minutes; then turn out of pan and let stand until cold. Wrap in waxed paper or aluminum foil. Store overnight to blend flavors and for easy slicing. Makes 1 loaf.

✿ MINCEMEAT BREAD

    1 cup prepared mincemeat, plain or brandied
    1 egg
    ½ teaspoon cinnamon
    3 tablespoons honey
    ¼ cup water
    1 package (1 pound 1 ounce) nut bread mix

Combine mincemeat and egg in large bowl; blend thoroughly. Stir in cinnamon, honey, and water. Add nut bread mix all at once and stir just until blended. Do not overmix. Pour into well-greased 9 x 5 x 3″ loaf pan, bake at 350° 50 to 60 minutes or until wooden toothpick inserted in center comes out clean. Cool ten minutes, remove from pan, and cool completely before slicing. Yield, 1 loaf.

❁ DATE BREAD

½ pound (1½ cups) dates, chopped fine
3 tablespoons margarine or butter
½ cup sugar
½ cup honey
1 cup boiling water
3 cups sifted flour
½ teaspoon salt
1½ teaspoons baking powder
1½ teaspoons soda
1 egg, slightly beaten
⅔ cup chopped nuts

Combine first five ingredients and let cool. Sift dry ingredients. Add egg to date mixture. Stir into dry ingredients, add nuts. Bake in well greased and floured 9 x 5 x 3" loaf pan at 350° 50 to 60 minutes or until done. Cool thoroughly. Yield, 1 loaf.

❁ FRUIT BRAN BREAD

1 cup whole bran cereal
1 cup cut and pitted dates or seedless raisins
½ cup honey
1 tablespoon shortening
1 cup boiling water
1 egg, slightly beaten
2 cups sifted regular flour
1 teaspoon baking soda
½ teaspoon salt
¼ cup sugar
½ cup chopped walnuts

Combine bran cereal, dates, honey, and shortening in mixing bowl; add boiling water, stirring until combined. Let stand until most of moisture is taken up, about 5 minutes. Stir in egg. Sift together flour, soda, salt, and sugar. Add to first mixture together with walnuts, stirring *only until combined*. Spread in greased 9½ x 5½" loaf pan. Bake in slow oven (325°) about 50 minutes or until done. Cool thoroughly before slicing. Makes 1 loaf.

✿ COUNTRY KITCHEN FANCY BREAD

    1 package (13¾ ounces) hot roll mix
    ½ teaspoon cinnamon
    ½ cup toasted diced almonds
    ¼ cup light or dark raisins
    1 egg
    ¼ cup honey
    ¼ cup melted butter

Combine flour mixture from hot roll mix with spice, almonds, and raisins. Dissolve yeast as package directs but decrease liquid ⅓ cup. Beat egg lightly, add honey; stir egg, honey, and butter into yeast. Blend into dry mixture. Cover bowl. Let stand in warm place until dough is doubled in volume. Turn onto floured board and knead down. Shape into small round loaf; place in greased 8-inch cake or pie pan. Grease top of loaf. Let rise 30 minutes. Bake in 350° oven about 40 minutes. Cut into wedges to serve. Makes one 8-inch round loaf.

✿ ROLLS, BASIC SWEET DOUGH

(Makes about 18 rolls.)

    3 tablespoons honey
    1½ cakes yeast (or 1 package granular yeast soaked according
        to package directions)
    1 cup milk, scalded and cooled to 80°
    1 tablespoon sugar
    5 tablespoons softened shortening
    1 egg, beaten
    1 teaspoon salt
    3 cups flour (approximate), sifted

Add honey and yeast to warm milk. Let stand 10 minutes. Add sugar, softened shortening, egg, salt, and enough flour to make a smooth elastic dough. Knead until smooth. Dough temperature should be about 85°. Place dough in lightly greased deep pan, cover with plastic wrap and let rise until double in bulk, about 2 hours. Divide into convenient-sized pieces and allow a 15-minute rest period. Shape into rolls or coffee cake as desired. Let dough double in size. Bake at 375° approximately 20 minutes.

YEAST-MAKING

Yeast, so common today, was often difficult for Great-grandma to get a century ago unless she lived near a brewery or bakery. Since this was rarely the case, she made her own yeast, which she believed was better than the "boughten." She used potatoes, hops, flour, sugar, and salt, and the process took about four days. This was a self-working. yeast. If she had some yeast on hand, she would use a gill of it with the other ingredients, but omitting the hops.

Into two quarts of cold water she put four large potatoes and a double handful of hops tied inside a coarse muslin bag, and salt. She boiled this mixture until the potatoes broke apart. Removing the potatoes with a perforated skimmer, she left the water still boiling, mashed the potatoes fine with a beetle (wooden pestle), and worked in flour and sugar. She moistened this mixture gradually with hop tea from the boiling pot, stirring it to a smooth paste. When the mixture was still slightly warm, she added some lively yeast to accelerate the process, and set it aside to "work." Later, she put it into earthen jars with small mouths which could be corked, or bottled it, and stored it in the icehouse or cellar.

If she wanted to make yeast cakes, she added Indian meal to the yeast mixture and dried the cakes, either in the hot sun or by putting them in a very moderate oven, or into the oven after the fire had gone down for the night, leaving them until the next morning. When entirely dry and cold, they were hung up in a bag in a cool, dry place. One cake three inches in diameter was used for a loaf of fair size, first soaking it in tepid water until soft, and adding a pinch of soda or saleratus, and mixing thoroughly. These cakes remained good for a month in summer or two in winter.

❁ CINNAMON FILLING

(For sweet rolls and coffee cake.)

Mix 4 tablespoons sugar, 4 tablespoons shortening, and ¼ teaspoon cinnamon together. Soften to spreading consistency with milk or egg whites.

Icing: Mix 1 cup powdered sugar, 1 tablespoon honey, 1½ tablespoons boiling water, and 4 drops flavoring until smooth. Keep warm until used.

HONEY BUNS

(*Makes 18 buns.*)

    1 13¾-ounce package hot roll mix
    ⅓ cup butter
    ⅓ cup brown sugar
    ⅓ cup honey
    ⅔ cup flaked coconut
    ½ teaspoon ground cinnamon or cardamom

Prepare hot roll mix according to package directions. Let rise. Cream butter and sugar; add honey and beat until well mixed. Add coconut. Roll dough to an 18 x 12″ rectangle. Spread with one-eighth the honey mixture; sprinkle with cinnamon. Roll as for jelly roll, starting with the long edge. Pinch end to seal. Cut into 1″ slices and place, cut side down, on a buttered baking sheet. Let rise. Press down the center of the buns with a spoon and fill each depression with 1 teaspoon of remaining honey mixture. Bake at 375° for 15 to 20 minutes or until golden brown. Remove from baking sheet while warm.

HONEY BUTTER CINNAMON BUNS

(*Makes 12 buns.*)

    ⅔ cup very warm water
    1 package active dry or compressed yeast cake
    ½ cup cinnamon honey butter (see note below)
    1 egg
    ½ teaspoon salt
    2 tablespoons dry milk powder
    ¼ cup chopped mixed candied fruit or raisins
    ¼ cup chopped pecans
    2 cups sifted flour
    Additional cinnamon if desired

Measure very warm water into large mixing bowl. Sprinkle or crumble yeast over water; stir until dissolved. Combine cinnamon honey butter, egg, salt, and dry milk. Add to yeast mixture; blend well. Add fruit, nuts, and flour. Stir to mix; then beat until batter is shiny and smooth, about 2 minutes. Scrape sides of bowl. Cover and let rise in a warm place, free from drafts, until double in size about 45 minutes. Stir down and drop by spoonfuls into greased 12-muffin pan. Let rise in warm place, free from draft, until doubled, about 30 minutes. Remove from pan. Serve warm.

Note: Look for commercial Cinnamon Honey Butter at your market in the dairy case or mix together ½ cup soft butter, ¼ cup honey, and 1 teaspoon cinnamon. Stir until well blended.

 ## CHERRY WHIRLIGIG ROLLS

(Best served warm. Makes 18 rolls.)

    1 cup warm water
    1 package active dry or compressed yeast cake
    ¼ cup honey
    1 teaspoon salt
    1 egg, beaten
    ¼ cup soft butter
    ¼ cup chopped, drained maraschino cherries
    3½ to 4 cups sifted all-purpose flour

Filling: Mix together ¼ cup flour, ¼ cup honey, ¼ cup butter, and maraschino juice to moisten.

Measure warm water in large mixing bowl. Sprinkle or crumble in yeast. Stir in honey, salt, egg, and butter. Blend well, then add cherries and slowly blend in flour. Grease fingers before kneading on lightly floured board until smooth and elastic; place in greased bowl, turning to bring greased side up, cover. Let rise in warm place until double in size, 1½ to 2 hours. Punch down, turn and let rise again until almost double in size, 30 to 40 minutes. Roll out on lightly floured board into rectangle 18 x 9″. Spread surface with filling. Roll up tightly. Seal well, cut into 18 slices. Put each slice in a greased muffin tin, cut side up. Cover, and let rise in warm place, until double in size, 35 to 40 minutes. Bake at 375° 20 to 25 minutes. Serve warm with coffee.

Note: Look in the frozen food department of your market for prepared, honey-sweetened, frozen bread dough. This may be used in many recipes to save time.

❁ HONEY TWISTS

(Serves 8 to 10.)

    1 cup milk, scalded
    ¼ cup sugar
    ¼ cup shortening
    1 teaspoon salt
    1 cake fresh or 1 package granular yeast
    1 egg, beaten
    3½ cups flour, sifted

Combine first four ingredients, cool to lukewarm. Soften yeast in this mixture. Add egg. Add flour and mix to soft dough. Cover. Let stand 10 minutes. Knead on lightly floured board. Place in greased bowl, cover, and let rise in warm place until double in size. Punch down and form dough in 1" rope. Coil to fit greased ten-inch pan, beginning at the outside and working to center. Cover, and let rise until double in size. Spoon Honey Topping over top. Bake in 350° oven for 1 hour.

Honey Topping: Blend ¼ cup honey, ¼ cup softened margarine, ¼ cup sugar, ¼ cup flour, ½ cup chopped nuts.

Or: Using dough above, roll out as for jelly roll, and spread with ½ cup margarine or butter, and honey. Seal well. Cut in 1" slices, and place in baking pan which has more butter and honey and pecan halves on bottom. Let rise until double. Bake in 375° oven for 20 to 25 minutes. Let rolls stand in pan one minute after baking before turning out. If greased muffin pans are used, place ½ teaspoon butter and 1 teaspoon honey in each, with a pecan half on top.

Or: Using any sweet roll dough, roll out after its first rising into a rectangle or sheet ½" thick. Spread with softened margarine and sprinkle with brown sugar, roll as for jelly roll, seal, and cut into 1" pieces. In baking pan, melt ¾ cup margarine, softened, add 1½ cups brown sugar, 1½ cups pecans, and ¾ cup honey. Place rolls, cut side down, in this mixture. Let rise until double, and bake at 375° 20 to 25 minutes. Cool in pans 5 minutes, then invert and cool. Makes about 16.

Or: In a saucepan bring to a hard boil ½ cup sugar, ½ cup margarine, and 2 tablespoons honey. Boil two minutes. Remove from heat and stir in ⅔ cup chopped nuts and ¼ cup light cream. Cool. Roll dough into rectangle shape. Spread with half of honey mixture. Roll as for jelly roll and cut into 16 pieces. Place slices cut side down in greased 9″ square pan. With fingers flatten each slice until they barely touch one another. Let rise about ten minutes. Pour remaining honey syrup over top and bake at 400° 20 to 25 minutes.

Or: Combine three tablespoons margarine, three tablespoons flour, three tablespoons honey, and ½ cup chopped pecans. Press dough into greased 8″ square pan, and spread with honey mixture. Let rise 20 minutes, and bake at 375° about 30 minutes. Makes about 16 pieces.

* * *

In Great-grandma's day, bread was truly the staff of life. Morning, noon, or night, a plate of some type of bread was a part of the table setting as surely as was butter and honey, or salt and pepper. Every housewife rose early at dawn, knowing that she must provide either hot biscuits, rolls, or any number of kinds of hot bread for her family. If it was to be a yeast-type bread, it had probably been "set" the day before. In the morning, she added perhaps an egg, some soda, the whole beaten, and put in greased pans to rise and bake. If biscuits, she brought out her large tin pan which always had flour in it, added liquid, a bit of shortening sometimes, and seasonings with a pinch of her expert fingers. She stirred flour into this from the sides of the pan, knowing just when her dough was perfect for pinching into pieces. She formed them deftly into biscuits (seldom did she use a cutter), and snuggled them closely in her favorite pan, darkened from use. Testing the oven with her hand, she knew when the temperature was exactly right. In a few minutes, with everyone gathered at the table, hot biscuits, browned to a golden color, light as a feather, were soon smothered in freshly churned butter and honey.

❀ FRUITED COFFEE CAKE

1¾ cups milk, scalded
⅓ cup honey
2 teaspoons salt
4 tablespoons margarine or butter
2 cakes yeast, soaked according to directions on package
1 egg, beaten
5 cups sifted flour
½ teaspoon nutmeg
½ cup candied fruit
¼ cup chopped nuts

Pour milk over honey, salt, and margarine. Cool to lukewarm. Stir in yeast and egg. Add half the flour and the nutmeg, and mix thoroughly. Add fruits and nuts. Add enough more flour to make a soft dough. Knead on lightly floured board until smooth and elastic, about 8 to 10 minutes. Place in greased bowl, turn once to grease other side. Cover and let rise in warm place until double. Punch down, cover and let rest 10 minutes. Divide dough in half, and divide each half again. Roll to form a rope ½″ in diameter. Twist, and pinch two sections together to form a rope. Starting at top, form a tree shape on a greased cookie pan. Repeat with other section. Brush with melted butter, cover and let rise in warm place until double in bulk, about 45 minutes. Bake in 350° oven 25 to 30 minutes or until brown. While still warm, brush with confectioner's sugar, and decorate if desired. Makes 2 trees.

*   *   *

Great-grandma often made her own baking powder by combining 1 ounce supercarbonate soda and 7 drams tartaric acid (in powder). This was rolled smoothly and mixed thoroughly, and kept in a tight glass jar or bottle. She used one teaspoon to a quart of flour. Sometimes she combined 12 teaspoons carbonate of soda and 24 teaspoons of cream of tartar instead.

DELICIOUS COFFEE CAKE

1¼ cups sifted flour
 3 teaspoons baking powder
½ cup sugar
¾ teaspoon salt
 1 egg, beaten
½ cup milk
 3 tablespoons melted shortening

TOPPING

⅓ cup margarine or butter
⅓ cup honey
 1 9-ounce can crushed pineapple, drained
¼ cup shredded coconut or nuts

Sift together dry ingredients. Combine egg, milk, and shortening; add to dry ingredients and mix till just smooth. Pour into greased 8 x 8″ baking pan. Cream margarine and honey. Spread pineapple over batter. Spread honey mixture over all. Sprinkle with coconut or nuts. Bake in 400° oven 30 minutes or till done. Serve hot. Serves 6.

*   *   *

While bread and rolls are now made in an afternoon, Great-grandma apportioned her time in such phrases as "While getting breakfast in the morning, as soon as the teakettle has boiled, take a quart tin cup . . ." or "At noon, the day before baking, take half a cup of corn meal and pour it over enough sweet milk . . ." or "In the morning, boil 2 ounces of the best hops in 2 quarts of water half an hour. . . ."

Her phrases to describe aspects of the cooking process included: warm as new milk; setting the sponge; blood warm; make a rising; stir in the wetting; putting the bread in sponge; tolerably hot oven; butter size of an egg or walnut; pretty hot oven; small teacupsful; pinch of salt or soda. It was the touch of her experienced fingers, the feel of the dough, the gauge of the cupful, the fragrance, and the color that told her so much more than the simple phrases.

✻ HONEY TWISTS

Make up your favorite sweet roll yeast dough. After it has risen, divide in two equal parts. Use one half to make Honey Twists. Use the other half for Muffin Puffs, below.

TWISTS

¼ cup honey
¼ cup sugar
2 tablespoons softened margarine or butter
2 tablespoons flour
½ cup chopped nuts

Form dough into roll 1″ thick; coil to fit greased 8″ cake pan, beginning at the outside and working to center. Cover and let rise in warm place until double in size, about 1 hour. Combine above ingredients and spoon over dough. Bake at 375° about 25 minutes. Makes one 8″ twist.

MUFFIN PUFFS

½ cup soft butter
1 teaspoon cinnamon (optional)
½ cup honey

With remaining dough, fill greased muffin pans half full of dough. Cover and let rise until double in bulk, about 45 minutes. Bake in 375° oven about 20 minutes. Drizzle combined honey and butter over hot muffins. Grated orange peel gives added flavor.

✻ ORANGE COFFEE CAKE

¼ cup soft butter
¼ cup honey
1 teaspoon orange peel
1 package refrigerated crescent rolls
Chopped pecans

Blend butter, honey, and peel. Separate rolls and spread about ½ teaspoon honey mixture over each. Sprinkle with pecans, then roll up as package directs. Place in greased 9″ cake pan, and bake at 375° 12 to 15 minutes or until golden brown. Serve hot.

✻ ORANGE NUT MUFFINS

    1½ cups bran
     1 cup milk
    ¼ cup orange juice
     2 teaspoons grated orange peel
    ¼ cup honey
     1 egg, slightly beaten
     3 tablespoons melted shortening
    1½ cups flour
    4½ teaspoons baking powder
    ¾ teaspoon salt
    ½ cup chopped nuts

Combine first five ingredients and let soak 15 minutes. Add egg and melted shortening. Sift together dry ingredients, add nuts, stir into first mixture just enough to moisten the dry ingredients. Do not beat. Fill greased muffin tins ⅔ full and bake in 400° oven 15 to 20 minutes or until done. Makes 15 to 18 medium-sized muffins.

Variation: Add ½ cup of raisins, dates, or currants to sifted dry ingredients.

For blender users: Combine all ingredients except dry ingredients in blender. Process at MIX until blended. Pour over dry ingredients in bowl and stir only until the flour is moistened. If using dates and nuts, add them after first mixture has been mixed. Stop the blender, then add, process at CHOP only until nuts and dates are chopped. Then pour mixture over dry ingredients.

*   *   *

Upkeep of ranges was always a chore a century ago. The mica oven window, when blackened with smoke, was taken out and washed with vinegar. Stovepipes had to be cleaned by putting a piece of zinc on the live coals in the stove; ashes or cinders were removed each morning, the outside brushed off with turkey wings, or, if greasy, washed with soda water with a piece of flannel, then blackened and polished. Rusted steel was cleaned with sweet oil or kerosene and polished with emery; brass with emery or brick; the hearth with hot water and soda, covering the grease spots first with hot ashes or live coals, or sprinkled with fuller's earth. And, as now, Great-grandma tried to protect her hands from such dirty labor. She used lard under her fingernails, and drew a small paper bag over her hand while polishing. Difficult work though it was, and never-ending, she considered a clean, shining stove as a mark of her pride in her cooking.

 ### BITSY BREAKFAST BREADS

    1 8-ounce package refrigerated biscuits, cut in half
    ⅓ cup honey
    ½ cup coconut (shredded or flaked) or ½ cup finely chopped pecans

Roll the cut biscuits into balls. Dip balls in honey and then roll in coconut or pecans. Grease four 2½ x 4½ x 1½″ loaf pans. Place 5 balls in each pan. Bake at 400° for 20 minutes. Remove from pans and serve immediately or cool and wrap in foil for reheating later. Makes 4 individual loaves.

 ### HONEY BRAN MUFFINS

(Delicious with sour milk or buttermilk.)

    1 cup flour
    1 cup all-bran cereal
    ¼ cup sugar
    2½ teaspoons baking powder
    ½ teaspoon soda
    ½ teaspoon salt
    ¾ cup sour milk or buttermilk
    1 egg, slightly beaten
    ¼ cup shortening, melted
    ¼ cup honey
    Honey

Combine dry ingredients in mixing bowl; make a well in center. Combine milk, egg, shortening, and honey. Add and stir only until dry ingredients are moistened. Fill greased muffin pans ⅔ full. Top batter with 1 teaspoon honey. Bake at 375° about 20 minutes. Makes 12 small or 8 large muffins.

FANCY DATE COFFEE CAKE

    1 cup dairy sour cream
    1 package active dry yeast
    ¼ cup warm water
    6 tablespoons soft margarine or butter
    1 teaspoon salt
    3 tablespoons sugar
 1½ teaspoons grated lemon rind
    ¾ teaspoon nutmeg
    1 egg, beaten
    3 cups flour (approximate)
    2 cups fresh dates
    ¼ cup plus 1 tablespoon honey
    2 tablespoons lemon juice

Warm sour cream over low heat. Dissolve yeast in water in large bowl. Add the cream, 2 tablespoons margarine, salt, sugar, 1 teaspoon lemon rind, ½ teaspoon nutmeg, egg, and 1 cup of flour. Beat until smooth. Beat in remaining flour until dough cleans sides of bowl. Knead on floured surface until smooth, about 10 minutes. Place in greased bowl, turn once to grease other side, cover, and let rise in warm place until double in bulk, about 1 hour.

Fasten 3″ strip of folded aluminum foil around 9 x 1½″ round pan to make collar. Grease pan and collar thoroughly. Cut dates into pieces, mix with ¼ cup of honey, lemon juice, the remaining margarine, rind, and nutmeg.

Punch down dough. Divide in half and roll into two 14 x 8″ rectangles and spread with date mixture. Roll as for jelly roll, starting at long edges. Cut each roll into 14 one-inch slices. Stand 9 slices around edge of pan, cut sides flat against side, and place remaining slices, cut side down, in center of pan, making two layers. Bake on low rack in 350° oven 1 hour. Cool 5 minutes, remove, and brush top with remaining honey. Serve warm, cut in wedges. Makes one 9″ cake.

❀ HONEY ALMOND CRANBERRY BREAD

3 cups prepared biscuit mix
½ teaspoon ground allspice
1 cup fresh cranberries, rinsed and drained
Grated rind of ½ orange
½ cup chopped blanched almonds
1 egg beaten
½ cup honey
¼ cup milk
¼ cup orange juice

Combine first five ingredients, add remaining ingredients, and beat until blended. Spoon mixture into greased and floured 9 x 5 x 3″ loaf pan. Bake at 350° 50 to 55 minutes or until done. Cool on rack.

❀ QUICK AND EASY ROLLUPS

½ cup milk
2 tablespoons honey
¼ cup butter, melted
2 cups biscuit mix

FILLING

½ cup honey
¼ cup soft butter
½ cup chopped nuts

Add milk, honey, and melted butter to biscuit mix. Mix thoroughly with fork. If too sticky, add a bit of biscuit mix but keep dough soft. Roll ¼″ thick, making an oblong 15 x 7″ (or a rectangle 10 x 12 ″). Mix filling ingredients. Spread one half over dough; roll like jelly roll. Cut into 9 slices. Place cut side down in 9″ square pan, buttered. Spread remaining honey mixture over rolls. Bake at 450° about 15 to 20 minutes or until golden. Yield, 9 rolls.

*   *   *

Heavy waffle irons a century ago had to be heated approximately an hour before using. Large families therefore made waffles only on special occasions, Sundays or, when, after the chores were done and before preparations for dinner began, the family found a little more time for leisure.

WAFFLES WITH ORANGE SAUCE

3 eggs
2 tablespoons honey
2 tablespoons butter, melted
1⅓ cups milk
2 cups biscuit mix

ORANGE SAUCE

1½ cups orange juice
½ cup honey
⅓ cup chopped nuts or dates

Beat eggs with honey, mixing thoroughly. Blend in butter and milk. Add biscuit mix and mix until smooth. Bake in preheated waffle iron; keep warm in oven. Make sauce: Combine orange juice, honey, and nuts or dates; simmer 5 minutes. Serve hot over waffles. Makes 4 waffles and 2 cups of sauce.

HONEY FRENCH TOAST

2 eggs, slightly beaten
¼ cup milk
¼ cup honey
¼ teaspoon salt
8 slices bread
Butter

LEMON HONEY BUTTER

1 cup honey
2 tablespoons lemon juice
2 tablespoons butter

Combine beaten eggs, ¼ cup milk, ¼ cup honey, and salt; dip bread in mixture and fry in butter until golden brown. Combine 1 cup honey, lemon juice, and 2 tablespoons butter, heat. Serve over toast.

✿ FABULOUS FRENCH TOAST

  9 slices dry white bread
  ¾ cup pancake mix
  ½ teaspoon vanilla
  2 eggs
  ¾ cup milk

  ½ cup honey
  ½ cup softened margarine or butter

Cut bread in half. Place mix, vanilla, eggs, and milk in bowl. Beat with rotary egg beater until smooth. Dip bread slices into batter. Fry in butter in skillet until golden brown. Serve with honey butter, made by beating together the honey and butter. Serves 6.

TOPPINGS FOR BREADS

✿ ORANGE HONEY BUTTER

  2 tablespoons honey
  ½ cup softened butter
  2 tablespoons frozen concentrated orange juice

Add honey to butter, beating till light and fluffy. Continue beating while slowly adding juice. Excellent on pancakes, waffles, French toast, or toasted English muffins. Makes ¾ cup.

✿ HONEY NUT BUTTER

Mix 4 tablespoons butter softened and ⅔ cup honey thoroughly. Add ¼ cup finely chopped almonds or walnuts. Garnish bowl with cinnamon if desired. Makes enough for 6 waffles or 15 pancakes.

✿ HONEY ORANGE

Beat together ½ cup butter or margarine, ½ cup honey, and 1 teaspoon grated orange peel. Makes ¾ cup.

✿ DATE HONEY SPREAD

Cut ½ cup dates or raisins into small pieces. Beat together 2 (3-ounce) packages cream cheese, 1 teaspoon grated lemon peel, 4 teaspoons lemon juice, and ¼ cup honey butter (equal parts of honey and butter), add to dates.

BEESWAX IN ARTS AND CRAFTS

Thousands of years before Christ, when ancient man first discovered bees, their importance to him could scarcely have been more than the pleasure of finding an unexpected treat as he hunted for food. But that discovery stimulated his curiosity, and for thousands of years to come, he was to delve into the secrets of the honeybee, his superstitions being gradually replaced by knowledge.

When early potters found that bees swarmed into their vessels, some 5,000 years ago, it was perhaps the beginning of beehives. Waterpots are still used as hives in some Mediterranean lands. Both in ancient Egypt and other nearby regions, craftsmen made pipe hives out of clay and other materials for their bees, laying them horizontally and piled together. Early basket makers made their beehives from coiled ropes of straw, the classic domed bee skeps which are used as a symbol for the bee.

As man's knowledge of the bee increased, he turned to its products for various needs. Before the invention of paper, wax tablets were used for making temporary records, and for correspondence. Horace, a Latin poet born sixty-five years before Christ, undoubtedly used such tablets, for he writes to other poets, "Turn often your style," which means literally to sharpen the stylus, or pointed instrument, used to inscribe characters on a wax tablet. Figuratively, however, Horace was probably advising a sharpening of writing style.

Early churches required that candlemakers use beeswax. No other wax was allowed the priests for their candles during ceremonies. In antiquity, the Church sought the purest sources of light for religious ceremonies, and used beeswax for candles and olive oil for lamps.

To sculptors and painters of long ago, bees meant beeswax for varnishing their work, material for modeling wax figures from which bronzes were cast. Stradivari and other famous violinmakers used beeswax in the varnish which gave their instruments such superb tone.

Early dentists used beeswax to make impressions for dentures. Even today it may be used in the form of impression wax, base plate wax, and in compounds. Early Europeans and their descendants for centuries used beeswax for polishing stairs and floors in ordinary houses and palaces. Tailors, shoemakers, and harness makers used it to wax their thread to make it smoother, stronger, and water-resistant. Cutlers used beeswax in a cement made of rosin and fine brick dust. The opening in the knife handle was filled with this and the heated blade forced into the cement. Lapidaries made their cement with wax, rosin, and whiting, using it to hold glass, gemstones, and other delicate objects while they cut and polished.

Beeswax is used in foundries to make wax fillets for rounding the corners of small patterns; in sheets of varying thickness for shims; as an ingredient of modeling compounds; and in the "lost wax" process for producing precision castings. It is also used in adhesive compositions such as crayons and chewing gum.

Great-grandma used beeswax to make tracing paper by dissolving white beeswax an inch in diameter in half a pint of turpentine. The paper was saturated with this mixture and then dried two or three days before using it.

Pure gold bronze was made by grinding gold leaf to a powder in pure honey, the whole diluted with clear water to let the gold settle. The water was poured off and the process repeated until the gold dust was clean. Pure silver bronze was made in the same way, substituting silver leaf for gold.

Propolis, the sticky substance made by bees to seal their hive inside, and to make seams and cracks watertight and airtight, was used by craftsmen as a varnish after dissolving it in alcohol. Filtered, it produced a beautiful polish for wood and, applied to tin, gave it a golden color. Gathered by the bees from the resinous buds and limbs of trees such as poplar, alder, birch, willow, pine, and fir, its sweet scent made it ideal for incense. Propolis was also used to attach gold leaf to decorations for walls, ceilings, moldings, and friezes when mixed with wood alcohol and filtered. Thus, through the ages, the bee and her products have brought riches to every culture.

CAKES AND COOKIES

CAKES, AND COOKIES, MOIST, AND FINE-FLAVORED, ARE TURNED out by the million every day in homes across the country. When honey is an ingredient in both cakes and cookies, texture, flavor, and keeping qualities are greatly enhanced.

The creation of cakes and cookies today is simpler than in Great-grandma's time. She often had to roll and sift the sugar, grind or pound the spices, pick over and remove such foreign objects as grit or stones from currants and raisins.

With no oven thermometer, her baking temperature was regulated by the feel of the heat on her arm or hand, or by throwing a tablespoonful of new flour on the floor of the oven. If the flour caught fire or quickly turned a dark-brown color, the temperature was too high; if the flour remained white after the lapse of a few seconds, the temperature was too low. She tested for doneness with a broom straw taken from the middle of the broom and inserted into the cake as we do a toothpick.

For special occasions, she decorated cakes with a glass syringe. Icings were colored pink with cochineal, blue with indigo, yellow with saffron or grated orange rind strained through a cloth, green with spinach juice, brown with chocolate, and purple with cochineal and indigo. Pink was also made with strawberry, currant, or cranberry juice.

Today, things are much simpler, whether you choose a from-scratch recipe or a quick one made with a mix. As an added suggestion, use two tablespoons of honey in your favorite cake mix, adding it in a fine stream to the batter as you beat. It gives a beautifully tender and less crumbly product. Remember, too, if you're baking goodies for children away at school or young men overseas or friends half a continent away, honey will help keep cookies oven-fresh. As an ingredient in your party desserts, honey will make them twice as fresh when made ahead of time. To measure honey accurately and easily, wet or oil the cup or spoon first.

PRINCESS CAKE

    ½ cup shortening
    ¾ cup white sugar
    ¾ cup honey
    2 eggs, beaten
    ½ teaspoon vanilla
    ½ teaspoon lemon peel
    3 cups sifted flour
    3 teaspoons baking powder
    ½ teaspoon soda
    ½ teaspoon salt
    1 cup milk

Cream shortening and sugar thoroughly. Add honey gradually, beating until well blended. Add eggs, vanilla, and lemon peel. Sift together dry ingredients and add alternately with milk to creamed mixture. Pour into 2 waxed-paper-lined 9-inch cake pans. Bake at 350° 35 to 40 minutes, or until done. Cool about a half hour before removing from pans. Frost with favorite icing.

❁ TENDER COCOA CAKE

½ cup shortening
¾ cup sugar
½ cup honey
2 eggs
½ teaspoon salt
3 teaspoons grated orange peel
2 cups sifted flour
⅓ cup unsweetened cocoa
1 teaspoon soda
½ teaspoon cinnamon
¼ teaspoon nutmeg
⅔ cup buttermilk
¾ cup chopped nuts
Cocoa Icing, below
¾ cup chopped nuts

In mixer, beat shortening, sugar, honey, eggs, and salt for 5 minutes on low speed. Add orange peel and blend. Sift dry ingredients together. Blend into creamed mixture alternately with buttermilk; add nuts. Turn into 2 greased and floured 9-inch cake pans and bake at 350° 25 to 30 minutes, or until done. Let stand about 30 minutes, turn out, and cool. Frost with Cocoa Icing, and sprinkle with ¾ cup nuts.

COCOA ICING

½ cup margarine
¼ cup unsweetened cocoa
1 pound confectioners' sugar
¼ cup milk
¼ teaspoon vanilla
¼ teaspoon orange peel

Melt margarine, add unsweetened cocoa, confectioners' sugar, and milk. Beat until smooth. Add vanilla and orange peel and more milk if needed.

✿ HONEY SPICE CAKE

⅓ cup shortening
1 cup brown sugar
½ cup honey
2 beaten eggs
2½ cups sifted flour
1½ teaspoons baking powder
½ teaspoon soda
½ teaspoon salt
½ teaspoon cinnamon
¼ teaspoon nutmeg
½ teaspoon clove
1 cup sour milk or buttermilk

In mixer, thoroughly cream shortening, sugar, honey, and eggs for 5 minutes on slow speed. Sift dry ingredients and add alternately with sour milk to creamed mixture. Pour into 2 waxed-paper-lined 9″ layer cake pans, and bake at 350° 25 to 30 minutes. Cool 15 to 20 minutes before removing from pans. Frost with icing below.

ICING

1 cup heavy cream
¼ cup honey
Dash of salt
¼ teaspoon vanilla
½ cup confectioners' sugar

Whip cream and add honey, salt, and vanilla. Mix gently. Add confectioners' sugar and blend. Best when used at once.

✿ TENDER WHITE CAKE

1 cup sugar
6 tablespoons light-colored honey
½ cup shortening
1 teaspoon salt
½ cup egg whites
2½ cups sifted cake flour
4½ teaspoons baking powder
⅓ teaspoon cream of tartar
¾ cup milk
1 teaspoon almond flavor

Beat together sugar, honey, shortening, salt and ¼ cup egg whites at low speed for 5 minutes in electric mixer. Sift dry ingredients together and add. Combine milk, almond flavor, and remaining ¼ cup egg whites, and add over 3-minute period. Continue beating 2 minutes at low speed. Bake in two layer pans lined on the bottom with waxed paper. Bake at 350° for 30 minutes. Cool and frost with favorite icing.

SOUR CREAM SPICE CAKE

  ½ cup margarine or other shortening
  ½ cup sugar
  ½ cup honey
  1 egg
  2 cups sifted flour
  ¼ teaspoon soda
  1 teaspoon baking powder
  ¼ teaspoon salt
  1 teaspoon cinnamon
  ½ teaspoon cloves
  ¼ teaspoon ginger
  ½ teaspoon allspice
  ½ cup water
  ⅔ cup chopped nuts
  1½ cups dairy sour cream
  ¼ cup honey
Nuts

Cream shortening, sugar, and honey until thoroughly blended. Add egg and beat. Sift dry ingredients and add alternately with the water, beating after each addition. Spoon into 8″ layer cake pans that have been greased and lined on the bottom with waxed paper. Bake at 350° for 25 to 30 minutes. Cool briefly, remove from pans, and finish cooling. Spread remaining ingredients together and smooth between and on top of cake. Or put on an icing made with confectioners' sugar, ¼ cup margarine, 3 tablespoons hot milk, a dash of salt, and 2 teaspoons lemon juice.

*   *   *

Since waxed paper was hardly heard of in Great-grandma's day, she buttered her cake tins, then cut a piece of letter paper to fit the tin exactly, buttered that on both sides, and placed it smoothly on the bottom. She then set the pan in the oven just long enough to warm the tin.

✽ BRAN HONEY CAKE

½ cup all-bran cereal
½ cup water
1¾ cups sifted flour
1½ teaspoons cinnamon
½ teaspoon each nutmeg and allspice
¼ teaspoon soda
¼ teaspoon salt
1 teaspoon baking powder
½ cup shortening
½ cup honey
½ cup sugar
1 egg
½ cup chopped nuts

Combine bran cereal and water and let stand until most of the water is absorbed. Sift together flour, spices, soda, salt, and baking powder, set aside. Thoroughly cream shortening, honey, and sugar for 5 minutes on low speed in mixer. Add egg and beat. Add nuts. Add dry ingredients alternately with bran mixture, mixing carefully. Pour into greased 13 x 9 x 2″ baking pan. Bake at 350° about 30 minutes or until done. Cool.

✽ CHOCOLATE LAYER CAKE

½ cup cake flour
6 tablespoons cocoa
1 cup sugar
6 tablespoons honey
½ cup plus 1 tablespoon shortening
1 teaspoon salt
2 whole eggs
1⅓ cups cake flour
2 teaspoons soda
1 cup milk
½ teaspoon vanilla
1 whole egg

Sift together ½ cup flour and cocoa. Blend with sugar, honey, shortening, salt, and 2 whole eggs by mixing 5 minutes at slow speed. Sift together the 1⅓ cups flour and soda and add to the above. Combine milk, vanilla, and whole egg, and add to above ingredients over a 2-minute period. Mix for another 2 minutes at slow speed. Spoon into 2 round layer pans lined on the bottom with waxed paper. Bake at 350° for 30 minutes or until done. Cool slightly for about 30 minutes, remove from pans. Ice as desired.

FEATHER ORANGE CAKE

    ¾ cup shortening
    1¼ cups sugar
    ¼ cup honey
     3 eggs
    2¼ cups sifted flour
    3½ teaspoons baking powder
    ½ teaspoon salt
    ¾ cup water
    ¼ cup chopped nuts
    ¼ cup orange juice
    1½ tablespoons grated orange rind

Cream shortening, sugar, honey, and eggs for 5 minutes on low speed in mixer. Sift together dry ingredients, and add alternately with water, nuts, juice, and rind. Bake in 2 waxed-paper-lined layer cake pans in 350° oven for 30 to 35 minutes, or until done. Cool, remove from pans. Ice with boiled or confectioners' sugar to which orange juice and peel have been added.

*   *   *

New shiny cake pans of tin were not as well liked for cake baking by Great-grandma as those which had been used long enough to become rather black. New tins, thought Great-grandma, could not produce a good crust. And the ideal cake-mixing spoon was a wooden one with a slotted bowl, as long as the distance from her fingertips to her elbow.

✿ PRUNE CAKE

¼ cup shortening
½ cup sugar
¼ cup honey
2 eggs, beaten
½ teaspoon vanilla
1¼ cups sifted flour
¼ teaspoon salt
1 teaspoon baking powder
¼ teaspoon soda
1 teaspoon cinnamon
½ teaspoon nutmeg
½ teaspoon allspice
¼ cup milk
¼ cup sour cream
½ cup chopped, cooked prunes, drained thoroughly
¾ cup chopped nuts

Thoroughly cream shortening, sugar, and honey for 5 minutes on low speed in mixer. Add eggs and vanilla, beating well. Sift together dry ingredients, add alternately with milk and sour cream. Add prunes and nuts. Pour into greased, waxed-paper-lined 9 x 5″ loaf pan. Bake at 350° for 50 to 60 minutes, or until done.

*   *   *

"Strong butter and eggs that are not absolutely fresh," said Great-grandma a century ago, "cannot have their flavor and smell hidden by the most liberal addition of vanilla."

Sugar icing, Great-grandma's style a century ago, went something like this: To one pound of extra-refined sugar add 1 ounce of fine white starch; pound finely together and then sift through gauze. Beat the whites of three eggs to a froth (to be successful with egg whites, beat long enough and always in one direction in the bowl), add the sugar gradually, and continue to whip for half an hour or longer. *Or:* To 1 pound of finest pulverized sugar add 3 wineglassfuls of water, letting it stand until it dissolves. Boil till it spins a thread. Beat 4 egg whites. Season with rose water, lemon juice, or vanilla.

APPLESAUCE CAKE

    ½ cup shortening
    1¼ cups sugar
    ¼ cup honey
    2 eggs, beaten
    1¼ teaspoons vanilla
    1 cup thick, unsweetened applesauce
    2 cups sifted flour
    1 teaspoon baking powder
    ½ teaspoon soda
    ¼ teaspoon salt
    1½ teaspoon cinnamon
    1 teaspoon cloves
    ¼ teaspoon allspice
    1 cup raisins
    ½ cup chopped nuts

Thoroughly cream shortening, sugar, honey, and eggs for 5 minutes at low speed. Add vanilla and applesauce, then sifted dry ingredients. Mix in raisins and nuts. Bake in greased 9″ square pan in 350° oven 45 to 60 minutes.

NUT CAKE

    ¾ cup shortening
    1¾ cups brown sugar
    ¼ cup honey
    3 eggs, beaten
    2¾ cups sifted flour
    1 teaspoon baking powder
    ½ teaspoon soda
    ½ teaspoon salt
    1 teaspoon cinnamon
    ½ teaspoon nutmeg
    ½ teaspoon allspice
    ¼ teaspoon ginger
    1 cup sour milk
    1½ cups chopped pecans
    1 teaspoon orange peel, grated

Cream shortening, sugar, and honey thoroughly. Add eggs, beat well. Add sifted dry ingredients alternately with milk. Add nuts and orange peel. Bake in 9 x 13″ pan, greased and floured lightly, at 350° for 50 to 60 minutes or until done.

*   *   *

Great-grandma made fruitcake in large quantities, using 3 pounds flour, 1 pound sweet butter, 1 pound sugar, 3 pounds stoned raisins, ¾ pound of sweet blanched almonds, 2 pounds currants, along with a pound of citron, 12 eggs, plus spices, and a wineglass each of wine and brandy.

BANANA CAKE

    ½ cup shortening
    1 cup and 2 tablespoons sugar
    2 tablespoons honey
    2 eggs
    1¼ teaspoons vanilla
    2½ cups sifted flour
    2½ teaspoons baking powder
    ½ teaspoon soda
    ½ teaspoon salt
    1¼ teaspoons cinnamon
    1 cup mashed bananas mixed with 2½ tablespoons milk

Cream shortening and sugar thoroughly. Add honey and beat thoroughly. Add eggs, beat, and add vanilla. Sift dry ingredients together, add to creamed mixture alternately with banana-milk ingredients, stirring only enough after each addition to blend thoroughly; pour into 2 greased 9-inch layer pans, and bake at 375° 25 minutes. Frost with desired icing, adding sliced bananas as decorations.

JIFFY FRUITCAKE

(*Starts with a mix.*)

    1 package date bar mix and filling
    ½ cup hot water
    ¼ cup honey
    3 eggs
    ¼ cup flour
    ½ teaspoon baking powder
    1 teaspoon cinnamon
    ¼ teaspoon nutmeg
    ¼ teaspoon allspice
    1 cup golden raisins
    1 cup candied cherries, halved
    ½ cup candied pineapple
    1 cup coarsely chopped nuts
    ¼ cup cranberry juice or brandy

In a large bowl, blend date filling from package of date bar mix with hot water. Add honey. Beat in eggs one at a time.

Combine dry date bar mix with flour, baking powder, spices, prepared fruits and nuts. Add alternately to mix with cranberry juice. Spoon into greased and lined, long (3½ x 12 x 4 inch) or tube (10-inch) angel food cake pan. Bake at 325° 60 to 70 minutes or until cake tests done in center. Let stand in pan 10 minutes before removing. Cool on cake rack. Cake must be thoroughly cold before wrapping for storing. Freeze if desired.

DELICIOUS FRUITCAKE

    2¼ pounds candied fruits
     ½ pound dates
      1 cup raisins
    1¾ cups flour
      1 cup pecans
    1½ cups walnuts
      1 cup shortening
     ½ cup sugar
     ½ cup honey
      5 eggs, beaten
      1 teaspoon baking powder
      1 teaspoon salt
    1¼ teaspoons cinnamon
     ½ teaspoon allspice
     ½ teaspoon mace
     ¾ teaspoon cloves
      6 tablespoons unsweetened pineapple juice

Dredge fruits in ¼ cup of the flour. Add nuts. Cream shortening with sugar, add honey and beat thoroughly. Add eggs and beat until smooth. Sift dry ingredients and add alternately with fruit juice, beat smooth. Pour batter over floured fruits and mix well. Line greased baking pans with heavy waxed paper, allowing ½ inch to extend above all sides of pan. Spoon batter into pans without packing. Bake at 250° 3 hours. Place pan of water on bottom shelf while baking to keep cake moist. Makes 5-pound cake.

HONEY SPICE CHIFFON CAKE

2 cups sifted flour
3 teaspoons baking powder
¼ teaspoon soda
1 cup sugar
¼ teaspoon salt
1½ teaspoons cinnamon
¼ teaspoon nutmeg
½ teaspoon allspice
½ teaspoon cloves
¼ teaspoon orange peel
½ cup salad oil
7 egg yolks
½ cup honey
⅔ cup water
½ teaspoon cream of tartar
1 cup egg whites

Sift together flour, baking powder, soda, ½ cup sugar, salt, spices, add peel. Make a well in center; add oil, yolks, honey and water. Beat at low speed until smooth. Add cream of tartar to egg whites, beat to soft peaks, add remaining sugar gradually, and beat until very stiff. Pour egg yolk mixture gradually over whites, blending carefully by folding with rubber spatula just until blended. Pour into 10" tube pan, and bake at 325° 60 to 70 minutes or until done. Invert and leave until cold. Loosen gently with spatula to remove. Frost as desired.

*   *   *

A long-ago recipe for Nut Cakes required 8 cupfuls sugar, 2 cupfuls of honey, 4 cupfuls milk or water, 1 pound almonds, 1 of English walnuts, along with 3 cents' worth candied orange peel, 5 cents' worth citron, and 3 of lemon peel, 2 large tablespoons soda, and spices. The milk, sugar and honey boiled for fifteen minutes, then skimmed, taken from stove, the nuts, spices, and fruit added. As much flour as could be mixed with a spoon was added. It was well to let it stand a few days after this before it was rolled out thicker than a cookie. An old German recipe, the cakes kept a year.

ORANGE HONEY CAKE

    1 cup milk
    1 cup all-bran cereal
    ¼ cup shortening, softened
    2 tablespoons honey
    3 teaspoons grated orange peel
    ¼ cup raisins
    ¼ cup chopped nuts
    1 cup sifted flour
    2 teaspoons baking powder
    ½ teaspoon salt
    6 tablespoons sugar
    3 tablespoons orange juice
    ¼ cup margarine
    ½ cup honey
    1 cup water

Combine milk and bran and let stand 5 minutes. Add shortening and honey and beat thoroughly. Add peel, raisins, and nuts. Sift dry ingredients together and add to bran mixture, stirring only until combined. Spoon into greased 8″ baking pan. Combine remaining four ingredients, bring to a boil, remove from heat. Spoon over batter, and bake at 350° 40 to 45 minutes. Cut in squares and serve warm. Serves 6.

"You should be too intelligent," was the advice given fifty years ago, "to share in the vulgar prejudice against labor-saving machines. A raisin-seeder costs a trifle in comparison with the time and patience required to stone the fruit in the old way. So with farina-kettles, syllabub churns, apple-corers, clothes wringers, and sprinklers and the like."

❀ HONEY LEMONY CAKE

½ cup shortening
½ cup butter
¾ cup sugar
¼ cup honey
5 eggs, separated
2 tablespoons lemon juice
2 teaspoons lemon rind
¼ teaspoon vanilla
2¼ cups sifted flour
¾ teaspoon baking powder
1 teaspoon mace
¼ teaspoon salt

Cream shortenings and sugar thoroughly. Add honey and beat well. Add egg yolks, lemon juice and rind, and vanilla, beat thoroughly. Fold in stiffly beaten egg whites, then sifted dry ingredients. Bake in 5½ x 9½" loaf pan, lined with waxed paper, in 325° oven 75 minutes.

*　　*　　*

"The discipline of failure is a stepping-stone to excellence," was long-ago advice. "Some failures are not irremedial, but others such as scorched soups and custards, sour bread, biscuit yellow with soda, and cake heavy as lead, come under the head of hopeless. They are absolutely unfit to be set before civilized beings and educated stomachs. Should such mishaps occur, lock the memory of the attempt in your own bosom, and do not vex or amuse your husband with the details."

❀ MERINGUED GINGERBREAD

¼ cup shortening
¼ cup boiling water
½ cup all-bran cereal
½ cup honey
1 egg
1 cup sifted flour
1 teaspoon soda
¼ teaspoon cloves
½ teaspoon ginger
¼ teaspoon cinnamon
¼ teaspoon salt
1 teaspoon orange peel

Combine first four ingredients in mixing bowl. Add egg and beat well. Let stand 5 minutes. Sift together dry ingredients;

add to bran mixture. Add peel. Spread in greased 8 x 8″ pan and bake in 350° oven about 25 minutes.

MERINGUE

2 egg whites
¼ cup sugar
1 cup coconut

Beat egg whites until frothy, add sugar gradually, beating until stiff but not dry. Spread over warm gingerbread, sprinkle with coconut. Broil 4 inches from broiler unit for 2 to 3 minutes or until coconut is brown. Cut into squares and serve. Serves 6.

Toppings and Icings

CHOCO-HONEY SAUCE

1 6-ounce package semisweet chocolate bits
½ cup honey
¾ cup evaporated milk

Melt chocolate bits in double boiler. Add honey and milk and stir until well blended. Serve warm or cold. Delicious with pound cake or puddings, milk shakes, and ice cream. Keeps indefinitely in refrigerator.

SPECIAL FOR GINGERBREAD

(*Easy and quick.*)

2 tablespoons cornstarch
¼ cup honey
1 cup orange juice
½ cup raisins

Blend cornstarch and honey. Heat with orange juice and raisins. Cook until thickened. Serve hot. Makes about 1½ cups.

❁ DELICIOUS LEMON-HONEY SAUCE
FOR CAKES

    1 package lemon pudding-and-pie-filling mix
    ½ cup honey
    3 cups water
    2 egg yolks

Combine mix, honey, and ¼ cup of the water in saucepan. Add yolks and blend well. Add remaining 2¾ cups water. Cook and stir until mixture comes to a full boil. Remove from heat and serve over cake.

❁ HONEYSCOTCH TOPPING

    ¼ cup sugar
    ¾ cup honey
    ¼ cup butter
    ¼ teaspoon salt
    ⅔ cup evaporated milk

Combine sugar, honey, butter, salt, and ⅓ cup of the milk in a saucepan. Cook over medium heat, stirring occasionally, to soft-ball stage (234°). Stir in remaining ⅓ cup milk and cook until thick and smooth, about 3 minutes. Makes 1½ cups. Serve hot or cold on gingerbread, cake, or pudding (or for a super sundae, on chocolate ice cream with toasted almonds).

❁ HONEY ICING

Heat 1 cup honey to 238° or until it shows a thread when a little is dropped from a spoon. Pour slowly into 2 egg whites, stiffly beaten. Continue beating until icing is fluffy and will hold its shape.

❁ MARSHMALLOW ICING

    ⅔ cup honey
    1 teaspoon sugar
    2 teaspoons plain gelatin
    ¼ cup water
    2 egg whites
    ⅓ cup sifted powdered sugar

Heat honey to 125° and place in mixing bowl. Blend sugar and gelatin. Bring water to boil, remove from heat, add gelatin-sugar mixture, and stir until dissolved. Place egg whites in mixing bowl together with all of the above ingredients, and whip. Add powdered sugar to mixture when thickening begins and continue to beat to a soft peak.

 ## NOUGATINE FROSTING

  2 egg whites, unbeaten
1½ cups sugar
  4 tablespoons water
  2 tablespoons light corn syrup
  2 tablespoons honey
  ¼ teaspoon cream of tartar
  ⅛ teaspoon salt
  ½ teaspoon vanilla
  ½ cup nuts, chopped
  2 tablespoons candied cherries, cut small

Put first 7 ingredients in top of double boiler and mix thoroughly. Place over rapidly boiling water and beat constantly with rotary egg beater until mixture will hold a peak (7 minutes). Remove from water, add vanilla, and beat until thick enough to spread. To ⅓ of frosting, add nuts and cherries and spread between layers. Spread plain frosting on top and sides of cake. Makes enough frosting for tops and sides of two 8″ layers.

COCONUT HONEY TOPPING

  ⅓ cup sugar
1⅓ cups flaked coconut
  ⅛ teaspoon salt
  ½ cup butter, melted
  3 tablespoons light cream
  ¾ cup honey
  ¾ teaspoon vanilla

Combine all ingredients and mix thoroughly. Spread carefully over baked hot cake in pan. Bake at 350° for 15 to 20 minutes or until topping is bubbly and brown. Cut and serve cake while still warm. Makes enough for 13 x 9″ cake. Especially good on butterscotch cake.

HAWAIIAN ICING

1½ cups sugar
½ cup Hawaiian-type punch
2 egg whites
Dash of salt
1 tablespoon honey

Combine and heat over water until peaks form. Excellent on cake or plain cupcakes. Garnish with coconut, mandarin orange sections, pineapple or cherries.

Quickie: Whip one cup of whipping cream until stiff. Fold in ½ cup dairy sour cream and ¼ cup orange honey. Delicious over spice or angel food cake.

 ### HONEY COCONUT TOPPING

3 tablespoons butter or margarine
¼ cup evaporated milk
½ cup honey
½ teaspoon vanilla
1 cup chopped coconut

Combine butter, milk, honey, and vanilla in saucepan. Bring to slow boil over low heat, stirring constantly. Remove from heat. Add coconut, blend, and spread over top of warm cake. Broil until coconut is lightly browned. Delicious with spice cake.

CHOCOLATE FUDGE ICING

1¾ cups powdered sugar
¾ cup cocoa
¼ teaspoon salt
3 tablespoons butter
1½ tablespoons honey
1 egg white
2 to 3 tablespoons hot milk

Sift dry ingredients together. Mix in warm bowl with remaining ingredients, except milk, until free of lumps. Add hot milk and mix until smooth. Keep in warm bowl (115°) until used, stirring occasionally. Too high a temperature causes icing to lose its shine.

✿ HONEY CRISP TOPPING

    3 tablespoons butter
    ⅓ cup honey
    ¼ cup shredded coconut
    ½ cup crushed dry cereals (Wheaties, for example)
    ½ cup drained crushed pineapple

Cream butter and honey until fluffy. Add other ingredients and mix in thoroughly.

Cookies

Cookies are as old as many ancient civilizations. Today many European countries serve sweets whose recipes have been handed down from Roman times, especially those prepared for certain celebrations such as Christmas. In Italy, in some areas, seasonal dishes are served, such as Christmas sweets of honey and ground nuts in lozenge shape, and an Easter cake made of eggs, certain cheeses, and honey. In Hungary, honey-cake valentines with inscriptions or designs on them are still made by itinerant bakers.

✿ OATMEAL BARS

    ½ cup shortening
    ½ cup sugar
    ½ cup honey
    1 egg
    1¼ teaspoons vanilla
    ⅔ cup sifted flour
    ½ teaspoon soda
    ½ teaspoon baking powder
    ½ teaspoon cinnamon
    ½ teaspoon salt
    1 cup rolled oats
    ½ cup raisins
    ½ cup cut-up nuts

Cream shortening, add sugar and honey, beating thoroughly. Add egg and vanilla, and beat. Sift together flour, soda, baking powder, cinnamon, and salt, and add to shortening mixture. Stir in oats, raisins, and nuts. Bake in 13 x 9" greased baking pan at 350° for 20 to 25 minutes. Cool, cut into bars. Makes about 25 bars.

❁ HONEY THUMBPRINTS

1 cup margarine
6 tablespoons sugar
2 tablespoons honey
1 egg yolk
1 egg
½ teaspoon vanilla
2 cups sifted flour
½ teaspoon salt
½ cup honey
1 3-ounce can coconut
2 teaspoons grated orange peel

Cream margarine, sugar, and honey thoroughly. Beat in egg yolk and egg, and vanilla. Sift together flour and salt, and add to creamed mixture. Shape into small balls, and bake on greased cookie sheet for 5 minutes at 375°. Take from oven, make a small dent with finger in each. Fill with combined honey, coconut, and orange peel. Bake another 4 to 5 minutes or until done. Makes 5 to 6 dozen.

❁ OATMEAL DROPS

½ cup shortening
1 cup sugar
⅓ cup plus 2 tablespoons honey
2 eggs
1¾ cups sifted flour
1 teaspoon soda
1 teaspoon salt
1 teaspoon cinnamon
½ teaspoon cloves
2 cups rolled oats
1 cup raisins
½ cup chopped nuts

Cream first four ingredients thoroughly. Sift together dry ingredients, and stir in. Add oats, raisins, and nuts. Drop rounded teaspoonfuls about 2 inches apart on lightly greased baking sheet. Bake 8 to 10 minutes. Makes about 5 dozen.

*   *   *

The cookie jar seemed never to be full enough for big families. An old recipe calls for 1 gallon dark honey, 15 eggs, 3 pounds sugar, 1½ ounces baking soda, 2 pounds almonds chopped up, 2 pounds citron, 4 ounces cinnamon, 2 each of cloves and mace, and 18 pounds of flour. The honey was brought almost to a boil, then cooled and all other ingredients added. After the cookies were cut out and baked, they were frosted with sugar and whites of eggs. We're not sure how many this made, but Great-grandma must have spent hours at her hot range.

 DELICIOUS ORANGE BARS

    ½ cup margarine or butter
    ½ cup sugar
    ½ cup honey
    1 egg
    ½ teaspoon salt
    1 teaspoon vanilla
    2 tablespoons orange juice
    1 tablespoon orange peel
    ⅔ cup flour
    ½ teaspoon baking powder
    ¼ teaspoon soda
    1 cup rolled oats
    1 package (4-ounces) shredded coconut, chopped
    ½ cup chopped pecans

Cream first three ingredients together thoroughly. Add egg, salt, and vanilla, orange juice and peel. Sift flour, baking powder and soda together, and add. Stir in remaining ingredients, and mix well. Spread dough into greased 6 x 12″ baking pan. Bake at 350° for 35 to 40 minutes or until done. While warm, cut into 24 bars.

HONEY ORANGED CHIPPERS

½ cup margarine
½ cup honey
1 egg
1 teaspoon vanilla
1 teaspoon grated orange peel
1¼ cups sifted flour
½ teaspoon soda
½ teaspoon salt
1 7-ounce package chocolate pieces
½ cup chopped nuts

Cream margarine and honey thoroughly, add egg, vanilla, and orange peel, and beat well. Sift dry ingredients together, and add. Add chocolate pieces and nuts. Drop rounded teaspoonfuls onto greased baking sheet. Bake at 375° for about 8 to 12 minutes. Makes 3 dozen cookies.

EASY FRUIT DROPS

½ cup shortening
½ cup brown sugar, packed
½ cup honey
2 eggs, beaten
½ teaspoon vanilla
2¼ cups sifted flour
2 teaspoons baking powder
¼ teaspoon soda
¼ teaspoon salt
½ cup pineapple juice
¼ cup chopped dates
¼ cup coconut
¼ cup candied orange or pineapple peel, cut fine
¾ cup chopped nuts

Cream shortening and sugar thoroughly. Gradually add honey, and beat well. Add eggs and vanilla. Sift together dry ingredients, and add alternately with juice. Stir in remaining ingredients. Drop from teaspoon onto greased cooking sheet. Decorate tops with nuts if desired. Bake at 375° for 12 to 15 minutes. Yield, 4 dozen.

SPICED FRUIT BARS

½ cup honey
2 eggs
⅓ cup melted shortening
¾ cup sifted flour
½ teaspoon soda
½ teaspoon salt
¼ teaspoon cloves
½ teaspoon cinnamon
½ teaspoon nutmeg
½ cup coconut
½ cup raisins
1 cup chopped walnuts

Add honey and eggs to shortening and beat well. Sift together dry ingredients, and add, mixing well. Stir in remaining ingredients. Spoon into greased 8 x 12″ cake pan, and bake in 350° oven 25 to 30 minutes or until done. When cool, cut into bars. Makes about 30 bars.

HONEY CRUNCHIES

1 cup shortening
1 cup brown sugar, packed
⅓ cup honey
2 eggs
1 teaspoon vanilla
¼ teaspoon lemon flavoring
2 cups flour
½ teaspoon soda
½ teaspoon baking powder
½ teaspoon salt
1 cup wheat cereal flakes
1 cup coconut

Cream shortening and sugar, add honey slowly and beat thoroughly. Add eggs and vanilla and lemon. Sift dry ingredients, and add. Stir in flakes and coconut. Drop by teaspoon on greased cookie sheet, 2″ apart, and bake at 350° for 10 to 12 minutes. Makes 4 dozen.

✻ DELICATE PUFFS

½ cup shortening
¼ cup honey
1 egg yolk, beaten
1 tablespoon orange peel
1 teaspoon lemon peel
1 teaspoon vanilla
1 cup sifted flour
Dash of salt
1 slightly beaten egg white
½ cup finely chopped pecans or almonds
Pecan halves or candied cherry halves

Cream shortening and honey thoroughly. Beat in yolk, add peels and vanilla. Add sifted flour and salt. Chill. Form into small balls, dip in egg whites, and roll in chopped pecans. Place on greased cookie sheet, decorate each with pecan or cherry halves, and bake in 325° oven 15 to 20 minutes. Makes 1½ dozen.

✻ FAVORITE HONEY COOKIES

1 cup margarine
½ cup brown sugar
½ cup honey
3 eggs
1 teaspoon vanilla
3 cups flour
1 teaspoon soda
½ teaspoon salt
1½ teaspoons cinnamon
½ teaspoon nutmeg
1½ cups chopped dates
½ cup raisins
⅔ cup chopped nuts

Cream margarine and sugar, add honey gradually. Beat in eggs, and vanilla. Sift together dry ingredients, and add. Stir in remaining ingredients and drop by teaspoon onto greased cookie sheet. Bake at 350° about 12 to 15 minutes or until done. Makes 4 dozen.

DELICATE HONEY-NUT BALLS

    1 cup butter
    ¼ cup honey
    1¾ teaspoons vanilla
    1 teaspoon orange peel
    2 cups sifted flour
    ½ teaspoon salt
    1¾ cups chopped nuts

Cream butter thoroughly, slowly add honey, add vanilla and peel. Sift together flour and salt, and add. Stir in nuts, and form into small balls. Bake on greased baking sheet at 350° for 12 to 15 minutes. Roll in confectioners' sugar while hot. Cool, and roll again. Makes 6 dozen.

*   *   *

Great-grandma agreed with a writer who said that, "in respect of the marvelous efficacy which fine and pure honey hath in preserving health, that gross and earthy stuff, sugar, is no whit comparable to this celestial nectar." Not long after the turn of the century, a firm in Wisconsin was using 10 tons of honey annually in making a cookie called Honey Jumbles. A single recipe called for 2 quarts of flour, 3 tablespoonfuls melted lard, 1 pint honey, ¼ pint molasses, 1½ level tablespoonfuls soda, along with salt, a pint of water, and vanilla.

ORANGE DROPS

    ¾ cup margarine or other shortening
    ¾ cup sugar
    ¼ cup honey
    2 eggs, beaten
    1½ cups sifted flour
    ½ teaspoon soda
    ¼ teaspoon salt
    ¾ cup orange juice
    1 cup chopped nuts
    1 cup coconut

Cream shortening with sugar thoroughly. Gradually add honey. Add eggs, and beat until smooth. Sift dry ingredients, and add alternately with juice, beating smooth after each addition. Add nuts and coconut, and drop onto greased cookie sheet. Bake at 375° for 10 to 15 minutes. Makes 4 dozen.

✿ MYSTERY DROPS

    1 6- or 7-ounce package semisweet chocolate pieces (1 cup)
    3 tablespoons honey
    3 cups confectioners' sugar
    1¼ cups chopped pecans
    2½ teaspoons instant coffee
    ⅓ cup hot water
    1¾ cups finely crushed vanilla wafers (3 to 4 dozen)
    1 large candy bar with nuts

Melt chocolate pieces over hot water, remove. Stir in remaining ingredients except candy bar. Mix thoroughly. Cut candy bar into small pieces, and form some of the above mixture around each piece. Let mellow for at least a day in a covered container. Makes 48.

*   *   *

Wines such as sherry, port, or Madeira were often used as flavorings in bakery products by our forefathers. One recipe calls for 1 cup of butter, 2 of sugar, 3 eggs, 1 wineglass of wine, along with a spoonful of vanilla and flour enough to roll dough as thin as a knife blade. These cookies kept a year in a tin box in a dry place if the family allowed them to.

✿ UNCOOKED FRUIT BALLS

    6 cups ready-to-eat protein cereal
    1¼ cups nuts
    7½ ounces pitted dates, about 1⅓ cups
    ¾ cup coconut
    ¾ cup candied fruits
    ¼ cup honey
    ⅓ cup sherry or other dessert wine
    ¾ teaspoon cinnamon
    ¼ teaspoon cloves
    ¼ teaspoon nutmeg
    Dash of salt
    Confectioners' sugar

Put cereal and next four ingredients through food chopper, using finest blade. Add honey and wine, spices, and salt to fruit. Form into small balls when thoroughly mixed. Roll in sugar, place in tightly covered container to ripen for several days. Roll again in sugar before serving. Makes about 60 balls.

Peanut butter and honey make a delicious combination as any child knows. A commercial company now adds honey to its peanut butter.

 ### PEANUT BUTTER GOODIES

    ¼ cup margarine
    ½ cup peanut butter
    ¼ cup white sugar
    ¼ cup brown sugar
    ½ cup honey
    1 egg
    ½ teaspoon vanilla
    1¼ cups sifted flour
    ½ teaspoon baking powder
    ¾ teaspoon soda
    ¼ teaspoon salt

Cream margarine, peanut butter, and sugars thoroughly. Add honey and beat well. Add egg and vanilla and mix. Sift together the dry ingredients and stir into creamed mixture. Form into balls and place 3″ apart on greased cookie sheet. Flatten with flour-dipped fork or with bottom of glass dipped in flour. Bake 10 to 12 minutes in 375° oven. Makes 4 dozen.

APPLE OATMEAL GOODIES

    ½ cup shortening
    ½ cup brown sugar
    ½ cup honey
    2 eggs, beaten
    1 cup chopped apple
    1 cup raisins
    ½ cup oatmeal
    1¾ cups sifted flour
    ½ teaspoon soda
    ½ teaspoon baking powder
    ¼ teaspoon salt
    ⅔ teaspoon cinnamon
    ¼ teaspoon cloves
    1½ cups chopped nuts

Cream shortening and sugar, gradually add honey, beating well. Add eggs and beat. Add fruits and oatmeal. Sift dry ingredients and add. Stir in nuts. Drop by teaspoon onto greased cookie sheet, and bake in 375° oven 10 minutes, or until done. Makes 5 dozen.

*   *   *

In order to have enough eggs for winter use (hens lay more eggs during March, April, May, and June on the farm), and to take care of the deluge of eggs during the peak laying months, Great-grandma preserved her own. She might have used mucilage made of gum arabic or gum tragacanth dissolved in water; albumen, or the white of egg; collodion, linseed oil, paraffin; shellac, or other varnish; saltpeter, lard, sugar syrup, finely powdered gypsum, or plaster of Paris, dry salt, and various solutions such as lime or soda, in water. The eggs, after having the solution brushed on, dried on a bed of dry sand or blotting paper, were then packed, with the small ends down, in pails, tubs, or cases in dry bran, meal, or flour.

HONEY FRUITCAKE COOKIES

```
    1 cup sifted flour
   ½ teaspoon soda
   ¼ teaspoon salt
   ½ teaspoon cinnamon
   ½ teaspoon cloves
   ½ teaspoon allspice
   ⅛ teaspoon nutmeg
   ¼ cup shortening
   ½ cup honey
   ¼ cup firmly packed brown sugar
    1 egg, beaten
    2 tablespoons milk
    2 tablespoons vinegar
   ¼ teaspoon imitation rum extract
   ¼ teaspoon vanilla extract
   ½ cup seedless raisins
   ½ cup currants
   ½ cup finely cut candied pineapple
   ½ cup finely cut candied citron
   ¾ cup sliced glacé cherries
   ¾ cup coarsely chopped pecans
```

Sift together flour, soda, salt, and spices. Cream shortening, honey, and sugar, beat till fluffy and light. Beat in egg, milk, vinegar, rum and vanilla extracts. Stir in dry ingredients gradually. Mix in fruits and nuts. Drop from teaspoon onto greased baking sheet. Bake in 325° oven about 20 minutes. Remove from pan immediately. When cooled, frost with confectioners' sugar frosting and garnish with glacé cherries or colored sugar sand. Makes 4 dozen.

LEBKUCHEN

    1 cup honey
    ¾ cup brown sugar, packed
    1 egg
    1 tablespoon lemon juice
    3 cups sifted flour
    ½ teaspoon soda
    ½ teaspoon salt
    1 teaspoon nutmeg
    1 teaspoon allspice
    1¼ teaspoons cinnamon
    1¼ teaspoons cloves
    1½ teaspoons grated lemon rind
    ⅓ cup finely chopped citron or ½ cup mixed candied fruit, finely cut
    ⅓ cup nuts, finely chopped
    2 cups confectioners' sugar for glaze

Warm honey in small saucepan and set aside. Combine sugar and egg and beat until smooth and fluffy. Add honey and lemon juice and beat well. Sift together flour, soda, salt, and spices. Add 1 cup of flour mixture and lemon rind to sugar-egg ingredients, and beat until smooth. Stir in remaining flour mixture until well blended. Add citron and nuts. Chill dough overnight, covered. Next day, heat oven to 375°. Lightly grease 2 cookie sheets. Roll ½ of dough at a time, keeping remainder chilled. Roll to ¼ inch thick on floured board. Cut with floured 2-inch round cookie cutter, place 2 inches apart on cookie sheet, bake 15 minutes. Remove from pan and cool slightly. Meanwhile make glaze, combining confectioners' sugar with 3 tablespoons water, stirring until smooth. Brush on warm cookies. Decorate if desired. Cool completely, then store, tightly covered, in a cool, dry place 2 to 3 weeks before using. A piece of bread may be put in the container to help keep the cookies moist. Change often to prevent molding. Makes 3 dozen.

*   *   *

Christmas at Great-grandma's house meant weeks of holiday baking, of fragrances filling the cozy kitchen, of a pantry filling gradually with tins and boxes of goodies, of glasses and jars freshly filled with preserves and last-minute jellies and golden honey. With snow swirling past her brightly decorated windows, great logs crackling in the fireplace, and a shiny pot of coffee gently bubbling on the back of the freshly polished wood range, Great-grandma's Christmas came with the spirit of homeyness, of a gathering family, of a faith so gentle and deep it comforted all who arrived at her door from out of the storm.

GLAZED CHRISTMAS COOKIES

        2 cups sifted all-purpose flour
        1 teaspoon salt
        1 teaspoon baking soda
        ½ cup soft butter or margarine
        1 teaspoon vanilla
        ½ teaspoon almond extract
        ⅔ cup honey
        1 egg, beaten
        ¼ cup vinegar
        ½ cup finely cut candied peel
        ½ cup finely cut red or green glacé cherries
        ½ cup shredded coconut
        1 egg white, slightly beaten
    Red sugar sand
    Blanched almonds

Sift together flour, salt, soda. Cream together butter, vanilla, almond extract, and honey. Beat until fluffy and creamy. Beat in egg and vinegar. Stir in sifted dry ingredients gradually, blend well. Mix in peel, cherries, and coconut. Chill dough several hours or overnight. Shape one quarter of the dough at a time, leaving remaining dough in refrigerator. Shape into balls ¾" in diameter. Place 2" apart on greased cookie sheet. Using a greased and floured tumbler (2" in diameter), press cookies, dipping tumbler in flour as needed. Brush cookies with slightly beaten egg white and sprinkle with red sugar sand. Arrange almonds in flower petal fashion on each. Bake in 375° oven about 12 minutes. Remove from pan immediately. Makes 6 dozen.

POINSETTIA BALLS

    3 cups sifted all-purpose flour
    ½ teaspoon baking soda
    ½ teaspoon salt
    1 cup butter or margarine
    ⅔ cup honey
    2 eggs, separated
    2 tablespoons grated orange rind
    1 tablespoon grated lemon rind
    2 tablespoons white vinegar
    1½ cups finely chopped pecans
    7 dozen red glacé cherries

Sift together dry ingredients. Cream together butter and honey, beat until light and fluffy. Beat in egg yolks, until well blended. Beat in fruit rinds and vinegar until blended. Stir in dry ingredients gradually, mix well. Chill dough one hour. Form into balls about 1 inch in diameter. Beat egg whites slightly. Dip balls in whites, then roll in pecans. Place 2 inches apart on greased baking sheet. Cut each cherry to form petals. Spread cut cherry on top of ball, spreading into a flower. Bake at 325° 18 to 20 minutes. Makes 7 dozen.

*   *   *

Great-grandma often used her spice or coffee mill for grating orange or lemon peel, and then ran rice or bread crumbs through to clean it.

HONEY CHEWS

    ¾ cup sifted flour
    ¼ teaspoon salt
    1 teaspoon baking powder
    ¼ teaspoon soda
    ½ cup sugar
    ½ cup honey
    ¼ teaspoon vanilla
    3 beaten eggs
    1 cup chopped dates
    1¼ cups chopped nuts

Sift dry ingredients. Add honey and vanilla to beaten eggs and beat thoroughly. Add to dry ingredients. Stir in dates and nuts, and blend well. Pour into greased 10 x 14″ pan. Bake in 300° oven 30 minutes or until done. Cool and cut into squares. Makes about 24, depending on size cut.

❁ SPICY BRAN COOKIES

½ cup shortening
½ cup brown sugar
½ cup honey
1 egg
½ teaspoon vanilla
½ cup milk
1 cup All-Bran (ready-to-eat cereal)
2 cups sifted flour
1 teaspoon soda
1½ teaspoons cinnamon
½ teaspoon ginger
½ teaspoon allspice
¾ teaspoon cloves
½ teaspoon salt

Cream shortening and sugar, add honey gradually and beat well. Add egg and vanilla and beat. Combine milk and bran and stir in. Add sifted dry ingredients, beating well. Drop by spoonfuls onto greased baking pan, bake at 375° for 10 to 12 minutes. Cool. Makes about 4 dozen. Cookies may be glazed with confectioners' icing, or brushed with egg white and sprinkled with colored sand.

*   *   *

Great-grandma's cooking "tins" were treated with great respect. To prevent rust, she placed them on the back of the range to dry after washing and wiping them. To protect new tinware, she rubbed lard over every part of the tin and set it in the oven until heated through. This made the tin permanently rustproof. Because new tins were often covered with rosin or other substances when bought, she prepared them by filling them with boiling water, then adding sal soda or aqua ammonia. They were then boiled and later scoured. To scour tins, she used sifted coal ashes moistened with kerosene, or whiting and kerosene. Sometimes she might use fine sand or bath brick, followed by whiting. Afterward, she washed them in soapsuds, rinsed and dried them. No chore was done easily a century ago!

CHRISTMAS FILLED BARS

⅓ cup shortening
⅔ cup sugar
⅓ cup honey
2 eggs, beaten
1 teaspoon vanilla
2 squares (1 ounce) unsweetened chocolate, melted
⅔ cup sifted flour
¼ teaspoon soda
¼ teaspoon salt
¼ cup raisins
⅓ cup chopped nuts
1 tablespoon milk

FILLING

1 cup confectioners' sugar
1 tablespoon hot milk
1 teaspoon butter
¼ teaspoon peppermint flavoring

Thoroughly cream shortening and sugar. Add honey, then eggs, and beat well. Add vanilla and chocolate. Add sifted dry ingredients, mixing well. Add raisins and nuts; stir in milk. Spoon into 2 waxed-paper-lined 8″ square cake pans. Bake at 350° for 20 minutes. Cool. Mix filling: Combine confectioners' sugar with hot milk, butter, and peppermint flavoring. Blend and spread between layers, cut into bars. Makes about 24 squares.

HONEY FRUIT DIAMONDS

(*Chewy and delicious*)

½ cup sugar
½ cup honey
3 eggs, beaten
1 teaspoon vanilla
1⅓ cups sifted flour
1 teaspoon baking powder
½ cup raisins
1 cup chopped dates or candied fruits
1 cup chopped nuts

Combine sugar, honey, eggs, and vanilla and beat thoroughly. Add sifted dry ingredients, fruit, and nuts, mixing well. Pour into well-greased 9 x 13″ pan, bake in 300° oven 25 to 30 minutes. Cool and cut into diamond shapes.

✿ FROSTED CHOCOLATE SQUARES

⅓ cup shortening
½ cup sugar
½ cup honey
2 eggs
1 teaspoon vanilla
2 1-ounce squares unsweetened chocolate, melted
¾ cup sifted flour
¼ teaspoon salt
½ teaspoon baking powder
1 cup chopped nuts

FROSTING

2 tablespoons water
1 tablespoon butter
¼ teaspoon vanilla
1 ounce square melted unsweetened chocolate
1 cup confectioners' sugar

Cream shortening, sugar, and honey thoroughly. Add eggs and beat well. Add vanilla. Blend in cooled, melted chocolate. Add sifted dry ingredients, blending well. Add nuts. Bake in greased 8-inch square pan in 350° oven for 35 minutes. Frost with your favorite chocolate icing, or use frosting recipe above. Heat water with butter, add vanilla and unsweetened chocolate. Add confectioners' sugar and beat till of spreading consistency. Makes 20 to 24 squares.

*   *   *

We often tend to think that traditions were born in our country alone. But traditions in baking go back many centuries in the old countries. When honey was the only sweetener and when spices were rare and expensive, when artistry became a legend in the preparation of exotic and treasured and often exhibited products of such peoples as the Swiss or the German or the French, traditions were born.

Some are still handed down from mother to daughter. Especially is this true in holiday cooking and baking. With the fragrance of rare spices, citrus peels, and other ingredients filling the air at Christmastime, surely every child then as now was drawn toward Mother and the pans of goodies coming fresh from the oven.

BIBERLI

(One of the old Swiss cookie recipes.)

1⅔ cups honey
1 cup sugar
1 teaspoon cinnamon
½ teaspoon cloves
½ teaspoon nutmeg
¼ teaspoon ginger
¼ teaspoon mace
1½ teaspoons grated lemon peel
2 tablespoons brandy, rum, or kirsch
4 cups sifted flour
½ teaspoon soda
1 teaspoon baking powder

FILLING

3 cups blanched, ground almonds
1 ounce candied citron peel, chopped fine
2 cups sugar
Juice of 1 lemon
3 egg whites, beaten stiff but not dry

In small saucepan, combine honey, sugar, spices, and heat just until sugar dissolves. Cool. Stir in lemon peel and brandy. Sift flour with soda and baking powder. Add honey mixture, mixing thoroughly, round into a ball and refrigerate, covered, at least a day, preferably two. When ready to roll, first prepare the filling:

For filling, blend the nuts and peel with the sugar, juice of lemon, and stiffly beaten egg whites. Set aside.

Divide dough in half, roll out on a well-floured board to a bit less than ¼ inch thick, cut into 2½″ rounds. Spoon on each a bit of filling, fold over to make a turnover. Bake at 350° in well-greased pan until light brown, about 15 minutes. Remove from pan immediately. Glaze with mixture of milk and egg yolk if desired. Bake remaining dough in any shape desired. Cool, and store in airtight containers to mellow for several weeks. Makes about 80.

HONEYBEES AND THE POET

The honeybee, organized, courageous, and apparently inde-
structible, has gone her own way, ignoring man's insatiable
curiosity about her. Challenged by her mystery, writers have
worshipped her, attributed supernatural powers to her, roman-
ticized and characterized her in literature, and naturalists
have devoted to her years of painstaking research.

Homer, speaking from about 850 B.C., said in *The Iliad*,
"Words sweet as honey from his lips distill'd." Aristotle and
Cato, centuries before Christ, studied the life of the bee and
wrote their impressions. Aristotle compared honey to "dew
distilled from the stars and the rainbow." In one of his *Epi-
grams*, Virgil wrote:

> *So you for others, oxen, bear the yoke;*
> *So you for others, bees, store up your honey. . . .*

In all great books of religion, references are made to the
bee or its honey. The Bible, in Exodus, speaks of "a land
flowing with milk and honey"; in Psalms, the goodness of the
Lord is described as "sweeter also than honey, and the
honeycomb." In Proverbs: "For the lips of a strange woman
drop as a honeycomb, and her mouth is smoother than oil:
But her end is bitter as wormwood, sharp as a two-edged
sword."

In Judges, Samson found a swarm of bees and honey in
the carcass of a lion he had killed. He made a bet with the
Philistines that they could not guess his riddle: "Out of the
eater came forth meat, and out of the strong came forth sweetness." Samson's wife, a Philistine, wheedled the answer out
of him, and the Philistines replied, "What is sweeter than
honey? and what is stronger than a lion?" So Samson lost the
bet.

In Matthew is this familiar sentence in the passage telling of John the Baptist wandering in the wilderness: "And his
meat was locusts and wild honey."

Many poets cited the bee in love songs such as *Rosalynde* by Thomas Lodge written about 1590:

> *Love, in my bosom, like a bee,*
> *Doth suck his sweet.*

In a Rose Garden, written by John Bennett in 1895, are these words:

> *A hundred years from now, dear heart,*
> *We shall not care at all.*
> *It will not matter then a whit,*
> *The honey or the gall.*

On the lighter side is Edward Lear's lilting, enchanting song about those famous lovers, the Owl and the Pussy-cat who "went to sea in a beautiful, pea-green boat," and "took some honey and plenty of money, wrapped up in a five-pound note."

Victor Hugo in *Ninety-Three* compares a bee to a soul. "It goes from flower to flower as a soul from star to star, and it gathers honey as a soul gathers light."

"A comely olde man as busie as a bee" said John Lyly in *Euphues and his England*, and one of William Blake's proverbs in *Proverbs of Hell* in the eighteenth century reminds us that a busy bee has no time for sorrow.

John Burroughs, in 1913, compared his life to that of the bee in *The Summit of the Years*: "I go to books and to nature as a bee goes to the flower, for a nectar that I can make into my own honey."

Abraham Cowley, in the seventeenth century, likened his city with its buzzing and stinging to a hive of bees, when he wrote "The Wish."

This familiar poem from Isaac Watts in *Divine Songs for Children* has been read by thousands of children even though written about two centuries ago:

> *How doth the little busy bee*
> *Improve each shining hour,*
> *And gather honey all the day*
> *From every opening flower!*

Shakespeare, too, felt the dignity of the bee. In *King Henry V*, he wrote:

> *For so work the honey-bees,*
> *Creatures that by a rule in nature teach*
> *The act of order to a peopled kingdom.*

In *Il Penseroso*, Milton sang of the bee in this way:

> *Hide me from day's garish eye,*
> *While the bee with honied thigh,*
> *That at her flowery work doth sing.*

Longfellow's Indian warrior in *Song of Hiawatha* takes note of this "white man's fly" and the white clover:

> *Whereso'er they move, before them*
> *Swarms the stinging fly, the Ahmo,*
> *Swarms the bee, the honey-maker;*
> *Whereso'er they tread, beneath them*
> *Springs a flower unknown among us,*
> *Springs the White Man's Foot in blossom.*

Tennyson wrote of the murmuring bees, along with the sweet sounds of rivulets hurrying through the lawn and the moan of doves in immemorial elms, in his poem, "The Princess."

Eugene Field, writing after the death of his granddaughter, reminds us of the superstition that bees knew when a member of the family had died because they would immediately gather on the coffin when it was brought from the house.

> *Out of the house, where the slumberer lay*
> *Grandfather came one summer day,*
> *And under the pleasant orchard trees*
> *He spake this wise to the murmuring bees:*
> *"The clover bloom that kissed her feet*
> *And the posey bed where she used to play*

Have honey store, but none so sweet
As ere our little one went away.
O bees, sing soft, and bees sing low;
For she is gone who loved you so."

This American tradition that "telling the bees" when a member of the family dies will keep the bees from swarming is beautifully told in the above poem previously quoted. A more famous poem on the same subject is "Telling the Bees" by John Greenleaf Whittier. The "chore-girl" drapes "each hive with a shred of black" and says " 'Stay at home, pretty bees, fly not hence!/ Mistress Mary is dead and gone!' "

William Butler Yeats in 1893 wrote "The Lake Isle of Innisfree." He hungered for a small cabin with nine bean-rows, and a hive for the honey-bee and to live alone in the bee-loud glade.

Nursery rhymes and ballads of forgotten poets have been handed down for years. A favorite is

The king was in his counting-house,
Counting out his money;
The queen was in the parlour
Eating bread and honey.

And the ballad: "Sugar in the gourd and honey in the horn, I never was so happy since the hour I was born," simple though it is, tells the importance of honey as interpreted by an unknown writer.

An old English stanza has this bit of advice:

A swarm of bees in May
Is worth a load of hay;
A swarm of bees in June
Is worth a silver spoon;
A swarm of bees in July
Is not worth a fly.

Whether in poetry or prose, words of wisdom concerning honey were often given by such early writers as Sir J. More,

London, who, around 1707, clearly shows the esteem in which the products of the bee were held:

> Natural wax is altered by distillation into an oyl of marvelous vertue; it is rather a Divine medicine than humane, because, in wounds or inward diseases, it worketh miracles. The bee helpeth to cure all your diseases, and is the best little friend a man has in the world. . . .

Not so poetic and far more practical, Charles Butler, a writer in the 1600s, gives this advice:

> If thou wilt have the favour of thy bees, that they sting thee not, thou must avoid such things as offend them; thou must not be unchaste or uncleanly; for impurity and sluttiness (themselves being most chaste and neat) they utterly abhor; thou must not come among them smelling of sweat, of having a stinking breath, caused either through eating of leeks, onions, garlick, and the like, or by any other means, the noisomeness whereof is corrected by a cup of beer; thou must not be given to surfeiting or drunkenness; thou must not come puffing or blowing unto them, neither hastily stir among them, nor resolutely defend thyself when they seem to threaten thee; but softly moving thy hand before thy face, gently put them by; and lastly, thou must be no stranger unto them. In a word, thou must be chaste, cleanly, sweet, sober, quiet and familiar; so they will love thee, and know thee from all others.

It is to the poets, the romanticists, and the research-writers and to all other writers who have felt the impact of the bee that her importance in man's life has become a part of literature.

six

PASTRIES, DESSERTS, AND CANDIES

Perhaps no dessert is as universally enjoyed as pie. This was no less true in Great-grandma's day. She rolled out pastry and filled a pie with a true feeling for flakiness, tastiness, and beauty.

To a large extent, the seasons determined the kind of pie that was made. In the summer, Great-grandma used fresh fruits from her own orchard and berry patches, and from the wilderness hills and valleys, and along the banks of lazy streams or fast-running rivers. She hunted out the wild sweet blackberry, whether in the cool hollows or on the sunny slopes of hillsides. Armed with tin pails, clean kerosene cans, lard buckets (the smaller ones tied to her waist so that both her hands would be free to pick), she went on forays lasting hours, knowing that what she picked today would go into jars to make pies in winter, or jellies and jams. In the early fall, she harvested the wild huckleberry before bears or an early frost stole the crop. Wild cap and other such berries were all gathered up.

In the winter, she utilized canned, dried, and root cellar fruits for pie filling, selecting them with care. Raisins as well as other dried fruits were picked over, seeded, stoned, and dredged with flour before using to keep them from sinking to the bottom of the pie. Almonds were blanched. Often in pounding them, she added a little rose or orange water with fine sugar to prevent their becoming oily.

Her oven was the correct temperature if she could hold her hand in it while she counted to twenty. To keep it that way was important. "If," she said, "you suffer the heat to abate, the under crust will become heavy and soggy and the upper crust will fall in."

Lard was her favorite shortening as it still is for many bakers. Puff paste required the freshest and finest of butter. For this, she half-filled a large bowl with cold water, and washed her butter in it with her hands until the butter was light and waxy, freed of salt and buttermilk. She used a yolk of one egg, the juice of a lemon, and half a saltspoonful of salt and a pound of butter for every pound of flour.

Always concerned with the attractive appearance of her handiwork, she took extra time to make her top crust beautiful by spreading butter over it, then lightly shaking sifted flour over that. Then, holding the pie in her left hand and a dipper of cold water in her right, she turned the pie in a slanting manner, and poured sufficient water over it to rinse off the excess flour. Enough flour remained on the butter, however, to fry into the crust, giving it a flaky appearance superior to rolling the butter into the crust.

Summer was indeed a busy time. In order to get all things accomplished, weeks were divided by Great-grandma into entire days devoted to routine jobs such as washing, ironing, sewing and mending, sweeping, which included cleaning the carpets with wet tea leaves, and general house cleaning. In between, she made soap for the family, toilet articles such as sachets, and did the baking and cooking.

Honey in berry pies brings out the natural flavor of the fruit, and adds variety to the taste of an otherwise ordinary pie.

✿ STRAWBERRY PIE

    2 (3-ounce) packages cream cheese
    2 tablespoons honey
Dash of salt
    ½ teaspoon milk to moisten cheese
    1 9-inch pastry shell, baked
    ½ cup honey
    ⅓ cup water
    1 tablespoon unflavored gelatin
    1 cup crushed strawberries (do not drain)
    2 to 3 drops red food coloring
1½ to 2 cups whole berries, hulled, halved or sliced

Cream together cheese, honey and salt, moisten with milk. Spread over bottom of pastry shell. Combine in a saucepan: honey, water, gelatin, crushed strawberries, and food coloring. Cook over medium heat, stirring constantly until slightly thickened and clear, 10 to 15 minutes. Cool until mixture mounds. Arrange sliced berries over cream cheese; spoon gelatin mixture over berries. Chill 2 to 3 hours.

*   *   *

Great-grandma made the most of her ripening fruit by using them in single varieties or in combinations or for extra flavor or to extend quantities. Crusts for her rhubarb pies were rolled a bit thicker than a silver dollar, and salt and a bit of grated nutmeg were added with the sugar.

✿ WALNUT CRUMB CRUST

    1 cup fine graham cracker crumbs
    ¼ teaspoon salt
    ¼ cup soft butter
    ½ cup chopped nuts
    1 tablespoon honey

Mix together all ingredients. Press into 9-inch pie pan. Bake at 375° for 5 to 7 minutes. Cool before adding pie filling. *Variety:* Lemon or gingersnap wafers may be used in place of graham cracker crumbs.

❀ RHUBARB CREAM PIE

1 cup honey
½ cup sugar
5 tablespoons flour
½ teaspoon nutmeg, optional
1 tablespoon margarine
2 well-beaten eggs
4 cups diced rhubarb
1 recipe pastry (see below)

Combine honey, sugar, flour, nutmeg, and margarine thoroughly. Add eggs and beat smooth. Pour over rhubarb in 9-inch pastry-lined pie pan. Cover with second crust. Bake in 450° oven 10 minutes, then at 350° about 30 minutes.

❀ PIE DOUGH

1 teaspoon salt
5 to 6 tablespoons milk
1½ teaspoons honey
1 cup shortening
2¾ cups all-purpose flour

Dissolve salt in milk and honey. Cut shortening into flour until pea-sized. Add all of liquid at once and mix until consistency of dough is uniform. Do not overmix. Roll to fit pan. Makes two crusts. If baked for shell, prick pastry thoroughly, and bake in 450° oven for 8 to 10 minutes.

❀ APPLE PIE

Pastry for two-crust pie
½ cup sugar
1 to 2 tablespoons flour
⅛ teaspoon salt
½ to 1 teaspoon cinnamon
¼ teaspoon cloves
¼ teaspoon allspice
2 tablespoons lemon juice
4 to 5 cups peeled, sliced apples
½ cup honey
2 tablespoons margarine

Prepare bottom crust of pie (9-inch); roll out top crust. Combine sugar, flour, salt, spices, and juice. Mix with apples, and spoon into pie crust. Pour honey over all, dot with margarine. Fit and seal upper crust. Bake on lower shelf in 425° oven 30 to 40 minutes, or until apples are tender.

✿ APPLE PECAN PIE

    6 apples, peeled and sliced (5 to 6 cups)
   ½ cup sugar
   ¼ cup honey
   2 tablespoons flour
   ½ teaspoon cinnamon
   ¼ teaspoon nutmeg
   ⅛ teaspoon salt
   2 teaspoons lemon juice
2½ tablespoons chopped pecans
   1 unbaked 9-inch pastry shell

TOPPING

½ cup brown sugar, packed
¼ cup butter or margarine
⅓ cup sifted flour
¼ cup chopped pecans
¼ teaspoon cinnamon

Combine apples with sugar, honey, flour, cinnamon, nutmeg, salt, and juice. Spread nuts over pastry shell, add apple mixture. Spread with topping above. To make: Combine brown sugar, butter or margarine, flour, chopped pecans, and cinnamon. Bake at 425° for 35 to 40 minutes.

✿ MINCE-APPLE PIE

Pastry for one-crust pie (9-inch)
  3 to 4 cups sliced apples
½ cup honey
 2 cups mincemeat
¼ cup sugar
½ cup flour
¼ cup margarine

Line pan with pastry. Combine apples with honey. Spread mincemeat on pastry, add apple mixture. Combine sugar, flour, and margarine, mixing until crumbs form. Sprinkle over apples. Bake on lower shelf in 425° oven 30 to 40 minutes. Serve warm.

FRESH BERRY PIE

(Blueberries, raspberries, loganberries, blackberries, or boysenberries.)

Pastry for two-crust pie (9-inch)
½ cup honey
¼ cup sugar
 3 to 4 tablespoons flour, depending on juiciness of fruit
¼ teaspoon lemon rind
 1 teaspoon lemon juice
⅛ teaspoon salt
½ teaspoon cinnamon, optional
¼ teaspoon nutmeg, optional
 4 cups fresh berries
 2 tablespoons margarine

Line pan with pastry, roll out top crust. Mix all ingredients thoroughly except berries and margarine. Put layer of berries on crust, add half the mix, then another layer of berries, ending with mix. Dot with margarine. Cover with crust. Bake at 425° for 40 to 45 minutes.

*   *   *

Great-grandma took a small cupful of the cream skimmed from the morning's milk, heated it to a boil, then stirred in the whites of two eggs beaten light, a tablespoon of sugar, and a teaspoonful of cornstarch "wetted" with cold milk. She boiled all this together for a few moments until smooth, cooled it, then, when the pies or tarts came hot from the oven, she poured this sauce through the slits in the top crust, and served them cold with powdered sugar sifted over the whole. It gave fruit pies and tarts a special flavor.

PECAN PIE

½ cup sugar
¾ cup light corn syrup
 2 tablespoons honey
 3 eggs, slightly beaten
 1 teaspoon vanilla
½ teaspoon salt
1½ cups pecan meats
Whipped cream if desired for topping
 1 9-inch pastry shell

Mix ingredients, reserving half the nuts. Pour into pie shell, top with remaining nuts. Bake at 350° 40 to 50 minutes.

SPECIAL BLUEBERRY PIE

4 cups blueberries
½ cup sugar
½ cup honey
3 to 4 tablespoons cornstarch
Dash of salt
¼ to ½ teaspoon cinnamon
¼ teaspoon nutmeg
1 tablespoon lemon juice
¼ teaspoon lemon peel
Pastry for 2-crust pie (9-inch)

Combine blueberries with remaining ingredients. Fill pastry-lined pie pan. Adjust top crust. Bake at 450° 10 minutes, then in 350° oven for 30 minutes.

ROSY CHERRY PIE

Red coloring
2 cups cherries, drained (canned or frozen)
⅔ cup honey
½ cup juice
2 tablespoons cornstarch
3 tablespoons water
1 tablespoon butter
⅛ teaspoon almond extract
Dash of salt
Pastry for 2-crust pie (8-inch)

Mix red coloring with drained cherries. Combine honey and juice in saucepan and boil one minute. Mix starch with water and add to hot honey mixture, continue stirring over warm heat until thick and clear. Add butter, extract, and salt. Gently mix with cherries. Cool. Pour into pastry-lined pie pan. Adjust upper crust. Bake at 425° 35 minutes or until filling is tender. May serve with cheese or ice cream, or whipped cream topping. Or try a dash of nutmeg in sour cream.

* * *

Pumpkins and squash were interchangeable at Great-grandma's house. At times, she might substitute sweet potatoes. With plenty of eggs and milk on hand, her pies were rich, and the amount plentiful to serve a large family. To one quart of stewed pumpkin pressed through a sieve, she used nine eggs with the yolks and whites beaten separately, two scant quarts milk, a teaspoon each of mace, cinnamon, and nutmeg, and for sweetening she either combined honey with white or brown sugar or used the sugars alone. She suggested a tablespoon of brandy to improve the flavor of pumpkin pie.

PUMPKIN PIE

1½ cups pumpkin
½ cup sugar
¼ cup honey
 2 eggs, beaten slightly
¼ teaspoon salt
 1 teaspoon cinnamon
½ teaspoon ginger
¼ teaspoon cloves
¼ teaspoon nutmeg
⅔ cup condensed milk
 1 cup water
 1 9-inch pastry shell

Combine pumpkin with sugar, honey, and eggs. Add salt and spices. Add milk and water and mix thoroughly. Pour into uncooked pastry shell. Bake in 425° oven for 15 minutes, reduce heat to 350° and bake 45 minutes more. Serve with whipped cream or whipped topping if desired. May add ½ cup chopped nuts 10 minutes before pie is done.

ALL-HONEY PUMPKIN PIE

1½ cups pumpkin
¾ cup honey
 3 eggs, beaten slightly
¾ teaspoon cinnamon
¼ teaspoon ginger
¼ teaspoon cloves
¼ teaspoon allspice
½ teaspoon salt
 1 cup milk
½ cup evaporated milk or cream
 1 9-inch pastry shell

Mix first three ingredients thoroughly, add spices and salt. Stir in milk and cream and mix thoroughly. Pour into uncooked pastry shell. Bake in 425° oven 10 minutes, reduce heat to 350° and bake 30 minutes more or until knife inserted in center comes out clean. Serve with whipped cream.

*   *   *

With cows freshening, adding copious amounts of milk and cream to the pantry, with hens laying eggs in the henhouse or a box nailed to a convenient wall and filled with straw and a china egg in it to encourage the hens, and with bees adding to the store of food, Great-grandma served custard and honey-flavored pies, tarts, and desserts often.

HONEY CUSTARD PIE

    4 eggs, beaten slightly
    ¼ cup sugar
    ½ cup honey
    ½ teaspoon salt
    3 cups rich milk, scalded
    1 teaspoon vanilla
    ¼ teaspoon cinnamon or nutmeg
    1 9-inch pastry shell

To eggs, add sugar, honey, and salt. Add scalded milk slowly, add vanilla and spice, or sprinkle spice on top of pie. Pour into uncooked pie shell. Bake on lower shelf of oven at 425° for 25 to 30 minutes or until custard is firm when tested. One-half cup of chopped nuts may be added before baking. They form a top crust as pie bakes.

LEMON CHIFFON PIE

    1 envelope gelatin, unflavored
    ¼ cup cold water
    4 beaten egg yolks
    ¾ cup honey
    ½ cup lemon juice
    ¼ teaspoon salt
    1½ teaspoons grated lemon rind
    4 beaten egg whites
    1 9-inch baked pie shell

Soften gelatin in cold water. Combine yolks, honey, juice, and salt, and cook over hot water, stirring constantly until thickened. Add gelatin, stir until dissolved. Add rind, and cool until partially set. Add beaten egg whites and fold into cooled mixture. Pour into baked pie shell, chill until firm. Spread with sweetened whipped cream.

*   *   *

Great-grandma's recipes were often confusing for the novice cook. She gave few directions about length of baking time, or the actual sequence of putting the ingredients together. Her recipes might read, "To every pound of flour for puff paste, allow the yolk of one egg, the juice of one lemon, cold water, half a saltspoonful of salt, one pound of fresh butter. . . ." To make her dollar go further, she often used crumbs of sponge cake in making her lemon pies or tarts. She combined them with lemon juice, rind, eggs, and sugar. Or she might use the whole lemons, peeled, and sliced thin, and layered with sugar and a bit of water and flour.

 ### LEMON MERINGUE PIE

  ½ cup sugar
  4 tablespoons cornstarch
Dash of salt
  2 tablespoons flour
1½ cups warm water
  2 egg yolks
  ½ cup honey
  2 tablespoons butter
  ⅓ cup lemon juice
  1 teaspoon grated lemon rind
  1 9-inch baked pie shell

MERINGUE

  2 egg whites
  ¼ teaspoon salt
  ¼ cup sugar

Mix sugar, cornstarch, salt, and flour in double boiler. Slowly stir in water, and cook until thick, stirring constantly. Beat egg yolks with honey until thick. Add a little hot mixture and stir into remaining mixture. Add butter and cook two minutes. Add juice and rind slowly. Cool, and pour into baked shell. Make meringue of egg whites, salt and sugar, beating in sugar gradually until meringue forms pointed peaks that don't curl over. Spread over pie so that it touches all inside edges. Bake at 425° about 4 minutes or 350° for 12 to 15 minutes.

ORANGE CHIFFON PIE

1 envelope unflavored gelatin
¼ cup cold water
4 well-beaten egg yolks
½ cup honey
½ teaspoon salt
½ cup orange juice
2 teaspoons grated orange peel
4 stiffly beaten egg whites
2 tablespoons honey
1 9-inch baked pie shell

Soften gelatin in cold water. Combine egg yolks with honey, salt, and juice. Cook in double boiler until mixture thickens, stirring constantly. Remove from heat, add gelatin and dissolve; add rind. Chill until partially set. Combine egg whites with 2 tablespoons honey and beat until mixture stands in peaks. Fold in gelatin mixture. Turn into pie shell. Chill until set. Top with whipped cream if desired.

PUMPKIN CHIFFON PIE

1 envelope unflavored gelatin
¼ cup cold water
2 egg yolks
¼ cup sugar
½ cup honey
1¼ cups canned or cooked pumpkin
½ cup milk
½ teaspoon salt
½ teaspoon nutmeg
½ teaspoon cinnamon
¼ teaspoon ginger
2 egg whites
1 9-inch baked pie shell

Soften gelatin in cold water. Beat yolks, sugar and half the honey until thick. Add pumpkin, milk, salt, and spices and cook in double boiler, stirring, until thick. Add gelatin, and mix thoroughly. Chill until mixture begins to thicken. Beat egg whites with the remaining honey, beating until peaks form. Fold in pumpkin mixture. Turn into shell and chill. Serve with whipped cream, sweetened, with a dash of orange peel added if desired.

PINEAPPLE MERINGUE PIE

For filling, follow recipe for Lemon Meringue Pie (p. 172) with these exceptions: Reduce sugar to ¼ cup, lemon juice to 4 teaspoons. Add ⅔ cup well-drained pineapple to hot filling.

*   *   *

A century ago, coconuts usually had to be prepared at home by cutting away the outer husk, splitting open the inner brown shell with an axe, grating the white meat. The grated coconut, which nowadays we get out of a box, was then mixed with milk and allowed to soak, or brought to a boil for a few minutes. Coconut pies could be very rich: eight eggs to a pound of coconut and a quart of milk. Wine, sugar, honey, melted butter, and nutmeg often made up the ingredients. A pie at Great-grandma's house was indeed a labor of love.

STRAWBERRY CREAM PIE

    1 cup powdered sugar
    1 quart strawberries
1½ tablespoons lemon juice
    ½ cup mild honey
    ½ teaspoon lemon rind, grated
Red food coloring
    1 package unflavored gelatin
¼ cup cold water
    1 9-inch baked pie shell
    1 cup whipping cream

Sprinkle powdered sugar over washed and hulled berries, and let set in refrigerator several hours or overnight. Press half the berries through a sieve, add the juice. Measure. If not 1½ cups of sieved berries and juice, add water. Mix lemon juice and honey and rind and add to the berries. Heat to boiling point and add few drops of red coloring. Add gelatin softened in water to the hot berries, stirring to dissolve. Refrigerate until mixture begins to thicken. Place whole berries in pastry shell; cover with thickened berry mixture. Chill. Whip cream and spread over pie.

CINNAMON CHERRY COBBLER

1 can (16 ounces) red sour pitted cherries (2 cups)
½ cup honey
2 tablespoons red cinnamon candies
1½ tablespoons cornstarch
2 tablespoons butter or margarine
1 package refrigerator cinnamon rolls

Drain cherries, reserving juice. If necessary, add water to make ¾ cup of liquid. In a saucepan combine juice, honey, cinnamon candies, and cornstarch. Cook and stir over low heat until candies melt and mixture is thick and clear. Add butter and cherries. Pour sauce into 8 x 8 x 2-inch baking pan. Arrange cinamon rolls on top. Bake at 375° 20 minutes or until rolls are done. Spread icing from package of rolls over top. Serve warm. Makes 8 servings.

CHOCOLATE PIE

3 squares (3 ounces) unsweetened chocolate
1 pint jar marshmallow creme
3 egg whites
¼ cup honey
Whipping cream if desired
Nuts, optional

CRUST

⅔ cup sifted flour
⅓ teaspoon salt
⅓ cup shortening
¼ cup rolled oats
2½ tablespoons finely chopped nuts
2 to 3 tablespoons cold water

Filling: Melt chocolate in double boiler; blend in marshmallow creme. Remove from heat and beat well. Beat egg whites and honey until stiff peaks are formed; fold into chocolate mixture. Pour into baked pie crust. Chill. Serve with whipped cream or chopped nuts.

Crust: Sift together flour and salt, cut in shortening. Add oats and nuts. Add water gradually, stirring to mix. Form into ball and roll to fit 8-inch pie pan. Prick well, and bake in 425° oven 10 to 12 minutes. Cool.

*   *   *

Dessert should be the crowning touch and the perfect end-ing to a well-planned meal. It need not be elaborate, but should appeal to the taste and to the eye. Here are recipes, some simple, some more complex, which owe their special flavor to honey.

DEEP DISH APPLE DESSERT

```
1  tablespoon flour
¼  teaspoon salt
½  teaspoon cinnamon
½  teaspoon nutmeg
2  teaspoons lemon juice
⅔  cup honey
4  cups sliced, peeled apples
1  tablespoon butter
1  cup biscuit mix
1½ tablespoons sugar
½  cup milk
```

Mix flour, salt, cinnamon, and nutmeg with lemon juice and honey. Combine with apples and put in an 8-inch pan or 1½-quart casserole. Dot with butter. Combine biscuit mix with sugar, add milk. Pour over apples. Bake uncovered, in 425° oven for 35 to 40 minutes, or until done. Serves 8.

*   *   *

Wild bees pollinated wild berries far from Great-grandma's house. For these berries which included wild blackberries, raspberries, and huckleberries, among others, she was grate-ful. Often she needed to replenish her stock of honey, too. If so, she sent Great-grandpa to the hills to find a bee tree filled with honey. It often took hours, or more than a day to trace the flight of the bees from flowers where they gathered nectar to their tree. To do this, he baited an old cigar box with honey. When the first roving bee stopped to sample the honey, he carefully dusted a bit of flour on her. He noted her flight pattern. As the dusted bee brought more workers, he dusted them, and having thus marked them, followed them toward their tree. Over hill and dale he walked, often pushing through brush and over logs until he found the tree, cut it down, and harvested the honey.

HUCKLEBERRY COBBLER

3½ cups huckleberries
¼ teaspoon grated lemon rind
½ cup honey
1 tablespoon flour
Dash of salt
1½ cups sifted flour
2 teaspoons baking powder
¼ teaspoon salt
2 tablespoons sugar
¼ cup shortening
½ cup milk
1 tablespoon butter

Combine berries with rind, honey, flour, and salt. Sift flour, baking powder, and salt and sugar together. Cut in shortening as for biscuits, add milk. Pour berries into greased 8-inch pan, dot with butter, and spoon over biscuit mixture. Sprinkle with sugar if desired. Bake at 425° 20 to 30 minutes. Serve hot. Serves 8.

HONEY COCONUT PIE

4 egg yolks, slightly beaten
1 cup water
½ cup honey
1 package lemon-flavored gelatin
3 tablespoons lemon juice
1½ teaspoons grated lemon rind
4 egg whites
Dash of salt
1 cup flaked coconut, toasted
1 9-inch baked pie shell

Combine yolks, water, and ¼ cup of honey in top of double boiler, mix well. Cook over boiling water 5 minutes or until thickened, stirring. Remove from heat, add gelatin, and stir until dissolved. Add juice and rind. Refrigerate until it begins to thicken. Beat egg whites with salt and remaining honey until they form very stiff peaks. Fold in gelatin mixture. Stir in ½ cup of coconut. Turn into pie shell. Sprinkle with remaining coconut. Chill until firm.

✿ APPLE BETTY WITH HONEY

    3 cups peeled, sliced apples
    1 tablespoon lemon juice
    ½ teaspon lemon rind
    ¼ teaspoon cinnamon
    ¼ teaspoon nutmeg
    ⅓ cup honey
    ⅓ cup water, warmed
    3 tablespoons melted butter or margarine
    1½ cups soft bread crumbs

Combine apples with juice, rind, and spices. Mix honey and warm water. Stir melted butter into crumbs. Place a layer of crumbs in greased 8-inch pan, add a layer of apples, moisten with honey-water. Repeat, ending with crumbs. Bake at 350° 30 to 45 minutes until apples are tender and crust brown. Cover during first 15 minutes. Serves 8.
Note: Add ½ cup of chopped nuts if desired.

✿ RHUBARB AND HONEY DESSERT

    ¼ cup margarine or butter
    ⅔ cup honey
    2 cups rhubarb, diced
    1 tablespoon flour
    ¾ teaspoon orange peel, grated
    1 teaspoon cinnamon
    ⅓ cup shortening
    ¾ cup sugar
    ¼ cup honey
    1 tablespoon grated orange peel
    1 egg, beaten
    1 teaspoon vanilla
    1¼ cups sifted flour
    2½ teaspoons baking powder
    ¼ teaspoon salt
    ¼ teaspoon soda
    ½ cup milk

Melt margarine in 8-inch square baking pan, add ⅔ cup of honey; arrange rhubarb over. Combine 1 tablespoon of flour, orange peel, and cinnamon, sprinkle over rhubarb. Cream shortening, add sugar gradually, beat well. Add ¼ cup of honey gradually, beat. Add orange peel and egg. Blend well. Add vanilla. Sift together flour, baking powder, salt, and soda.

Add alternately with milk to egg mixture, stirring only enough after each addition to blend thoroughly. Pour batter over fruit and bake in 350° oven 45 to 50 minutes. Invert pan, let remain in inverted pan 1 minute to allow syrup to drain onto cake. Serve with whipped cream. Serves 6. If desired, may add grated orange peel to whipped cream.

FRUITED PUDDING

    1 cup water or juice
    ¼ cup shortening
    ½ cup sugar
    ½ cup honey
    1½ cups raisins
    ¾ teaspoon nutmeg
    1 teaspoon cinnamon
    ½ teaspoon cloves
    ½ teaspoon vanilla
    1¾ cups sifted flour
    ½ teaspoon soda
    1 teaspoon salt
    1½ cups chopped dates
    ½ cup chopped dried apricots
    ⅔ cup chopped nuts

Combine water, shortening, sugar, honey, raisins, and spices. Cook 3 minutes. Cool, add vanilla. Sift dry ingredients, and add. Stir in fruits and nuts. Pour into 8 x 12-inch waxed-paper-lined pan and bake in 325° oven for 50 to 60 minutes. Cool. Serve with dollop of whipped cream. Makes 16 2 x 3-inch pieces.

HONEYED BREAD PUDDING

    2 cups bread cubes
    ¼ to ½ cup chopped raisins, dates, figs, or nuts, if desired
    3 tablespoons butter
    ⅓ cup honey
    Dash of salt
    ½ teaspoon vanilla or lemon extract
    3 eggs, beaten
    2 cups milk, scalded

Use day-old bread, cut into cubes. Place with fruits in a 1- or 1½-quart baking dish. Add butter, honey, salt, and extract to eggs. Add milk slowly. Pour over cubes. Set baking dish in pan of hot water and bake at 350° 45 to 55 minutes, or until set. Serves 6.

✿ PEAR CRUNCH

    3 fresh pears
    1 tablespoon lemon juice
    1 tablespoon flour
    ½ teaspoon cloves
    ½ teaspoon cinnamon
    ½ teaspon grated lemon rind
    2 tablespoons honey
    ⅓ cup margarine or butter
    ⅓ cup brown sugar, packed
    2 tablespoons honey
    ¾ cup sifted flour
    ¼ teaspoon soda
    ¼ teaspoon salt
    ¾ cup rolled oats

Peel, core, and slice pears, put in 8-inch square pan. Sprinkle with lemon juice. Combine 1 tablespoon of flour with spices, add rind, and spread over pears, drizzle with honey. Combine shortening, sugar, and honey and beat until fluffy. Sift together flour, soda, and salt, add to creamed mixture. Add oats, mixing with hands if necessary. Spread over pears, pressing down slightly. Bake at 350° for 25 minutes or until lightly browned. Serve warm with ice cream. Serves 6.

✿ BAKED CUSTARD

    ⅓ cup honey
    ¼ teaspoon salt
    ½ teaspoon vanilla
    4 eggs, slightly beaten
    2½ cups scalded milk
    Nutmeg

Add honey, salt, and vanilla to eggs. Gradually add scalded milk, stirring constantly. Pour into custard cups, sprinkle with nutmeg. Place in pan of water. Water should be almost to top of the cups. Bake at 325° for 50 minutes or until a knife inserted in center comes out clean. Remove from water. Serve with more honey and toasted coconut if desired. May also bake custard in 1-quart casserole or mold. Place in pan of water as above. Bake until done.

❊ DATE PUDDING

1 cup boiling water
1 teaspoon soda
1 cup dates
2 tablespoons butter or margarine
½ teaspoon salt
½ teaspoon vanilla
1 egg, beaten
¼ cup honey
1½ cups sifted flour
¼ teaspoon baking powder
¾ cup sugar
½ cup chopped nuts

Combine boiling water, soda, dates, and butter. Cool while preparing remainder of pudding. Add salt and vanilla to egg, mixing well. Beat in honey thoroughly. Sift together flour and baking powder, add sugar, add to egg alternately with date mixture, beating well after each addition. Add nuts. Bake in greased 9 x 13-inch pan in 350° oven for 25 to 35 minutes, or until done. Top with whipped cream when ready to serve. Makes 10 to 12 servings.

❊ SPECIAL DATE PUDDING

3 eggs
½ cup sugar
½ cup honey
¼ cup sifted flour
⅓ teaspoon salt
½ teaspoon soda
½ teaspoon vanilla
1 pound dates, pitted and chopped
1 cup chopped nuts

Beat eggs, add sugar and honey and beat until well mixed. Sift together dry ingredients, and add. Add vanilla. Stir in dates and nuts. Turn into greased 8-inch square pan and bake at 325° for 45 minutes or until done. Serve warm with honey-sweetened whipped cream. Serves 8.

HONEY KUCHEN

3 tablespoons margarine or butter
⅔ cup honey
¾ cup chopped walnuts or pecans
¼ cup sugar
⅔ cup milk
2 cups biscuit mix
¼ teaspoon grated lemon or orange rind
1 egg, beaten
⅓ cup chopped dates or raisins

Heat oven to 400°. Melt margarine in 8-inch square pan, add honey. Spoon nuts over mixture. Add sugar and milk to biscuit mix; add rind and egg. Stir in fruit. Spread over honey mixture. Bake in 400° oven for 20 to 25 minutes. Invert and serve warm. Serves 8.

DELICIOUS LEMON BAVARIAN

1 package (3 ounces) lemon-flavored gelatin
1¼ cups boiling water
¼ cup honey
¼ teaspoon salt
¼ teaspoon lemon extract
½ teaspoon vanilla
⅓ cup chopped pecans
1 cup heavy cream

Combine gelatin and water, stir in honey and salt. Mix well. Cool. When mixture begins to thicken, add lemon extract, vanilla, nuts, and whipped cream. Turn into mold and chill until firm. Serves 6.

* * *

Studies in bee pollination show that bees are more important than our forefathers thought. Prune growers in one California county lost $1 million a year for five years because not enough bees pollinated the orchards. As many as 50,000 colonies of bees may be required to pollinate 16,000 to 17,000 acres of alfalfa. Alfalfa is an important feed crop for beef and other livestock.

❁ HONEY BAVARIAN MOLD

    1 tablespoon (1 envelope) gelatin
    2 tablespoons cold water
1¾ cups milk, scalded
    ½ cup honey
    ⅛ teaspoon salt
    2 eggs, separated
    1 teaspoon vanilla
    ¼ cup chopped candied ginger
    1 cup heavy cream or evaporated milk

Soften gelatin in cold water. Place milk in double boiler, add softened gelatin, honey and salt, stir to dissolve thoroughly. Beat egg yolks slightly, stir in a little of the hot milk mixture, add remaining mixture. Cook over hot water until thickened, stirring constantly. Add vanilla and ginger. Remove from heat and cool. Beat egg whites to stiff peaks, fold in cool mixture. Add whipped cream. Turn into 5-cup mold or individual molds and chill several hours or overnight. If desired, serve with fresh or frozen fruit. Makes 6 servings.

❁ HONEY MOLDED DESSERT

    1 package lemon or orange flavored gelatin
    ¾ cup boiling water
    ½ cup honey
    3 tablespoons lemon juice and rind of one lemon
    ⅛ teaspoon salt
1¼ cups prepared whipped topping
    ½ cup chopped pecans
    ½ pound vanilla wafers

Dissolve gelatin in boiling water. Add honey and lemon juice, rind, and salt. Cool until slightly congealed. Fold in whipped topping and nuts. Pour into 8-inch square pan lined with half the crushed vanilla wafers. Cover with remaining crumbs. Serves 6.

*   *   *

Fruit and honey not only make a beautiful picture, but are a healthy combination as our forefathers well knew. Honey's energy-producing value is second to few foods because of the way it is used by the body. While cane and beet sugars must be broken down into simpler sugars before they can be absorbed into the bloodstream and assimilated into the tissues, the sugars in honey are mainly already broken down, and therefore require little digestion before absorption takes place. For athletes and active people it gives virtually instant energy without putting any strain on the digestive system. This also makes it a fine food for the elderly as well as the young.

✿ HONEYED RICE PUDDING

    2 cups cooked rice
    ¼ cup honey
    Dash of salt
    1 tablespoon butter
    1 cup chopped dates
    1 teaspoon grated lemon rind
    2 eggs, slightly beaten
    1 cup milk

Grease 1-quart casserole. Combine first 6 ingredients, pour into casserole. Combine eggs and milk and pour over. Bake in pan of hot water at 350° 45 to 55 minutes or until set. Makes 5 servings.

✿ CRUNCHY COCONUT SQUARES

    1⅓ cups coconut
    ¼ cup butter or margarine
    1½ cups wheat-flake cereal, slightly crushed
    1 package (3 ounces) strawberry-flavored gelatin
    1 cup boiling water
    ¼ cup cold water
    ½ cup honey
    1 teaspoon lemon juice
    1½ cups whipped topping

Brown coconut in butter, stirring constantly. Combine with cereal, press half in 9-inch square pan. Stir gelatin into boiling water until dissolved, add cold water, honey, and juice. Chill until slightly thickened, fold in whipped topping. Pour over coconut mixture, and top with remaining mixture. Chill until firm. Serves 8.

✿ SYLLABUB

Syllabub was a rich dessert a century ago. It required a quart of warmed rich milk or cream, a cup of wine, and half a cup of sugar. After the sugar was dissolved in the wine, the lukewarm milk, held high, was poured into it. To make it frothy, the mixture was poured back and forth several times. A little nutmeg grated over it enhanced the flavor. A little honey dissolved in the milk before adding to the wine (and using less sugar if desired) added another flavor.

✿ HONEY MOUSSE

    4 eggs, separated
    1 cup honey
1½ cups heavy cream, whipped
    ⅓ cup chopped pecan or pistachio nuts

Drop egg yolks into double boiler and beat until light. Beat in honey slowly, mixing thoroughly. Heat over hot water, beating, until thickened. Cool, and chill mixture. Beat egg whites until stiff and fold into mixture. Fold in whipped cream, and freeze several hours or overnight. Sprinkle with nuts before serving. Serves 6 to 8.

*   *   *

With ripe fruits filling her cellar, and pears ripening into mellowness, Great-grandma abandoned making cakes and rich pies, substituting simple but elegant fruit dishes.

✿ HONEY PEARS

    8 unpeeled pears
2¾ cups pineapple juice
    ½ cup brown sugar
    ¼ teaspoon lemon extract
    1 teaspoon vanilla
    ⅔ cup chopped pecans
    ½ cup honey

Halve and core pears, trim bottoms flat and put in baking dish. Pour over juice to prevent discoloration. Mix sugar, lemon extract, and vanilla, and sprinkle over pears. Spoon on nuts, and pour honey over all. Bake at 350° for 30 minutes.

* * *

Since approximately 80 percent of pollination of all fruits and vegetables and other crops is done by the honeybee, modern agriculture has come to depend greatly on it to fulfill the pollination needs. However, the honeybee cannot compete with killing sprays and thoughtless destruction of the environment. Even as Great-grandma knew, a land without a busy bee is a land without promise.

LAYERED PINEAPPLE DESSERT

- ⅔ cup sugar
- ⅓ cup honey
- 2 eggs, separated
- 2 cups milk
- 1 package lemon-flavored gelatin
- 1 1-pound can crushed pineapple, drained
- 2 cups heavy cream
- 1 large angel food cake
- 1 cup toasted coconut

Combine sugar, honey, egg yolks, and milk, and cook over hot water until smooth. Pour over gelatin and stir until dissolved. Cool until it starts to congeal. Add stiffly beaten egg whites. Add drained pineapple, and fold in whipped cream. Cut cake into thin pieces, arrange in large pan, pour over half the gelatin mixture. Add a layer of cake, and another layer of gelatin. Top with toasted coconut. Refrigerate several hours or overnight. Serves 8 to 10.

STUFFED DATES

- ½ cup honey
- ¼ cup chopped candied pineapple or other fruit
- 1¼ cups chopped nuts
- 1 pound pitted dates

Combine honey, fruits, and nuts and mix well. Stuff dates, roll in sugar, and store in tightly closed container. Serves 4.

* * *

With harvesting of the food over, the holidays meant a change of pace for Great-grandma. Roasted nuts meant an extra fillip, especially almonds which were at that time a fashionable appetizer and deserved her best ornamental dishes.

Roasted chestnuts and peanuts were often salted, and then dusted with cayenne to give them a what-is-it flavor. Almonds, however, were small indeed or the shells were empty if for some reason the honeybees had not been able to pollinate the flowers during the blooming season.

 ### STRAWBERRY TORTE

BOTTOM LAYER

¾ cup butter or margarine
1 cup sifted flour
¼ teaspoon salt
½ cup sugar

FILLING

3 tablespoons cornstarch
¾ cup sugar
2 (10-ounce) packages frozen strawberries, thawed
¼ cup honey
Few drops of red coloring, if desired

TOPPING (MERINGUE)

4 egg whites
⅛ teaspoon cream of tartar
⅛ teaspoon salt
½ teaspoon almond extract
8 tablespoons sugar

For bottom layer, thoroughly cut shortening into combined flour, salt, and sugar. Press in bottom of 9 x 13-inch pan. Bake at 350° for 10 to 15 minutes, or until lightly browned. Cool. For filling, combine cornstarch and sugar in saucepan. Add berries and honey and cook, stirring constantly, until mixture comes to a boil and is clear. Cool slightly. Pour over bottom layer. For meringue, combine egg whites, cream of tartar, salt, and extract. Beat until foamy. Add sugar slowly, beating after each addition. Spread over filling, brown in 350° oven 15 minutes. Makes 10 to 12 servings.

COOKIE CHOCOLATE DESSERT

    1 egg white
    ½ cup honey
    1 teaspoon vanilla
    2 cups finely chopped nuts
    1 tablespoon flour
    ½ teaspoon salt
    2 packages chocolate chips
    1 can sweetened condensed milk
    1 cup sifted flour
    ¼ teaspoon salt
    ¼ teaspoon soda
    1 tablespoon butter or margarine
    1 cup chopped nuts
    1 teaspoon vanilla

Beat egg white to stiff peaks, add honey gradually, add vanilla. Mix in 2 cups nuts, 1 tablespoon flour, and ½ teaspoon salt. Melt chocolate chips in double boiler, add the sweetened milk, remove from heat. Sift together the flour, salt, and soda. Add butter to milk mixture, then dry ingredients, chopped nuts, and vanilla, mixing well. Spread ¾ of mixture in greased 9-inch pan, spread egg-white mixture on top, cover with remaining flour mixture. Bake in 350° oven for 30 to 35 minutes, or until done. Cut into serving pieces when cool. Serve with whipped cream if desired. Makes about 20 pieces, depending on size cut.

ANGEL YULE LOG

    4 egg yolks
    ¾ cup honey
    ¼ teaspoon salt
    ½ cup lemon juice
    1 teaspoon grated lemon peel
    1 envelope (1 tablespoon) plain gelatin
    ⅓ cup sweet sherry wine
    4 egg whites
    ¼ cup honey
    ½ cup diced candied cherries
    1 (12-ounce) baked angel food cake

Beat egg yolks well; continue beating while adding ¾ cup honey in a fine stream. Add salt, lemon juice, and peel; cook and stir over low heat until mixture thickens. Soften gelatin in sherry; dissolve in hot mixture. Beat egg whites to stiff peaks. Continue beating while slowly adding ¼ cup honey. Gently fold into custard; add cherries. Break angel food cake into bite-size pieces. Combine with custard. Turn into a buttered loaf pan about 10 x 4 x 3 inches (1¾-quart capacity) or use an angel food pan. Chill in refrigerator 6 hours or overnight. Unmold and garnish if desired with additional whipped cream and cherries. Makes 12 servings.

CHRISTMAS FRUITCAKE LOAF

(No aging needed.)

⅓ cup shortening
1¾ cups boiling water
1 cup sugar
1 cup honey
2 cups pitted, chopped dates
1 cup raisins
3 cups flour
1 teaspoon salt
1¼ teaspoons soda
1 teaspoon cinnamon
¾ teaspoon cloves
¼ teaspoon nutmeg
½ cup chopped walnuts
½ cup chopped almonds, blanched
1 (3-ounce) package candied fruits (lemon peel, orange peel, pineapple, citron, and cherries)

Combine first 6 ingredients, cook over low heat 20 minutes. Cool. Add sifted dry ingredients. Fold in nuts and fruits. Bake in greased 7½ x 12-inch pan in 325° oven 1½ hours, or until done. Serve with whipped cream.

*　　*　　*

To waken flagging appetites, a simple fruit bowl is both appealing to the eye and nutritious. Use any combination your family enjoys, using summer fruits, or winter canned ones mixed with available fresh beauties. Oranges, apples, bananas, avocados, and grapes are year-round favorites. Add a bit of coconut, a few chopped dates, perhaps a few chopped nuts, and you have a delectable combination. Use equal parts of honey and orange (or other juice) or wine to toss them in. Or add a bit of candied ginger to your dressings. Lemon juice added to a bit of honey makes an excellent dressing. Chill about two hours before using. Longer marinating may make the fruits soft. As a dessert following a heavy meal, such a serving of fruit will be appreciated by your guests.

Toppings and Sauces for Pastry, Cakes, Pies, and Desserts

- For an extra-delicious flavor, just before serving pumpkin pie, spread with equal parts of honey and chopped pecans, cover with whipped cream. Or use whipped cream sweetened with honey, using 1 cup heavy cream to 2 tablespoons honey. Whip cream until slightly thickened, add honey, and continue beating until thick. Makes enough for one pie. Extra garnish for pies may include shaved chocolate curls from a bar of baking chocolate. Using a vegetable parer to skim off the curls is a quick and easy method.

- For pies such as lemon, sweeten a cup of dairy sour cream with 2 tablespoons honey. For cream pies such as banana, beat an egg white with a dash of salt, and ¼ teaspoon vanilla. Beat until soft peaks form, add ⅓ cup honey gradually, beating until mixture forms stiff peaks. Makes 1¼ cups topping.

- For simple, gelatin-type pies, try a berry topping to spread on after the pie is chilled and firm. Thaw and drain a 10-ounce package of strawberries, using the liquid for sauce. Combine 1 tablespoon sugar with 1 tablespoon cornstarch in saucepan, add 1 tablespoon honey, and juice from berries. Add 3 drops food coloring if desired. Cook over medium heat, stirring constantly until clear and thickened.

- For desserts or hot puddings, combine ½ cup orange juice with 1 cup honey, pinch of salt, and 2 tablespoons grated orange peel. Makes 1½ cups. Use other juices if desired. Or, whip ⅓ cup cream, then add slowly combined ½ cup honey and 1 teaspoon lemon juice, dash of salt, and continue beating. Or, 1¾ cups honey, heated, and combined with nuts or a bit of cinnamon. For custards or rice pudding or ice cream, beat together a 1-pound can of whole cranberry sauce with ⅓ cup honey and 2 teaspoons lemon juice.

- Lemon sauce for date pudding is excellent. Mix 2 tablespoons of cornstarch with ¼ cup water. Add 1½ cups water, ¾ cup honey, 1 well-beaten egg, ¼ teaspoon salt, and blend well. Cook and stir until mixture thickens and comes to a boil. Remove from heat; stir in ¼ cup juice and 2 teaspoons grated peel. Makes 2¾ cups.

- A delicious fudge sauce for ice cream or other desserts may be made by melting ½ cup butter; remove from heat. Mix ½ cup cocoa with 2 tablespoons cornstarch; stir into butter. Pour 1 cup honey and 1 cup water into chocolate mixture. Heat, stirring constantly, until mixture comes to a boil and thickens. Remove from heat; add 1 cup miniature marshmallows and ½ teaspoon salt. Stir until marshmallows are melted. Makes 2½ cups.

*   *   *

Great-grandma knew the value of intriguing, tasty sauces for her cakes and puddings. A recipe a century ago called for leaves of roses, gathered while the dew was still on them, and as soon as they opened flat, put into a wide-mouthed bottle. When the bottle was full, the best French brandy was poured over them. It was fit for use in three or four weeks, and could be replenished often. It was often preferable to wine as a flavoring in pudding sauces.

Children of all ages like candy, just as they did in Great-grandma's time. A century ago, however, candy was a treat, whether it was homemade or "boughten," and not a casual sweet as it is so often today. Parties often began with, "Come over for a taffy pull," and ended with great hilarity as young people, coming from near and far, sang and danced, ate from a large table set out with platters of food, and finally, reluctantly, turned homeward, walking with lighted lanterns across field and meadow and over narrow bridges and rushing streams.

❀ MAPLE-HONEY PULL TAFFY

  1 cup maple-honey syrup
1¾ cups light corn syrup
  2 tablespoons butter
  1 tablespoon vinegar
  ¼ teaspoon soda
  2 teaspoons vanilla

Combine first four ingredients in a heavy saucepan. Bring to a boil over medium heat, stirring until well blended. Continue cooking until small amount of syrup forms a hard ball in very cold water (260°). Remove from heat, add soda and vanilla. Beat quickly until it turns smooth and creamy. Pour into buttered plate. When cool enough to handle, butter hands and pull candy until satiny and light in color. Pull into long strips ¾-inch wide in diameter; cut strips into 1-inch pieces. Wrap pieces in wax paper. Makes 1½ pounds hard taffy or 4 dozen pieces.

❀ CHOCOLATE FUDGE ROLLS

  3 squares unsweetened chocolate
  2 tablespoons butter
  3 cups sugar
  ¼ teaspoon salt
  1 cup dairy sour cream
  ¼ cup honey
  1 teaspoon vanilla
  ½ cup finely chopped walnuts

Melt chocolate and butter together in a deep saucepan. Add sugar, salt, sour cream, and honey. Bring to boil over medium heat, stirring until blended. Cover and boil 2 minutes. Remove cover, continue cooking, stirring often until a small amount forms a soft ball in very cold water (240°). Remove from heat, let stand until lukewarm before adding vanilla and nuts. Beat until mixture is thickened and loses its gloss. Turn onto buttered plate. When cool enough to handle, knead until creamy. Shape into 5 rolls about 5 inches long. Let stand until firm and cut each roll into 8 pieces. Makes about 1½ pounds. May be wrapped and frozen.

HONEY CARAMEL CHEWS

1 cup undiluted evaporated milk
¼ cup butter
1½ cups sugar
½ cup honey
¼ teaspoon salt
1 teaspoon vanilla
1 cup coarsely chopped nuts

In a saucepan, heat milk and butter until butter is melted. Set aside. Mix sugar, honey, and salt in a heavy 2-quart saucepan. Cook and stir constantly over medium heat until mixture comes to a boil and sugar is dissolved. Boil, stirring often, to firm ball stage (250°). Continue boiling and very slowly add hot milk and butter so that sugar mixture does not stop boiling. Cook and stir until candy again reaches the firm ball stage (250°). Remove from heat; stir in vanilla and nuts. Pour into well-buttered 8 x 8-inch pan. When cool, cut into 40 squares. Wrap each caramel chew in wax paper.

HONEY DIVINITY DROPS

¼ cup honey
2½ cups sugar
⅔ cup water
¼ teaspoon salt
2 egg whites
1 teaspoon vanilla

In a 2-quart saucepan combine honey, sugar, water, and salt. Stir over low heat until sugar is dissolved. Continue cooking slowly without stirring, to 265° on candy thermometer, or until a small amount of the mixture forms an almost brittle ball in cold water. Meanwhile in a large mixer bowl, beat egg whites at high speed until very stiff. Slowly pour in hot syrup, beating constantly, at high speed until mixture loses its gloss and a small amount dropped from spoon holds its shape. Add vanilla. Drop by teaspoonfuls onto buttered shallow pan. Makes about 3½ dozen pieces of divinity.
Variety: For rainbow divinity, divide divinity into three bowls. Add small amount of food coloring to each batch just before dropping candy onto buttered pan.

✿ *NOUGAT*

  1 cup sugar
  ⅓ cup honey
  ⅓ cup light corn syrup
  ¼ cup water
  ¼ teaspoon salt
  2 egg whites
  ¼ teaspoon vanilla
  1 cup chopped nuts

Combine sugar, honey, corn syrup, and water. Cook, stirring only until sugar dissolves, to hard-ball stage (260°). Add salt to egg whites and beat until stiff. Gradually pour syrup over whites, beating constantly until thick. Add vanilla and nuts. Drop from teaspoon on greased pan or pour into greased pan; cool and cut in pieces. For chocolate nougat, dip pieces in melted dipping chocolate. Makes 24 pieces.

✿ *HONEY BUTTER BRITTLE*

  1 cup coarsely chopped toasted walnuts
  1 cup butter
  ½ cup brown sugar, firmly packed
  ½ cup honey
  Dash of salt
  1 teaspoon vanilla

Spread walnuts on cookie sheet and toast at 350° 15 to 20 minutes. Combine butter, brown sugar, honey, and salt in saucepan; bring to a boil, stirring, then add ½ cup chopped walnuts. Continue cooking, stirring frequently to hard-crack stage (300°); add vanilla. Pour candy onto well-buttered 8-inch cake pan. Cover top with balance of toasted walnuts. Press nuts down into candy. When candy is cold, turn out of pan; break into small irregular pieces.

Variety Hint

  1 package (6 ounces) butterscotch pieces
  2 tablespoons butter
  ½ cup finely chopped toasted walnuts

Melt the butterscotch pieces with 2 tablespoons butter. While candy is still warm, spread half of butterscotch mixture on it. Cover with ¼ cup finely chopped toasted walnuts. When candy is cold, turn out of pan and spread bottom with remaining butterscotch mixture. Cover with ¼ cup toasted walnuts.

CHOCOLATE NUT TOFFEE

    ¾ cup blanched almonds
    1 cup sugar
    ¾ cup cream
    ⅟₁₆ teaspoon salt
    1½ tablespoons butter
    ¾ cup honey
    ½ teaspoon vanilla
    4 squares sweet chocolate

Cut up and toast almonds. Cook sugar, cream and salt to 230°, add butter and honey and continue cooking to 258°. Remove from fire, add vanilla and ½ cup of the nuts. Pour into greased pan, cool slightly, pour melted chocolate over toffee and sprinkle with remaining almonds. When cold, cut into squares. This is a soft honey toffee.

HONEY CARAMELS

    ¼ cup cream or evaporated milk
    1 teaspoon flour
    ¼ teaspoon salt
    2 tablespoons butter
    ½ cup honey
    ½ teaspoon vanilla
    ½ cup chopped nuts

Mix first three ingredients in heavy saucepan. Add and mix in butter and honey. Heat, stirring constantly, until mixture reaches 258° or until syrup when dropped in cold water forms a firm ball (about 15 minutes). Add vanilla and nuts; pour into buttered dish. When cool, cut into squares and wrap in waxed paper. *Note:* A pecan roll can be made by putting a layer of chopped nuts on a buttered 8 x 10-inch pan, covering with a ¼-inch layer of hot caramel. When cool, cover the caramel with a slightly thicker layer of marshmallow or nougat flavored with vanilla. When cool, cut into 4½-inch-wide strips and shape into rolls. Wrap in waxed paper or aluminum foil.

✿ HONEY CANDY ROLLS

1 cup dry milk powder
1 cup plain or chunk-style peanut butter
1 cup honey
½ teaspoon vanilla
Additional peanuts if desired

Mix all ingredients together. Shape into bite-size rolls. Keep a supply handy in refrigerator for snacking.

*   *   *

Great-grandma made candies for reasons other than for sweets. Her horehound candy was good for coughs and was made by boiling the horehound, a bitter mint, in a little water until the juice was extracted, then it was strained through cheesecloth. Sugar was dissolved in a tiny bit of water and stirred into the juice. After working the sugar mixture against the pan until it was creamy and thick, she poured it in a buttered pan, cooled it, then marked it into squares and let it dry.

Pine-tree-tar cough candy was also a favorite. It contained sugar, tar which was made by dissolving 1 tablespoon of tar in 2 tablespoons of alcohol, 1 tablespoon of oil of capsicum, 1½ tablespoons of oil of wintergreen. It was rolled into round sticks and cooled.

Because she liked colored and flavored candies, she often made her own colorings, using 1 ounce of cochineal with ½ pint of boiling water for red. After it boiled 5 minutes, she added 1 ounce of cream of tartar, ½ ounce of powdered alum, and continued to boil about ten minutes or until a clear color. When done, 2 ounces of sugar were added.

Indigo stone was dissolved in warm water for blue, and for yellow she might use the heart of a yellow lily in warm water. If she had saffron, she often steeped a bit of it in soft water for 24 hours.

Spinach gave a pretty green color, and carmine moistened with rose water made pink. Sugars were often colored with these for a prettier look.

She often flavored her candies with essential oils of rose, wintergreen, peppermint, cloves, and others, dropped them on lump sugar, pulverized the sugar with a rolling pin, and carefully preserved it in tightly closed bottles until needed.

To make cinnamon sugar, she pulverized ½ ounce of cinnamon with ½ pound of loaf sugar by grinding in a mortar or with a suitable piece of hard wood. Other sugars such as orange, lemon, clove, ginger, and vanilla were usually handy in her cupboards.

Just when Great-grandma rested is difficult to determine. She had little or no time to pity herself, nor did she want to. Her family's health and well-being were her first concern. But surely the little verse, "Man may work from sun to sun, but woman's work is never done" applied to all the Great-grandmas of her time.

HONEY IN ANCIENT CIVILIZATIONS

From the beginning of recorded history, civilizations have valued honey and its products as a food, a medicine, a trading commodity, and a social and religious offering. Deeply enmeshed in superstition and idolatry, religions and cultures wove a web of sacredness around the honeybee for centuries, abandoning beliefs slowly as research attempted to pierce the innermost heart of the life of the honeybee.

Earliest man, with little to give, offered honey as an appeasement to his gods, and as a sacrifice, which indeed it must have been for him. In death, it was used as a shroud for heroes. Left beside the body or in the tomb, it provided food in the hereafter.

For the living, it warded off evil spirits, or bestowed the gifts of health, eloquence, and poetic inspiration, happiness, and peace.

In many ceremonies, honey played a leading role. It was used to consecrate holy land, to pay taxes demanded by conquerors, to bless brides, and to feed kings, heroes, and gods.

Honey was also significant to early romantics and in religion. Amor, the god of love, dipped his arrows into it. The Hindus believed their god of love had a bow whose string was a chain of bees, symbolizing the sweetness and the sting of love. According to Mohammedan teaching, the bee was the only creature directly spoken to by the Lord.

Man's interest in bees gave rise to many quaint superstitions. Pliny the Elder thought that if a person carried the bill of a woodpecker on his person he would never be stung. In Greece, a swarm of bees rising from a hive meant strangers would arrive. In the British Isles, if a swarm landed on a house, good luck would follow. However, the landing of a swarm on a rotten branch meant misfortune, and on a dead tree, a death. In Central Europe, it was believed that an unfaithful lover would be stung if led past beehives.

Honey as a food was highly prized. Many Roman and Greek chefs became famous for their honey recipes, and guests were honored by being offered honey. "Here," they were told "is honey which the gods provided for your health."

Hives of bees were taken on great military expeditions for more than their honey; they became lethal weapons during some of the great battles. It is said that an emperor of Turkey, having besieged a city and made a breach in the wall, found the breach defended by bees whose hives had been placed in the rubble. The bravest militia of the Ottoman empire, the Janissaries, refused to clear the obstacle. And again, once when a large Turkish galley was pursuing a small corsair with only forty or so men aboard, and the Turks were about to board her, the defenders threw earthen hives of bees into the galley. The enemy, frightened and defenseless against the stings, gave up without much resistance, and the men who were attacked, having donned masks and gloves, took over the galley.

Before man studied bees, it was thought that bees sucked their young from flowers, that they could predict rain, and finally that swarms developed within decaying bodies of oxen.

Honey was responsible for man's first-known alcoholic drink, mead. It was the prized drink of the Middle Ages and was taken as a love potion. In Norse mythology, Odin and Thor drank mead in Valhalla with heroes slain in battle.

Thus has the honeybee followed man throughout history, playing various roles in his daily life, yet scrupulously keeping her own house in order, defending it as she has done for thousands of years, unaware that she has spurred man's imagination from the dawn of history, becoming as she did so, a part of his heritage.

BEVERAGES PAST AND PRESENT

WHETHER FOR SOCIABILITY OR THE SIMPLE SLAKING OF THIRST, beverages were as much a part of life in ancient times as they are today. Although the greater variety of drinks today is in marked contrast to the fewer known in times past, all civilizations concocted their favorite beverages. Some were alcoholic, some were not, and then as now such beverages were used in the celebration of special occasions, ceremonies, or in the honoring of heroes.

One of the most fascinating early alcoholic drinks known was mead or honey wine. So ancient is its origin that we can only speculate that prehistoric man first used it thousands of years before Christ. Certainly the Aryans, Greeks, Romans, Anglo-Saxons, Vikings, and the people of India drank it.

The Old English poem *Beowulf* refers often to mead, as well as to mead halls and benches. During the seventh and eighth centuries, the finest meads were offered only to great rulers and warriors. Legends tell of the effects of this love potion on honeymooners and wedding guests.

Mellow first-grade honey makes the best mead. Exact proportions and methods of handling the mixture were followed by generations of families. When grape wines were introduced, many people turned to the newer wine. Still, many beekeepers stubbornly maintained their own supplies. With their own honey, they could produce it cheaply and at their convenience. Furthermore, they enjoyed its flavor.

People are discovering this old but new honey wine flavor once more. Both here and abroad, old-time mead is increasingly being made and used.

Mead was not the only honey beverage used by peoples long ago. Honey "tea" is one of the oldest. Basically hot water and honey, it continues to be used. While Great-grandma considered it a laxative, a treatment for intestinal troubles, a cure for sore throats and colds and innumerable other ailments when lemon or barley water was added, it is basically a warming, energy-giving drink.

Peasants in many countries believed that honey prevented tuberculosis. The Scots believed that honeysuckle, a favorite plant of the bees, contained a life substance. The Gaels gave honey to their children regularly as the best possible tonic. Spiced honey was the Turks' favorite. The nomadic Arabs, the Bedouins, fed their children buttermilk with honey, a drink filled with energy and food value.

Today, honey still adds flavor and energy to our beverages. Although canned and bottled beverages abound, it is fun to add subtle flavors to familiar drinks.

With this in mind, we've included recipes for simple but elegant tea and coffee variations, milk shakes, hot and cold punches, holiday or special occasion suggestions, as well as recipes for ginger beer and mead.

Giving guests a beverage to sip is offering hospitality in a charming and time-honored way. Whether a friend drops in for a chat or guests arrive for brunch, lunch, or a casual or more formal dinner, beverages bring warmth of atmosphere and relaxation. Whether you plan to serve a cool drink, a hot stimulating one, a before-dinner freshener, or one to end a meal, make it imaginative, unusual, challenging, or glamorous.

Coffee is a favorite at almost any time, so it is apt to become too routine. Serve it the following way either at the table following dinner or in the living room in demitasse cups and spoons, put out cream and sugar, and pour from a suitably decorative pot.

HONEY DEMITASSE WITH SESAME

    2 cups water
    1⅓ tablespoons honey
    1⅓ tablespoons sugar
    1⅓ tablespoons sesame seeds
    2 tablespoons instant coffee

Mix first three ingredients and bring to a boil. Cover and simmer 2 or 3 minutes. Remove from heat, add instant coffee, and strain into demitasse cups. Serves 8.

COFFEE COOLER

    6 tablespoons honey
    2 tablespoons sugar (or to taste)
    4 cups strong coffee
    ½ cup cream
    ¼ teaspoon ginger
    2 egg whites

Dissolve honey and sugar in hot coffee and chill. Put all ingredients in blender for 15 seconds, or beat thoroughly. Pour over cracked ice. Serves 4 to 6.

*   *   *

Great-grandma used beverages to combat various ailments. While Great-grandpa could get along on hot tea or coffee with a little whiskey added to stave off a cold, the children could not. So Great-grandma boiled a quart of spring water, put in as much camomile as could be grasped in three fingers, and added honey. The patient then sat with his head over the vapors rising from the kettle with a woolen cloth over his head, and inhaled deeply. He was then put into a warm bed.

As a remedy against tapeworms, Great-grandma made an emulsion of peeled pumpkin seeds, honey, and water. The patient took two doses half an hour apart before breakfast. After three hours, he swallowed two ounces of castor oil. This was guaranteed to kill the tapeworm before it killed the patient.

COFFEE AND COCOA

3 cups hot cocoa
¾ cup hot coffee
Honey to taste
¾ teaspoon vanilla
Whipped cream

Combine cocoa, coffee, and honey, and chill. Add vanilla and pour over ice. Garnish with whipped cream. Serves 4.

RICH MOCHA

4 tablespoons hot coffee
2 squares chocolate
½ cup sugar
1 cup honey
3 cups water
¾ teaspoon vanilla
Whipped cream

In the hot coffee melt chocolate. Add sugar, honey, and water. Heat to boiling and strain. Cool and add vanilla. Pour into glasses in which you have placed 1 tablespoon whipped cream and a little shaved ice. Or serve hot, substituting milk for water and putting cream on top.

MILK AND COFFEE

4 eggs
4 tablespoons honey
5 tablespoons instant coffee
4 tablespoons sugar
8 cups cold milk
½ teaspoon vanilla

Beat eggs, add honey and mix thoroughly. Beat in coffee and sugar until dissolved. Add milk and vanilla, beating thoroughly. Chill. Serves 8.

✿ COFFEE ZIP

4 ounces unsweetened chocolate
1 teaspoon cinnamon
¼ cup honey, or to taste
4 cups strong coffee
4 cups milk
Whipped cream

Melt chocolate over hot water. Add cinnamon, honey, and coffee and blend. Add milk; pour over cracked ice and serve with a dollop of whipped cream and a dash of cinnamon. Serves 8.

✿ COFFEE NOG

2 eggs, separated
2 tablespoons sugar
3 tablespoons instant coffee
2 tablespoons honey
3 cups milk

Beat egg whites until they form peaks, gradually add sugar, then 1 tablespoon coffee, beating until stiff. Beat yolks with remaining coffee, blend in honey. Add ⅓ cup milk, and beat until smooth. Blend in remaining milk, and fold in egg-white mixture. Serves 6.

*   *   *

Simple syrups have always been popular to sweeten beverages. By making them ahead and chilling them, they save much time.

✿ CHOCOLATE SAUCE

4 squares unsweetened chocolate
1¼ cups hot water
¼ cup sugar
¾ cup honey
Dash of salt
½ teaspoon vanilla

Combine in saucepan all ingredients except vanilla. Bring to gentle boil and simmer 2 minutes. Add vanilla, cool, and refrigerate. Makes about 2 cups.

✿ COCOA SYRUP

1 cup unsweetened cocoa
½ cup sugar
Dash of salt
2 cups boiling water
1¾ cups honey
Vanilla

Combine cocoa and sugar, add salt. Add water gradually, stirring until smooth. Add honey. Cook over medium heat, boil 1 minute without stirring. Remove from heat, add vanilla. Store covered. Yield, approximately 4 cups.

✿ MINT SYRUP

3 tablespoons sugar
1½ cups water
¾ cup honey
1 bunch fresh mint

Cook sugar and water about 10 minutes, add honey and blend. Pour over bruised mint. Cool, and strain out mint. Yield, 1½ cups. Very good added to tea.

*   *   *

Nonfat dry milk was never heard of in Great-grandma's day. Her extra skimmed milk (left from separating the cream from whole milk) was used for making cheese, drinking, and often for feeding the pigs. Now and then she poured surplus milk around a favorite rosebush.

✿ MOCHA COOLER

1 cup nonfat dry milk
4 cups cold water
3 teaspoons instant coffee
4 to 5 tablespoons Chocolate Sauce (see page 203)
Whipped cream
Nutmeg

Sprinkle milk on water, add the coffee and syrup, and beat until smooth. Top with whipped cream and a dash of nutmeg. Refrigerate until ready to serve. Serves 4.
Variation: Whole milk may be substituted for the nonfat dry milk and the cold water; beat well, and serve as above.

✿ HONEY-SWEETENED SIMPLE SYRUP

    3 cups honey
    3 cups water

Combine, and bring to a boil, stirring to blend. Simmer gently 5 minutes. Cool. Store in refrigerator, covered. Makes approximately 5¾ cups.

*   *   *

Orange syrup was often added to coffee drinks a century ago. The syrup could be bought but if an orange came Great-grandma's way, she cut it, covered it with sugar, and later drained off the juice. Cooled, honey-sweetened coffee was poured into cups with a tablespoon of orange syrup and one of partially whipped cream allowed for each serving.

✿ COFFEE COOLER

    1 cup Chocolate Sauce or Cocoa Syrup (see pages 203, 204)
    1 cup strong coffee, chilled
    5 cups milk

Beat or blend all ingredients until foamy. Pour over ice and serve with a dollop of whipped cream if desired. Serves 8.

Tea

Tea was as popular in Great-grandma's day as it is today. Hot or cold, sweetened or spiced, or added to other ingredients, it served as a refresher for company or family or as a base for medicines.

Making good tea is as important now as a century ago. Use freshly boiling water, measure accurately, heat the teapot before adding the tea, let steep 3 to 5 minutes, and strain if necessary. Iced tea may be cleared, if cloudy, by adding a little boiling water. Hot brewed tea should not be refrigerated.

To make cloudless tea, put 3 teabags to every ¾ cup cold

water in a pitcher or other glass or china container. Cover and refrigerate for 12 to 24 hours. Strain and add ice, and serve as usual. Flavor will be excellent.

SPICY HOT TEA

    8 cups water
    1¼ sticks cinnamon
    1¼ teaspoons whole cloves
    3 tablespoons tea
    ½ to ¾ cup mild honey
    2½ tablespoons lemon juice
    1 cup orange juice

Bring water, cinnamon, and cloves to a boil. Remove from heat, add the tea, stirring briefly. Cover and steep five minutes. Strain, and add honey. Bring juices to a boil, and stir into hot tea. Serve at once. Serves 8.

PINEAPPLE TEA PUNCH

    2 cups water
    1 cup grated pineapple
    1 cup honey
    1 cup sugar
    ½ cup hot tea
    Juice of 3 lemons
    Juice of 3 oranges
    1 cup grape juice
    2½ quarts water

Boil 2 cups of water and the pineapple for 15 minutes. Strain through a cheesecloth, pressing out all the juice. Add the honey, sugar, tea, fruit juices, and finally the remaining water. Serve over ice. Serves 10 to 12.

*   *   *

Honey's energy is as important to the working bee as it was to Great-grandma. Unlike Great-grandma, the weary bee always has a "house bee" ready and willing to feed her when necessary. She needs and deserves it, for a worker with a life span of 4 to 6 weeks during harvesttime, may contribute the sum total of half a teaspoon of honey and in so doing literally beat her wings to shreds.

HONEY FRUIT TEA

    1¼ quarts boiling water
    1½ teaspoons tea
      5 whole cloves
    1¼ cups orange juice
      1 quart lime juice
    ½ cup lemon juice
    ½ cup honey

Pour boiling water over tea and cloves. Cover, steep for 5 minutes, strain. Combine tea with other ingredients and pour over cracked ice to chill. Garnish with thin orange slices, red cherries, or mint leaves. Makes about 12 cup servings.

PINK PUNCH

    ¼ cup sugar
    3 cups diced rhubarb
    3 cups water
    ¾ cup honey
    1¼ cups pineapple juice
    3 tablespoons lemon juice
    1 pint ginger ale

Cook sugar, rhubarb, and water together until rhubarb is tender. Add honey and chill. Blend, ½ at a time, in blender until all rhubarb is liquefied. Add remaining ingredients and pour over ice in punch bowl. Serves 8.

PINK PUNCH FOR A CROWD

    4¼ cups cranberry juice cocktail
    ¾ cup honey
    ¾ cup sugar
    1 quart pineapple or grapefruit juice
    2 quarts ginger ale

Heat 1 cup cranberry juice cocktail, add honey and sugar to dissolve; cool. Add remaining chilled juices. Refrigerate until ready to serve. Pour into punchbowl, add chilled ginger ale. Makes 32 punch-cup servings.

✤ SPICED TEA COOLER

    1½ cups boiling water
    ¼ teaspoon each, nutmeg, allspice, cinnamon
     2 tablespoons tea or 6 tea bags
    ½ to ¾ cup honey
    ⅓ cup lemon juice
    2¼ cups cranberry juice cocktail
    ½ cup orange juice

Pour boiling water over spices and tea, steep for 4 minutes, strain. Add honey. Cool, add remaining ingredients. Refrigerate. Pour into 6 tall glasses. Serves 6.

*　　*　　*

Great-grandma had an "inexpensive drink" which often took the place of lemonade. She measured 1 cupful of pure cider vinegar, half a cupful of good molasses, a bit of honey, and put them into a quart pitcher of ice water. She might add a tablespoon of ground ginger to add flavor and health.

Rhubarb was a health food used as a tonic in the early spring. Combined with citrus juices, today it adds up to more than the simple tonic of a century ago.

✤ HONEY AND CITRUS JUICE

    16-ounce can each, frozen orange and grapefruit juice
    ½ cup honey
     6 cans cold water

Blend frozen fruit juices, honey, and water in a blender or beat with rotary beater. Makes about 6 cups.

✤ GINGER ALE TEA

     2 tea bags or 2 teaspoons tea
     1 cup boiling water
    ¼ cup honey
     1 cup orange juice, fresh or frozen
    ¼ cup lemon juice, fresh, frozen, or canned
     1 12-ounce can apricot nectar
    ¾ quart ginger ale

Pour boiling water over tea and steep 3 to 5 minutes, strain if using tea leaves. Add honey and stir. Add juices and nectar. Refrigerate. Add ginger ale when ready to serve. Makes 1½ quarts.

❁ DELICIOUS TEA PUNCH

     4 quarts boiling water
     ½ cup tea
     1 cup honey
     3 cups sugar
     10 cups pineapple juice
     2¼ cups lemon juice
     1 quart cold water
     Ice

Pour boiling water over tea and steep 5 minutes, strain. Add honey and sugar, stir to dissolve. Add remaining ingredients except ice and refrigerate. Serve in punch bowl over block of ice. Makes 8 quarts.

❁ OLD-FASHIONED TEA PUNCH

     1 quart boiling water
     4 tablespoons tea
     1 cup honey
     Juice of 4 lemons
     ½ pint Apollinaris (a German mineral water)
     Handful of mint sprays

Make tea in the usual way, add honey and lemon juice. Cool and pour over cracked ice in punch bowl. Add Apollinaris and strew mint over surface just before serving.

❁ TEA PUNCH FOR THIRTY

     ½ cup honey
     ½ cup sugar
     1 quart strong tea
     1 cup lemon juice
     ¾ quart grape juice
     2¼ cups orange juice
     1 quart cold water
     ½ quart ginger ale
     Ice

Dissolve honey and sugar in hot tea, add juices and water, and refrigerate. When ready to serve, add ginger ale and pour over block of ice. Serves 30.

*   *   *

Although Great-grandma made many variations of tea for guests, one of the simplest and most delicious was a cup of hot tea mixed with an equal amount of rich prune juice and sweetened with honey. Lacking prune juice, she substituted equal parts of chilled apple juice, often coloring it with a small amount of maraschino cherry juice. A wild strawberry floated atop each cup.

 ## TEA PUNCH, FRUITED

    1 cup water
    1¼ cups honey
    1½ cups pineapple juice
    3¼ cups orange juice
    1 cup lemon juice
    1 cup bottled raspberry syrup
    3 cups strong hot tea
    1 quart soda water, refrigerated
Ice

Heat water, add honey to dissolve. Add juices, raspberry syrup, and tea. Refrigerate. Before serving, add soda water, and pour over ice in punch bowl. Makes 15 cups.

DELICIOUS ICED TEA

    4 oranges
    4 lemons
    ½ cup sugar
    4 quarts water
    4 tablespoons tea
    2 quarts boiling water
    ½ cup honey

Squeeze oranges and lemons. To skins and juices, add sugar and 4 quarts water. Boil together for 10 minutes. Add tea to 2 quarts boiling water. Strain the juice mixture into the tea and steep 5 minutes. Strain and add honey. Refrigerate when cool. When ready to serve, pour over ice cubes in tall glasses with lemon slice on top. The mixture is cloudy from orange and lemon skins which give the delicious flavor. Makes 6½ quarts.

PARTY TEA PUNCH

Delicious and pretty

1 cup strong hot tea
¼ cup honey
5 tablespoons sugar
¼ cup lemon juice
½ cup orange juice
½ pint ginger ale, chilled
½ pint orange sherbet

Combine tea, honey, and sugar, add juices. Chill. Just before serving place mixture in punch bowl, add ginger ale, and spoon in sherbet. Makes 8 punch-cup servings.

Some More Punches

PUNCH FOR FIFTY

2 sticks cinnamon
1 tablespoon whole cloves
¾ cup sugar
2 cups water
2 cups honey
1 quart grapefruit juice
2 quarts orange juice
1 quart lemon juice
2 quarts soda water

Heat spices and sugar in water for 10 minutes. Add honey to dissolve. Cool and remove spices; add juices. Just before serving, add chilled soda water, and pour over ice.

HOLIDAY PUNCH

1½ cups honey
2 cups boiling water
2 cups orange juice
1 cup lemon juice
4 cups cranberry juice cocktail
1 quart ginger ale

Dissolve honey in boiling water, chill. Combine all ingredients except ginger ale, chill. Before serving add ginger ale. Rum may be added if desired. Makes 20 punch-glass servings.

*   *   *

Eggnogs were a prime beverage in Great-grandma's day. When nothing else seemed just right to give to an ailing child or to Great-grandpa when he was recovering from an illness, a quickly beaten-up egg-milk mixture, seasoned a bit and cold, was taken to the bedside. Fresh eggs from the henhouse and fresh milk from the just-filled pail, cooling now in the well, made this extra delicious. Sweetening with honey gave it additional flavor and nutrition.

HONEY EGGNOG

    2 eggs
    2 to 4 tablespoons honey
    1 quart milk

Beat eggs until light. Add honey and mix well. Pour over milk and mix thoroughly. Sometimes Great-grandma added a bit of flavoring such as vanilla. And if she thought a child needed more nourishment, she added more eggs, approximately one to a glass of milk. Serves 4.

RICH-FLAVORED EGGNOG

    4 eggs, well beaten
    ½ cup honey
    2 quarts bottled chocolate milk or drink
    ¼ cup cream, whipped (1 cup)

Add beaten eggs to honey, add chocolate milk and beat. Reserve a few tablespoons of whipped cream, fold in the remainder. Pour into pitchers, garnish with reserved cream. Makes 3 quarts.

REFRESHING LEMONADE

    ½ cup honey
    Juice of 4 lemons
    4 cups cold water
    Lemonade ice cubes (see below)

Mix honey and lemon juice, add cold water. To make cubes, add lemon juice to water in ice cube tray. Freeze, tucking a cherry or mint leaf in each. Pile the cubes in a bowl and let guests help themselves.

HOT HONEY LEMONADE

Great-grandma had great faith in hot lemonade with honey for relieving grippe or a cold or weariness. For one glass, she combined 2 tablespoons lemon juice with 2 tablespoons of honey and mixed them into 1 cup spring water heated to boiling. If it were summertime, she often made cold drinks, adding fruit juices to the honey lemonade.

HONEY FRUIT LEMONADE

    1 cup honey lemonade (your favorite lemonade sweetened
        with honey)
    6 tablespoons orange juice
    1¼ tablespoons pineapple juice
    1 tablespoon fresh crushed strawberries sweetened with 1
        tablespoon honey

Combine in blender, then pour over cracked ice. Serves 1.

HONEY FRUIT ALE

    1 cup lemonade
    1 cup unsweetened fruit juice
    ¼ cup honey
    2 cups ginger ale

Combine all ingredients except ginger ale in a shaker and mix thoroughly. Add ginger ale and pour over ice. Makes 1 quart.

*   *   *

Few items were tossed out a century ago. Cocoa nibs or shells were made into a beverage by wetting 2 ounces of them in a little cold water, adding a quart of boiling water, and boiling them for an hour and a half. After straining them, a quart of fresh milk, heated just below the boiling point was added with honey to sweeten just before serving.

In measuring honey, Great-grandma found it easier if she measured the liquid ingredients first so less honey would stick to the measuring implement. For her, the ordinary coffee cup held half a pint and was the common standard of domestic measure. Ten drops made a saltspoon, and 4 saltspoons equaled a teaspoon in liquid measure. Two of her basting spoons equaled a gill, and 2 gills filled a cup. Also, 1 basting spoon equaled 4 tablespoons.

PINEAPPLE MILK

6 tablespoons honey
3¼ cups fresh diced pineapple
3¼ cups milk
1½ cups cracked ice

Put in blender for about a minute. Serves 6.

PUNCH AND CANDY CANES

A delicious way to use Christmas candy canes

1 6-ounce can frozen orange juice concentrate
¼ cup lemon juice
¼ cup honey
1 egg white
4 peppermint candy canes
6 hard peppermint candies
Ginger ale

Put all ingredients except candy canes and ale into blender. Turn to LIQUEFY and blend until candy is liquefied. Pour into 4 glasses, fill with ginger ale and mix briefly. Use candy canes as garnish and to stir.

*   *   *

"Virgin honey" to Great-grandma was honey that dripped freely from the comb without pressure or heat. This was her best quality.

ICY FRUIT FROST

⅔ cup chilled, unsweetened grapefruit juice
¾ cup unsweetened pineapple juice
⅔ cup honey
1 cup finely crushed ice

Quickly whirl all ingredients in blender until mixture is frothy. Serve in chilled glasses. Makes 6 servings. *Note:* Fruit Frost may be poured into ice cube trays and frozen until thick.

✿ ORANGE REFRESHER

    2 eggs
    3 tablespoons honey
    2 tablespoons lemon juice
    1 6-ounce can frozen orange juice concentrate
    2¼ cups cold water

Beat eggs lightly, add honey. Combine other ingredients and mix with eggs and honey thoroughly. Pour over ice. Serves 6.

✿ PEACH HONEY FLOAT

    2 cups crushed fresh peaches
    ½ cup honey
    1 quart milk
    ½ teaspoon almond extract
    1 quart vanilla or cherry-vanilla ice cream

Combine fresh peaches and honey. Add half of milk; beat or blend, then add balance of milk, extract, and half of ice cream. Beat until smooth. Pour into tall glasses; top with balance of ice cream. Makes 6 servings.

✿ STRAWBERRY VELVET

    2 cups milk
    2 cups fresh strawberries, mashed
    ¼ to ½ cup honey
    4 scoops vanilla ice cream

Combine milk, berries, and honey. Whip until smooth, then pour into cold glasses. Add a scoop of vanilla ice cream to each glass. Makes 4 servings.

✿ HONEY MILK SHAKE

    2 cups milk
    ¼ to ⅓ cup honey
    2 scoops ice cream

Warm ½ cup milk and add honey. Add remaining milk. Whip in half the ice cream until smooth. Pour into glasses, and top with remaining ice cream. Serves 2.

*   *   *

Great-grandma clarified honey now and then by beating up the white of an egg to a stiff froth and whipping it into 4 or 5 pounds of honey. She then stirred in pure water to make a syrup of the consistency of cream, and boiled it until the white of egg could be removed with a skimmer. She then poured out the honey into a milk can or other receptacle having a spigot or faucet at the bottom, and let it stand for about a month. She could then draw off the clarified honey from the spigot. Sometimes she used strong linen strainers covered with clear white sand through which to filter the hot honey. Afterward she allowed the excess water to evaporate with gentle heat.

BANANA EGGNOG
(Great-grandma's children seldom ate bananas except as a special treat when they were ill.)

2 cups milk
3 ripe bananas
2 to 3 tablespoons honey
1 egg
Nutmeg or cinnamon

Combine all ingredients except spice in blender or electric mixer bowl. Blend or mix at high speed until eggnog is smooth and frothy. Pour into 4 glasses, top with spice, and serve.

*   *   *

Great-grandma was not alone in believing honey was good for her family and thus worth all her work of storing it for future use. Years ago the pale and ailing girls of Denmark and Hanover were sent to the country, it is said, to exercise and eat honey.

ORANGE SHERBET PUNCH

2⅔ cups orange juice (may be reconstituted)
¼ cup honey
¼ cup sugar
1 quart orange sherbet
Milk
Soda water

Blend all ingredients except sherbet and pour into 8 tall glasses. Add ¼ cup milk to each glass and stir to blend. Top each with 1 scoop of orange sherbet, and fill glass with soda water. *Note:* May use all honey instead of sugar. Makes 8 glasses.

Variations: Substitute soft fruits such as diced peaches for orange juice, add lemon juice for tartness, and put the whole in blender until thick and fluffy.

❈ WASSAIL

    2 lemons
    2 oranges
    1½ quarts cold water
    ¾ tablespoon whole allspice
    2 sticks cinnamon
    1 cup honey
    1 gallon cider

Extract juice from lemons and oranges and set aside. Boil orange and lemon rinds and spices in water for 1 hour. Strain, add honey. Combine cider, orange, and lemon juice and boiled strained liquor. Serve hot. Approximately 6 quarts.

❈ MOCHA DRINK

    ¼ cup sugar
    ½ cup honey
    2½ tablespoons instant coffee
    1½ cups rich milk
    1½ pints vanilla ice cream
    Dash of salt
    Carbonated water

Put all ingredients except carbonated water in blender briefly. Pour into glasses and add carbonated water. Serves 6.

❈ HONEY AND BANANA FLOAT

    ½ cup honey
    1 banana
    1½ teaspoons instant coffee
    2½ cups milk
    1 pint vanilla ice cream, softened

Mash bananas with fork or in blender. Blend in honey and coffee. Add milk and softened ice cream. Beat until frothy and blended. Makes 1¼ quarts.

❁ SIMPLE HOT SPICED PUNCH

Grape juice or loganberry juice
1 tablespoon honey to each quart or to taste
½ teaspoon allspice to each quart

Heat juice, using 2 parts juice to 1 part water. Add honey
and allspice, mix thoroughly. The recipe may be varied by
adding 2 tablespoons lemon juice to each quart.

*   *   *

Our forefathers probably knew of only one soda drink, a
remedy for stomach disorders, which consisted of soda dissolved in water. However, they did know ice cream, and they
would have approved heartily of sodas as we know them.

❁ COFFEE SODA

4 cups water
2¾ tablespoons instant coffee
½ cup sugar
½ cup honey
Coffee or vanilla ice cream
Soda water

Boil water, add coffee and sugar, and boil 5 minutes. Add
honey and refrigerate. When cold place scoops of ice cream
in 8 tall glasses, add coffee syrup and soda water.

❁ COCOA SODA

½ cup cream
½ cup cocoa mix
2¾ tablespoons Honey-Sweetened Simple Syrup (see page 205)
Chocolate or vanilla ice cream
Soda water

Blend cream, cocoa mix, and syrup and divide among 8 tall
glasses. Add scoops of ice cream and fill to tops with soda
water.

*   *   *

Honey was used to sweeten still another kind of beverage
in Great-grandma's day. The Ginger Beer old-fashioned recipe
below, served with pride to guests, gave a casual moment
charm and warmth and a chance to sit for a spell.

OLD-FASHIONED HOT PUNCH

¼ pound sugar
1 large lemon
1 pint boiling water
2 tablespoons honey
½ pint rum
½ pint brandy
½ teaspoon nutmeg

Rub the sugar over the lemon until it has absorbed all the yellow part of the skin, then put the sugar into a punch bowl; add juice of lemon (free of pips) and mix these two ingredients together well. Pour over them the boiling water, add honey, stir to blend; add the rum, brandy, and nutmeg. Mix thoroughly and the punch will be ready to serve. To ensure success, the processes of mixing must be diligently attended to.

MILK PUNCH

4 large lemons
1 quart rum or brandy
1½ pounds loaf sugar
2 or 3 tablespoons honey
2 nutmegs, grated
1 quart water
1 quart boiling unskimmed milk

Pare yellow rind from lemons and steep 24 hours in rum or brandy. Mix with juice of lemons, loaf sugar, honey, nutmeg, water, and milk. Strain the whole through a jelly bag. Can be used immediately or bottled and kept for several months.

HOT TODDY

4 teaspoons honey
1 cup cream sherry
2⅔ cups boiling water
Grated nutmeg
Cinnamon sticks

Place honey in heated mugs. Add sherry and water, stir. Sprinkle lightly with nutmeg and stir with cinnamon sticks. Serves 4.

❀ GINGER BEER

  6 ounces bruised ginger
  6 quarts water
  5 pounds loaf sugar
  ¼ pound honey
  ½ cup lemon juice
  17 quarts cold water
  1 egg, slightly beaten
  2 teaspoons essence of lemon

Boil ginger in 6 quarts of water for half an hour, add sugar, honey, lemon juice, the 17 quarts cold water, and strain through a cloth. When cold, put in the egg and essence of lemon. After standing three or four days it may be bottled.

Mead

Honey wine recipes often were handed down from generation to generation. Honey wine or mead was an ancient and popular drink thousands of years before Christ. It is thought to be the first alcoholic drink known and used by man, becoming a part of his ancient rituals of celebration.

There are many methods known, and many types made. At the turn of the century, one method suggested was to add spring water to new honey, put a whole egg into it, and boil this liquor till the egg swims above the liquor. Strain, and pour into a cask. To every 15 gallons add 2 ounces of white Jamaica ginger, bruised, 1 ounce of cloves and mace, 1½ ounces of cinnamon, all bruised together and tied up in a muslin bag. Accelerate the fermentaton with yeast. When worked sufficiently, bung up. In six weeks draw off into bottles.

Another method: Boil the combs from which the honey has been drained with sufficient water to make a tolerably sweet liquor; ferment this with yeast and proceed as in the preceding recipe.

Sack mead was made by adding a handful of hops and sufficient brandy to the comb liquor. However, true mead is simply a fermentation of honey and water. When spices, fruit juices, and such are added, it is not true mead but metheglin (spiced), pyment (grape juice sweetened with honey), hippocras (spices add to pyment), melomel (apple juice sweetened with honey and fruit juices).

Beekeepers in Britain as well as those in our own country are turning once more to mead-making in small quantities. Not only do they consider this wine excellent but they also "save" by utilizing honey "capping washes" from the honey-straining process. This is the basis of their "must," the mixture of honey and water from which mead is made. The delicately flavored mild honeys make the best mead.

In making mead, if one desires a medium sweet wine, the proportions are approximately 4 pounds of honey to 1 gallon of water, or a gravity reading on the hydrometer of about 1.098. If the gravity reading is higher, the resulting mead will be drier. If too low, the mead will not keep.

The must should be brought to a boil and held there 30 seconds to sterilize. It is then put into a container (not metal) to begin fermentation. A wine yeast is added when the must has cooled to 65 degrees. Cover tightly with muslin, and let ferment until all activity has ceased, about three weeks to a month. Decant into clean containers for more fermentation. Choose those containers into which traps or fermentation locks can be fitted, for air must be kept out during this period or the mead may spoil. Let it ferment until activity stops, then bottles should be stored for two or three years to allow subtle flavor and aroma to develop fully.

In our country, the Internal Revenue law provides that the head of any family may, without payment of tax, produce 200 gallons of mead per year for use of his family, and not for sale, if he registers to do so. No charge is made for the permit.

"Wine," it has been said, "can be made by anyone, but only beekeepers can make mead."

Honey: Its Varieties and Flavors

Hundreds of years before Christ, when honey was used primarily for the pleasures and purposes of kings, gods, and the privileged, little or no attention was given its flavor, color, and texture. Worshipped as a nectar of the gods to give solace and peace, it held a unique position.

Today, however, homemakers are becoming as discriminating in purchasing honey as was Isaac Bromley who wrote in the poem "Our Chauncey":

Bring me honey of Hymettus, bring me stores of Attic salt;
I am weary of the commonplace, to dulness call a halt!

The choice is wide, not only in flavor but in color and texture as well. The homemaker will find flavors ranging from mild, to aromatic, spicy, fragrant, pungent, bitter, harsh, or medicinal; colors from near-white through yellow, yellow-green, gold, amber, dark brown or red to nearly black; textures from thin to heavy. She may also choose from various types, which include liquid, comb, cut comb, solid (granulated or crystallized), and chunk.

Liquid honey is obtained by uncapping the combs and extracting the honey from the cells by centrifugal motion. Granulated or "sugared" honey is partially or wholly solidified. Although the liquid is usually preferred, the granulated is becoming more popular here as it is in Canada. Comb honey differs from liquid honey only in the presence of the comb. It is the honey as stored by the bees. It may be served as is, or cut into smaller chunks. Cut-comb honey (or honey chunks) is little chunks of sealed comb honey about 4 inches long and 1½ inches wide, wrapped in cellophane and packed in individual cartons. Chunk honey consists of pieces of comb honey put into containers, with liquid honey poured over and around them. Mild liquid honey is most often preferred for cooking and baking.

Flavor depends on the floral source. However, soil, climatic conditions, and other environmental factors that affect the growth of the plant may also affect the flavor. Clover honey may, for example, taste superb in one area of the country but be of unimpressive flavor in another. Whether the area is desert, temperate, or swampland affects the kind of nectar a plant gives.

There are also honeys that are used exclusively as food for bees because of their unpalatable flavor. Beekeepers welcome these honeys as winter food for bees, and, since most of this type of honey is stored in hives in late fall and consumed by the bees, the honey produced early in the year is marketable.

Honey from a few plants may affect people adversely. Honey from a species of rhododendron which grew four centuries before Christ poisoned the Greek soldiers of Xenophon. Generally speaking, however, honey poisoning is rare and need not concern us.

Although many hundreds of kinds of honey are produced in this country, only about twenty-five to thirty are commercially available. Nectar and pollen plants such as the clovers, sweet clover, and alfalfa, together with the less important ones which include the citrus plants (such as orange, grapefruit, lemon, limes, tangelos), cotton, sage, and tupelo, furnish the greatest part of the nation's commercial honey.

On the average, white honeys are more widely accepted because of their mildness. More than half the honey produced in this country is light-colored and mild-flavored clover, sweet clover, or alfalfa honey. On the other hand, they are considered lacking in flavor by many connoisseurs of honey.

Light and dark honeys may be blended by producers and processers to produce a golden honey. In some localities the lack of sufficient supplies in one color prompts this blending.

The desired flavor and color of honey vary from area to area. People often prefer the kind that is harvested locally. Distinctly flavored honeys come from citrus blossoms, wild sage, tupelo trees of the South, buckwheat, mints such as horsemint, spearmint, and thyme, basswood, and tulip trees. Buckwheat, a favorite in New York State, is probably the darkest table honey.

Dark honey usually contains more minerals. Generally speaking, the eastern and southern honeys are darker than the average, the north-central higher than average in moisture content, as well as lighter than average, the intermountains honey lighter than average but more heavily bodied with the greatest tendency to granulate. South Atlantic states' honey shows the least tendency to granulate.

Following are a few of the kinds of honey found, their flavor and color:

ALFALFA: Much of the honey crop of Utah, Nevada, and other Rocky Mountain states comes from this source. It is mild and near-white when gathered pure. Bees often desert it for other flowers, and therefore it may be diluted with other honeys.

ALSIKE CLOVER: In the northern states it is often the leading source of surplus honey (honey offered for sale). It is mild and light-colored, and may be mixed with honey from white clover.

BASSWOOD OR LINDEN: This honey is extra white and has a slight bite when pure, but is usually mixed with clover honey.

BLACK LOCUST: Extra white and of very high quality.

BLACK MANGROVE: Abundant along the coasts of Florida, it yields a light honey with a thin body having a slightly brackish taste.

BLACK SAGE OR BALL SAGE: This is perhaps the source of most sage honey, and the best honey plant in California. It has a distinctive flavor.

BLACKBERRY: Reddish brown or near-wine in color, it is somewhat more flavorful than clover.

BUCKBUSH: In the hilly country of the eastern United States, it is often called coralberry and produces a light-amber honey with a good flavor. In the Rocky Mountains a white berried species called snowberry also yields good honey.

BUCKWHEAT: This produces a purple to black honey with a very pronounced flavor much liked by residents of the buckwheat area. In California, sage-buckwheat honey is a favorite. Surpluses of more than 500 pounds of buckwheat honey per colony were common at one time, but other crops have crowded out much of the acreage once given to buckwheat. Manufacturers of various foods prize this honey.

CATSCLAW: An important honey plant in the Southwest where it produces a white honey.

CLOVER, SWEET: Yields so much nectar that beekeepers often establish their apiaries near it. Honey is white and has a mild flavor.

CLOVER, WHITE: This is usually the leading honey plant east of the Mississippi River. The honey is white to extra-light amber with a mild, delicious flavor.

COTTON: Less cotton honey is produced than formerly, perhaps due to soil depletion. Spraying for boll weevil may have affected it too. Most cotton honey is now produced on the black lands of Texas which are still very rich in soil nutrients. It is light-colored and usually of a mild flavor.

DANDELION: Honey is yellow with strong flavor.

GALLBERRY: Common from the Carolinas southward into Florida and along the Gulf Coast. Light amber with a pleasant aromatic flavor. Since it doesn't crystallize, it is excellent for chunk honey.

GOLDENROD: Honey is much esteemed in local areas where grown including the northern states and eastern Canada. Rich, yellow honey, it may be mixed in various areas with other fall plants when bees are gathering nectar.

HORSEMINT: White to light amber honey with a minty flavor and odor which may be quite strong.

MAPLE: Light amber to slightly darker. Good flavor.

MESQUITE: Honey is light amber to white and is usually mixed with that of other nearby plants such as catsclaw and soapbush. The tree spread northward from the Southwest in former times, into Texas, Oklahoma, Arizona, and New Mexico, and eastern California.

ORANGE AND OTHER CITRUS CROPS: A major source of honey in California, Arizona, Florida, and Texas. Beekeepers often move their hives to the groves where large surpluses are produced. Honey is mild, white, and with a delicate aroma of citrus blossoms. Flavor is distinctive, and not always preferred by those not living in the area.

RASPBERRY: White honey with a delicious flavor. Produced in the northern states and southern Canada.

SAW PALMETTO: Chief source of palm honey, a rich yellow honey often preferred in the Southeast. Often considered the best honey in Florida.

SOURWOOD: Water-white honey with a mild, delicious flavor. Because the combs are so white and delicate that the honey cannot be extracted, the honey is sold as comb honey or as chunk comb honey. Many experts agree this is the most delicious honey in the eastern states. Most of it is sold in the areas where it is produced, in the southern Alleghenies from West Virginia and southern Pennsylvania to northern Georgia, and brings premium prices. If mixed with tulip tree honey, it is darkened. Often it is sold as sourwood honey even though mixed with other kinds.

SPANISH NEEDLES: Honey is golden yellow with a pronounced flavor highly esteemed in local areas. The plant grows in swampy places in the central states from Maryland to Georgia, and west to Missouri and Arkansas. Honey may be mixed with white clover honeys and vetch to obtain a mild, golden-tinted honey.

SUMAC: Honey is a light amber with an excellent flavor.

SWEET PEPPER BUSH: Honey is light yellow with a mild flavor and odor of the bloom. It is marketed under the scientific name, Clethra. The plant is abundant in southeastern Massachusetts.

TULIP TREE: One of the chief honey plants in many parts of the South Atlantic Coast states. Honey is red-amber and of good flavor.

TUPELO: Perhaps the leading honey plants in parts of Georgia and Florida. Honey is mild in flavor and light amber, and, if pure, never granulates.

WHITE BRUSH: Shrub of the arid Southwest. Honey is white with a very heavy body and a mild flavor.

VETCH: Water-white, mild honey with a wide selection of flavors, colors, and textures.

Although this by no means exhausts all the varieties of honey, it will give you an idea of the kinds that are most readily available. By trying them, you will discover which flavors you prefer. But whichever ones become your favorites, you will have the satisfaction of knowing that you are using a natural food, delicious and healthy, that man, with all his additives and chemical processes, has not been able to improve upon.

INDEX

A

All-Honey Pumpkin Pie, 170
Angel Yule Log, 188–89
Apple Betty with Honey, 178
Apple Oatmeal Goodies, 149
Apple Pecan Pie, 167
Apple Pie, 166–67
Applesauce Cake, 131
Applesauce Nut Bread, 103
Apple-Topped Pork Chops, 16
Apricot-Nectar Dressing, 90
A Taste of Island Dressing, 79
Avocado Fruit Dressing, 89
Avocado-Orange-Grapefruit Salad, 80
Avocado Salad, 73
Avocado Salad Dressing, 85

B

Baked Beans, Canned, 57
Baked Beans, Spanish Style, 56–57
Baked Custard, 180
Baked Lamb Shoulder, 27
Baked Lamb, Western Style, 26
Baking soda, 112
Banana Cake, 132
Banana Dressing Luscious, 91
Banana Eggnog, 216
Banana Fruit Salad, 82
Barbecued Bear, 28
Barbecued Spareribs Supreme, 20
Beans, dried, 57
Beef
    Chili, Gourmet Style, 26
    Dressed-up Steak, 21
    Grilled Steak, 21
    Hamburgers Royal, 25
    Honey Glazed Short Ribs, 24
    Oriental Pot Roast, 22
    Preserving, 22–24
    Steak and Honey, 22
    Succulent Rolled-Beef Roast, 20–21
    Zesty Meat Loaf, Muffin Style, 25
Beeswax in arts and crafts, 121–22
Berry Topping, 190
Beverages
    Banana Eggnog, 216
    Cocoa Soda, 218
    Coffee and Cocoa, 202
    Coffee Cooler, 201, 205
    Coffee Nog, 203
    Coffee Soda, 218
    Coffee Zip, 203
    Ginger Beer, 220
    Honey and Banana Float, 217
    Honey and Citrus Juice, 208
    Honey Demitasse with Sesame, 201
    Honey Eggnog, 212
    Honey Fruit Ale, 213
    Honey Fruit Lemonade, 213
    Honey Milk Shake, 215
    Hot Honey Lemonade, 213
    Hot Toddy, 219
    Icy Fruit Frost, 214

    Milk and Coffee, 202
    Mocha Cooler, 204
    Mocha Drink, 217
    Orange Refresher, 215
    Peach Honey Float, 215
    Pineapple Milk, 214
    Refreshing Lemonade, 212
    Rich-Flavored Eggnog, 212
    Rich Mocha, 202
    Strawberry Velvet, 215
    Wassail, 217.
        See also Punch and Tea
Biberli, 157
Biscuits, 111
Bitsy Breakfast Breads, 116
Boneless Glazed Shoulder Butt, 14
Bran Honey Cake, 128
Bran Raisin Nut Bread, 99
Bread
    Applesauce Nut, 103
    Bitsy Breakfast Breads, 116
    Bran Raisin Nut, 99
    Country Kitchen Fancy, 106
    Date, 105
    Enriched White, 98
    Fabulous French Toast, 120
    Fresh Orange, 104
    Fruit Bran, 105
    Honey Almond Cranberry, 118
    Honey French Toast, 119
    Honey Prune, 103
    Honey Rye, 100
    Mincemeat, 104
    Savory Cheese, 101
    Swedish Rye, 102
    Whole Wheat, 99
    Yeast-making, recipe for, 107.
        See also Rolls
Broiled Chicken, Wined, 34
Broiled Ham Slices with Honey, 11
Butter, honey and, 45

C

Cabbage Delight, 55
Cabbage, leftover, 55
Cake
    Applesauce, 131
    Banana, 132
    Bran Honey, 128
    Chocolate Layer, 128–29
    Christmas Fruitcake Loaf, 189
    Delicious Fruitcake, 133
    Feather Orange, 129
    Fruitcake, 132
    Honey Lemony, 136
    Honey Spice, 126
    Honey Spice Chiffon, 134
    Jiffy Fruitcake, 132–33
    Meringued Gingerbread, 136–37
    Nut, 131, 134
    Orange Honey, 135
    Princess, 124–25
    Prune, 130

Sour Cream Spice, 127
Tender Cocoa, 125
Tender White, 126–27
Canadian Bacon, Honeyed, 15
Candy
Chocolate Fudge Rolls, 192
Chocolate Nut Toffee, 195
Great-grandma's, 196–97
Honey Butter Brittle, 194–95
Honey Candy Rolls, 196
Honey Caramel Chews, 193
Honey Caramels, 195
Honey Divinity Drops, 193
Maple-Honey Pull Taffy, 192
Nougat, 194
Stuffed Dates, 186
Canning, 61–62
Carrots and Honey, 44
Carrots, Delicious, 46
Carrots, glaze, 47
Carrots, Simple Hints for, 47
Cherry Whirligig Rolls, 109
Chicken
Broiled Chicken, Wined, 34
Chicken Breast with Sesame Seed, 31
Chicken Delicious, 31
Chicken Diablo, 33
Chicken, Honey Roasted, 30
Cleaning, 31–32
Glazed Baked Chicken, 32–33
Honey Barbecue Chicken, 35
Honey Glazed Chicken, 35
Oven-Barbecued Chicken, 33
Chili, Gourmet Style, 26
Choco-Honey Sauce, 137
Chocolate Fudge Icing, 140
Chocolate Fudge Rolls, 192
Chocolate Layer Cake, 128–29
Chocolate Nut Toffee, 195
Chocolate Pie, 175
Chocolate Sauce, 203
Christmas Filled Bars, 155
Christmas Fruitcake Loaf, 189
Cinnamon Cherry Cobbler, 175
Cinnamon Filling for Bread, 107
Cinnamon Honey Butter, 109
Cocoa Icing, 125
Cocoa Soda, 218
Cocoa Syrup, 204
Coconut Honey Topping, 139
Coffee and Cocoa, 202
Coffee Cake
Delicious, 113
Fancy Date, 227
Fruited, 112
Orange, 114
Coffee Cooler, 201, 205
Coffee Nog, 203
Coffee Soda, 218
Coffee Zip, 203
Coleslaw Piquant, 76
Colorful Vegetable Salad and Dressing, 75
Cookie Chocolate Dessert, 188
Cookies
Apple Oatmeal Goodies, 149
Biberli, 157
Christmas Filled Bars, 155

Cookie Chocolate Dessert, 188
Delicate Honey-Nut Balls, 147
Delicate Puffs, 146
Delicious Orange Bars, 143
Easy Fruit Drops, 144
Favorite Honey, 146
Glazed Christmas, 152
Honey Chews, 153
Honey Crunchies, 145
Honey Fruitcake, 150–51
Honey Fruit Diamonds, 155
Honey Oranged Chippers, 144
Honey Thumbprints, 142
Lebkuchen, 151
Mystery Drops, 148
Oatmeal Bars, 141
Oatmeal Drops, 142
Old recipes, 143
Orange Drops, 147
Peanut Butter, 149
Poinsettia Balls, 153
Spiced Fruit Bars, 145
Spicy Bran, 154
Uncooked Fruit Balls, 148
Cookout Bean Salad, 77
Corn, drying, 54–55
Cottage Cheese, 82–83
Country Kitchen Fancy Bread, 106
Cream Cheese, 80
Crisp Salad Bowl, 73
Crunchy Coconut Squares, 184
Crunchy Ham, 9

D

Date Bread, 105
Date Honey Spread, 120–21
Date Pudding, 181
Deep Dish Apple Dessert, 176
Delectable Fruit Salad Mold, 87
Delicate French Dressing, 90
Delicate Honey-Nut Balls, 147
Delicate Puffs, 146
Delicious Coffee Cake, 113
Delicious Fruitcake, 133
Delicious Iced Tea, 210
Delicious Lemon Bavarian, 182
Delicious Lemon-Honey Sauce for Cakes, 138
Delicious Orange Bars, 143
Delicious Tea Punch, 209
Desserts
Angel Yule Log, 188–89
Apple Betty with Honey, 178
Baked Custard, 180
Christmas Fruitcake Loaf, 189
Cinnamon Cherry Cobbler, 175
Cookie Chocolate Dessert, 188
Crunchy Coconut Squares, 184
Date Pudding, 181
Deep Dish Apple Dessert, 176
Delicious Lemon Bavarian, 182
Fruit Bowl, 189–90
Honey Bavarian Mold, 183
Honey Bread Pudding, 179
Honey Rice Pudding, 184
Honey Kuchen, 182
Honey Molded Dessert, 183
Honey Mousse, 185

Honey Pears, 185
Huckleberry Cobbler, 177
Layered Pineapple Dessert, 186
Pear Crunch, 180
Rhubarb and Honey Dessert, 178–79
Special Date Pudding, 181
Strawberry Torte, 187
Syllabub, 185
Dressed-up Steak, 21

E
Earliest Spring Salad, 72
Easy Fruit Drops, 144
Easy Ham and Rice, 14
Easy Lima Beans, 59
Eggs, preserving of, 150
Enriched White Bread, 98

F
Fabulous French Toast, 120
Fancy Date Coffee Cake, 117
Favorite Honey Cookies, 146
Feather Orange Cake, 129
Fluffy Honey Dressing, 81
Fluffy Sauce, 21
French Dressing, 73
Fresh Berry Pie, 168
Fresh Corn Sauté, 54
Fresh Orange Bread, 104
Frosted Chocolate Squares, 156
Frosted Fruit, 85
Frozen Fruit Delicious, 84
Frozen Fruit Delicious Salad Dressing, 84
Fruit Bowl, 189–90
Fruit Bran Bread, 105
Fruit Ring Salad, 81
Fruit Salad Dressing, 82
Fruit Salad, Supreme, 79
Fruit with Fluffy Dressing, 81
Fruitcake, 132
Fruited Coffee Cake, 112
Fudge Sauce, 191

G
Game
    Barbecued Bear, 28
    Honeyed Venison Roast, 28
    Roast Quail, 29–30
    Sauces for game, 30
    Wildfowl, 29
Gelatin, 87
Ginger Ale Tea, 208
Ginger Beer, 220
Glamorous Beets, 48
Glazed Baked Chicken, 32–33
Glazed Christmas Cookies, 152
Glazed Winter Squash, 53
Glazes
    Carrots, glaze, 47
    Great-grandma's Glazes, 11
    Honey Glazed Chicken Glaze, 35
Gourmet Ham Balls, 13
Green Beans, 59–60
Green Beans Delicious, 76
Grilled Steak, 21

H
Ham
    Boneless Glazed Shoulder Butt, 14
    Broiled Ham Slices with Honey, 11
    Crunchy Ham, 9
    Curing and smoking, 11–12
    Easy Ham and Rice, 14
    Gourmet Ham Balls, 13
    Ham Loaf, Muffin Style, 12–13
    Honey Orange Glazed Ham, 9
    Honey-Spiced Glazed Ham, 10
    Lazy Day Ham, 13
    Whole Ham, Honey Glazed, 10
Hamburgers Royal, 25
Ham Loaf, Muffin Style, 12–13
Harvest Moon Salad, 77
Hawaiian Topping, 140
Heavenly Salad, 84
Holiday Punch, 211
Honey
    As medicine, 62–68
    Clarifying, 216
    Harvesting, 33–34
    History of, 1–6; In ancient civilizations, 197–98
    Measuring, 213–14
    Varieties and flavors, 5, 222–27
        Alfalfa, 224
        Alsike Clover, 224
        Basswood or Linden, 224
        Blackberry, 224
        Black Locust, 224
        Black Mangrove, 224
        Black Sage or Ball Sage, 224
        Buckbush, 224
        Buckwheat, 223–24, 225
        Catsclaw, 225
        Chunk, 222
        Clover, 223
        Clover, Sweet, 225
        Clover, White, 225
        Comb, 222
        Cotton, 225
        Dandelion, 225
        Dark, 223
        Gallberry, 225
        Goldenrod, 225
        Horsemint, 225
        Light, 223
        Liquid, 222–23
        Maple, 225
        Mesquite, 226
        Orange and Other Citrus, 226
        Raspberry, 226
        Saw Palmetto, 226
        Sourwood, 226
        Spanish Needles, 226
        Sumac, 227
        Sweet Pepper Bush, 227
        Tulip Tree, 227
        Tupelo, 227
        Vetch, 227
        White, 223
        White Brush, 227
Honey-Almond Carrots, 44–45
Honey Almond Cranberry Bread, 118
Honey and Banana Float, 217
Honey and Citrus Juice, 208

Honey Avocado Ring, 88
Honey Baked Beans, 58
Honey Barbecue Chicken, 35
Honey Bavarian Mold, 183
Honeybees
    Drones, 38
    In literature, 158–62
    Queen, 38–39, 41–42
    Royal jelly, 39, 41
    Workers, 38–42
Honey Bran Muffins, 116
Honey Bun Carrots, 46
Honey Buns, 108
Honey Butter Brittle, 194–95
Honey Butter Cinnamon Buns, 108
Honey-Buttered Carrots, 46
Honey Candy Rolls, 196
Honey Caramel Chews, 193
Honey Caramels, 195
Honey Cheese Dressing, 89
Honey Chews, 153
Honey Coconut Pie, 177
Honey Coconut Topping, 140
Honey Crisp Topping, 141
Honey Crunchies, 145
Honey Custard Pie, 171
Honey Demitasse with Sesame, 201
Honey Divinity Drops, 193
Honey Dressing 1, 88
Honey Dressing 2, 89
Honey Dressing 3, 91
Honeyed Acorn Squash, 52–53
Honeyed Bread Pudding, 179
Honeyed Duckling, 37
Honeyed Parsnips, 61
Honeyed Rice Pudding, 184
Honeyed Venison Roast, 28
Honey Eggnog, 212
Honey French Dressing, 70
Honey French Dressing, 83
Honey French Toast, 119
Honey Fruit Ale, 213
Honey Fruitcake, 150–51
Honey Fruit Diamonds, 155
Honey Fruit Dressing, 80
Honey-Fruited Pork Chops, 17
Honey Fruit Lemonade, 213
Honey Fruit Tea, 207
Honey Ginger Yams, 51
Honey Glazed Chicken, 35
Honey Glazed Short Ribs, 24
Honey-Glazed Sweet Potatoes, 50
Honey Grapefruit Mold, 87
Honey Icing, 138
Honey Kuchen, 182
Honey Lemony Cake, 136
Honey Milk Shake, 215
Honey Molded Dessert, 183
Honey Mousse, 185
Honey Nut Butter, 120
Honey Orange, 120
Honey Oranged Chippers, 144
Honey Orange Glazed Ham, 9
Honey Pears, 185
Honey Prune Bread, 103
Honey Rye Bread, 100
Honey-Sauced Beets, 47
Honeyscotch Topping, 138

Honey Spice Cake, 126
Honey Spice Cake Icing, 126
Honey Spice Chiffon Cake, 134
Honey-Spiced Glazed Ham, 10
Honey-Sweetened Simple Syrup, 205
Honey Thumbprints, 142
Honey Topping, 110
Honey Twists, 110–11, 114
Honey vinegar, 48
Hot Honey Lemonade, 213
Hot Toddy, 219
Household hints, 91–96
Hubbard or Acorn Squash, Honeyed, 52
Huckleberry Cobbler, 177

I

Icing
    Chocolate Fudge, 140
    Cocoa, 125
    Honey, 138
    Honey Spice Cake, 126
    Marshmallow, 138–39
    Nougatine Frosting, 139
    Sugar, 130
Icy Fruit Frost, 214

J

Jiffy Fruitcake, 132–33

L

Lamb
    Baked Lamb Shoulder, 27
    Baked Lamb, Western Style, 26
    Preserving, 27
Layered Pineapple Dessert, 186
Lazy Day Ham, 13
Lebkuchen, 151
Lemon Chiffon Pie, 171
Lemon Honey Butter, 119
Lemon Meringue Pie, 172
Lemon Sauce, 191
Lima Bean Casserole, 58
Lima Beans, Sauced, 59
Lime-Mint Fruit Salad Dressing, 90

M

Mandarin Pork Chops, 17
Maple-Honey Pull Taffy, 192
Marshmallow Icing, 138–39
Mead, 199–200; preparation of, 220–21
Meringued Gingerbread, 136–37
Milk, 82
Milk and Coffee, 202
Milk Punch, 219
Mince-Apple Pie, 167
Mincemeat Bread, 104
Mint Syrup, 204
Mocha Cooler, 204
Mocha Drink, 217
Moon Glow Sauce, 32
Muffins
    Honey Bran, 116
    Orange Nut, 115
Mystery Drops, 148

N

Nougat, 194
Nougatine Frosting, 139

Nut Cake, 131, 134

O

Oatmeal Bars, 141
Oatmeal Drops, 142
Old-Fashioned Hot Punch, 219
Old-Fashioned Tea Punch, 209
Onions, 55
Onions en Casserole, 56
Orange and Lemon Beets, 48–49
Orange Chiffon Pie, 173
Orange Coffee Cake, 114
Orange Drops, 147
Oranged Sweet Potatoes, 49
Orange Honey Butter, 120
Orange Honey Cake, 135
Orange Nut Muffins, 115
Orange Pineapple Dressing, 86
Orange Pineapple Ring, 86
Orange Refresher, 215
Orange Sauce, 119
Orange Sherbet Punch, 216–17
Oriental Pork with Vegetables, 18
Oriental Pot Roast, 22
Oven-Barbecued Chicken, 33
Oxcheek Salad, 76

P

Party Tea Punch, 211
Peach Honey Float, 215
Peanut Butter Cookies, 149
Pear Crunch, 180
Pecan Pie, 168
Perfect Salad Dressing, 90
Perk-up Salad Dressing, 78
Piecrust
    Walnut Crumb, 165
Pie Dough, recipe for, 166
Pie(s)
    All-Honey Pumpkin, 170
    Apple, 166–67
    Apple Pecan, 167
    Chocolate, 175
    Fresh Berry, 168
    Honey Coconut, 177
    Honey Custard, 171
    Lemon Chiffon, 171
    Lemon Meringue, 172
    Mince-Apple, 167
    Orange Chiffon, 173
    Pecan, 168
    Pineapple Meringue, 174
    Pumpkin, 170
    Pumpkin Chiffon, 173
    Rhubarb Cream, 166
    Rosy Cherry, 169
    Special Blueberry, 169
    Strawberry, 165
    Strawberry Cream, 174
Pineapple Meringue Pie, 174
Pineapple Milk, 214
Pineapple Tea Punch, 206
Pink Punch, 207
Pink Punch for a Crowd, 207
Piquant Salad, 71
Poinsettia Balls, 153
Poppy Seed Dressing, 79

Pork
    Apple-Topped Pork Chops, 16
    Barbecued Spareribs Supreme, 20
    Canadian Bacon, Honeyed, 15
    Honey-Fruited Pork Chops, 17
    Mandarin Pork Chops, 17
    Oriental Pork with Vegetables, 18
    Pork Chops Supreme, 18
    Salting down, 15–16
    Sausage-making, 18–19
    Spareribs, Oh So Simple, 19
    Spareribs on the Grill, 19
    Suckling Pig, 14–15
Pork Chops Supreme, 18
Princess Cake, 124–25
Prune Cake, 130
Pumpkin, 52, 169–70
Pumpkin Chiffon Pie, 173
Pumpkin Pie, 170
Punch(es)
    Delicious Tea, 209
    Holiday, 211
    Milk, 219
    Old-Fashioned Hot, 219
    Old-Fashioned Tea, 209
    Orange Sherbet, 216–17
    Party Tea, 211
    Pineapple Tea, 206
    Pink, 207
    Pink Punch for a Crowd, 207
    Punch and Candy Canes, 214
    Punch for Fifty, 211
    Simple Hot Spiced, 218
    Tea Punch for Thirty, 209
    Tea Punch, Fruited, 210
Punch and Candy Canes, 214
Punch for Fifty, 211

Q

Quick and Easy Rollups, 118
Quick Casserole, 51

R

Radishes, 77
Refreshing Lemonade, 212
Rhubarb and Honey Dessert, 178–79
Rhubarb Cream Pie, 166
Rich-Flavored Eggnog, 212
Rich Mocha, 202
Roast Quail, 29–30
Rolls
    Basic Sweet Dough, 106
    Biscuits, 111
    Cherry Whirligig Rolls, 109
    Honey Buns, 108
    Honey Butter Cinnamon Buns, 108
    Honey Twists, 110–11, 114
    Quick and Easy Rollups, 118
Rosy Cherry Pie, 169

S

Salad Dressing(s)
    Apricot-Nectar, 90
    A Taste of Island, 79
    Avocado Fruit, 89
    Avocado Salad, 85
    Banana Dressing Luscious, 91
    Colorful Vegetable Salad, 75

Delicate French, 90
Fluffy Honey, 81
French, 73
Frozen Fruit Delicious, 84
Fruit, 82
Honey 1, 88
Honey 2, 89
Honey 3, 91
Honey Cheese, 89
Honey French, 70, 83
Honey Fruit, 80
Lime-Mint Fruit, 90
Orange Pineapple, 86
Perfect, 90
Perk-up, 78
Poppy Seed, 79
Spring Salad Bowl Dressing, 71
Sweet-Sour, 75
Tangy French, 72
Tart Honey, 91
Whipped Cream, 81
Yogurt, 74
Zippy Dip, 78
Zippy Honey, 80
Salad for Children, 83–84
Salad Greens with Yogurt Dressing, 74
Salad(s)
    Avocado, 73
    Avocado-Orange-Grapefruit, 80
    Banana Fruit, 82
    Coleslaw Piquant, 76
    Colorful Vegetable, 75
    Cookout Bean, 73
    Crisp Salad Bowl, 73
    Delectable Fruit Salad Mold, 87
    Earliest Spring, 72
    Frosted Fruit, 85
    Frozen Fruit Delicious, 84
    Fruit Ring, 81
    Fruit Salad Supreme, 79
    Fruit with Fluffy Dressing, 81
    Green Beans Delicious, 76
    Harvest Moon, 77
    Heavenly, 84
    Honey Avocado Ring, 88
    Honey Grapefruit Mold, 87
    Orange Pineapple Ring, 86
    Oxcheek, 76
    Piquant, 71
    Radishes, 77
    Salad for Children, 83–84
    Salad Greens with Yogurt Dressing, 74
    Spinach Garden Toss, 72
    Spring Salad, 71
    Summer Fruit Special, 85
    Sweet-Sour, 75
    Tossed Salad, Divine, 70
    Tossed Salad with Sesame, 70
    Vegetable Salad with Sour Cream, 74
    Yuletide, 88
Sauce(s)
    Chocolate, 203
    Fluffy, 21
    Fudge, 191
    Game, 30
    Lemon, 191
    Moon Glow, 32

Orange, 119
Zesty, 25
Savory Cheese Bread, 101
Simple Hot Spiced Punch, 218
Sour Cream Spice Cake, 127
Spareribs, Oh So Simple, 19
Spareribs on the Grill, 19
Special Blueberry Pie, 169
Special Date Pudding, 181
Special for Gingerbread Topping, 137
Spiced Fruit Bars, 145
Spiced Tea Cooler, 208
Spicy Bran Cookies, 154
Spicy Hot Tea, 206
Spinach Garden Toss, 72
Spinach Ring, 53
Spring Salad Bowl, 71
Spring Salad Bowl Dressing, 71
Steak. See Beef
Steak and Honey, 22
Strawberry Cream Pie, 174
Strawberry Pie, 165
Strawberry Torte, 187
Strawberry Velvet, 215
Stuffed Dates, 186
Succulent Rolled-Beef Roast, 20–21
Suckling Pig, 14–15
Sugar Icing, 130
Summer Fruit Special, 85
Swedish Rye Bread, 102
Sweet and Sour Green Beans, 60
Sweet Potatoes, Leftover, 50
Sweet Potatoes Royal, 49
Sweet Potatoes, Canned, 50–51
Sweet-Sour Salad, 75
Sweet-Sour Salad Dressing, 75
Syllabub, 185
Syrups
    Chocolate Sauce, 203
    Cocoa Syrup, 204
    Honey-Sweetened Simple Syrup, 205
    Mint Syrup, 204

T
Tangy French Dressing, 72
Tart Honey Salad Dressing, 91
Tasty Honey Beans, 57
Tea
    Delicious Iced, 210
    Delicious Tea Punch, 209
    Ginger Ale Tea, 208
    Honey Fruit Tea, 207
    Old-Fashioned Tea Punch, 209
    Party Tea Punch, 211
    Pineapple Tea Punch, 206
    Preparation, 205–6
    Spiced Tea Cooler, 208
    Spicy Hot Tea, 206
    Tea Punch for Thirty, 209
    Tea Punch, Fruited, 210
Tender Cocoa Cake, 125
Tender White Cake, 126–27
Topping(s)
    Berry, 190
    Choco-Honey Sauce, 137
    Coconut Honey, 139
    Date Honey Spread, 120–21

Delicious Lemon-Honey Sauce for Cookies, 138
Hawaiian, 140
Honey, 110
Honey Coconut, 140
Honey Crisp, 141
Honeyscotch, 138
Special for Gingerbread, 137
Topping(s), Bread
Date Honey Spread, 120
Honey Nut Butter, 120
Honey Orange, 120
Lemon Honey Butter, 119
Orange Honey Butter, 120
Topping(s): Pastry, Cakes, Pies, Desserts, 190–91
Tossed Salad, Divine, 70
Tossed Salad with Sesame, 70
Turkey with Rice, 36

U
Uncooked Fruit Balls, 148

V
Vegetables
Baked Beans, Canned, 57
Baked Beans, Spanish Style, 56–57
Beans, Dried, 57
Cabbage Delight, 55
Cabbage, Leftover, 55
Carrots and Honey, 44
Carrots, Delicious, 46
Carrots, Simple Hints, 47
Company Sweet Potatoes, 50
Corn, Drying, 54–55
Easy Lima Beans, 59
Fresh Corn Sauté, 54
Glamorous Beets, 48
Glazed Winter Squash, 53
Green Beans, 59–60
Honey-Almond Carrots, 44–45
Honey Baked Beans, 58
Honey Bun Carrots, 46

Honey-Buttered Carrots, 46
Honeyed Acorn Squash, 52–53
Honeyed Parsnips, 61
Honey Ginger Yams, 51
Honey-Glazed Sweet Potatoes, 50
Honey-Sauced Beets, 47
Hubbard or Acorn Squash, 52
Lima Bean Casserole, 58
Lima Beans, Sauced, 59
Onions, 55
Onions en Casserole, 56
Orange and Lemon Beets, 48–49
Oranged Sweet Potatoes, 49
Pumpkin, 52, 169–70
Quick Casserole, 51
Spinach Ring, 53
Sweet and Sour Green Beans, 60
Sweet Potatoes, Canned, 50–51
Sweet Potatoes, Leftover, 50
Sweet Potatoes Royal, 49
Tasty Honey Beans, 57
Vegetable Salad with Sour Cream, 74
Vinegar, 72

W
Waffles with Orange Sauce, 119
Walnut Crumb Crust, 165
Wassail, 217
Whipped Cream Dressing, 81
Whole Ham, Honey Glazed, 10
Whole Wheat Bread, 99
Wildfowl, 29

Y
Yeast-making, 107
Yogurt Dressing, 74
Yuletide Salad, 88

Z
Zesty Meat Loaf, Muffin Style, 25
Zesty Sauce, 25
Zippy Honey Dressing, 80
Zippy Dip Dressing, 78